Understanding Psychological Contracts at Work

A Critical Evaluation of Theory and Research

Neil Conway

Rob B. Briner

OXFORD
UNIVERSITY PRESS

OXFORD
UNIVERSITY PRESS

Great Clarendon Street, Oxford OX2 6DP

Oxford University Press is a department of the University of Oxford.
It furthers the University's objective of excellence in research, scholarship,
and education by publishing worldwide in

Oxford New York

Auckland Cape Town Dar es Salaam Hong Kong Karachi
Kuala Lumpur Madrid Melbourne Mexico City Nairobi
New Delhi Shanghai Taipei Toronto

With offices in

Argentina Austria Brazil Chile Czech Republic France Greece
Guatemala Hungary Italy Japan Poland Portugal Singapore
South Korea Switzerland Thailand Turkey Ukraine Vietnam

Oxford is a registered trade mark of Oxford University Press
in the UK and in certain other countries

Published in the United States
by Oxford University Press Inc., New York

British Library Cataloguing in Publication Data

Data available

Library of Congress Cataloging in Publication Data

Data available

Typeset by SPI Publisher Services, Pondicherry, India
Printed in Great Britain on acid-free paper by Biddles., King's Lynn, Norfolk

ISBN 978-0-19-928064-3
ISBN 978-0-19-928065-0 (pbk.)

▨ PREFACE

We have been thinking about writing this book for a long time. For almost a decade the psychological contract has provided us with excellent material for numerous arguments—most of which remain completely and happily unresolved and continue to stimulate and frustrate in almost equal measure. The stimulating part is the way in which the psychological contract appears to give genuine insights into the workings of relationship between employee and employer. In particular, the concept does seem to shed light on the implicit nature of many of the beliefs surrounding this relationship, the ways in which these beliefs are shaped by, and shape, the behaviours of both parties, and how the relationship can go wrong. The frustrating part is how poorly the concept performs once we dig a little deeper and try to move beyond these initial insights. Rather than discovering additional layers of helpful theoretical elaboration, we have instead found inconsistencies, confusions, gaping holes, and much uncharted territory. The psychological contract is perhaps a good example of a concept that ultimately raises more questions than it answers—which is of course not necessarily a bad thing.

So, overall, is the idea any good? Does it raise many more questions than it answers so that it just creates problems rather than providing important insights? Do the strengths of the concept outweigh the weaknesses and limitations? What do we really know about the psychological contract? Does existing research tell us much? How can the idea be used practically? It was our desire to address these sorts of quite fundamental questions that led to the idea of the book. While there are a few places where it is possible to find critiques of some aspects of the concept, and a few other places where research findings are reviewed, there has been so for no attempt to draw this material together and provide a more detailed critical evaluation.

Thinking about writing a book and having a general idea about its contents is, of course, the easy bit. We encountered many obstacles when we actually started to write. While most of these were self-erected, some were a consequence of what can best be described as gaping holes in existing research. Even in those places where we had hoped to be able to simply report and describe what others had done in relation to some fairly basic aspects of the concept, we found that there just was not enough literature to review in many instances. Rather than leaving these gaps we felt they should be acknowledged and at least partially filled by our own speculation and guesswork. This proved to be more difficult than we anticipated.

Another obstacle we encountered—which can partly be blamed on the existing literature, but probably more on our own intellectual shortcomings—was the problem of describing and explaining in detail some of the fundamental ideas within the psychological contract concept. Even when writing about ideas that are relatively well developed within the field, and that we felt we knew pretty well, it soon became apparent that our knowledge was just not as detailed or as clear as we had thought. This led to many more discussions about whether our failure to clearly and easily articulate these ideas was more a reflection of a confused literature than our inability to grasp ideas. At the time of writing it remains too close to call.

Even though the idea is now almost forty years old, it is, as they say, still in its infancy. We do believe that the idea has great potential but that it is yet too early in its development to say much about where it is heading and what kinds of contribution to understanding behaviour at work it may eventually make. However, we are also certain that further critical scrutiny of various kinds is essential if the concept is to fulfil its potential.

We would like to thank numerous friends and colleagues who have all in various ways contributed to our thinking and the development of the ideas we present here. These include Vincent Cassar, Jackie Coyle-Shapiro, David Guest, and Denise Rousseau. Also, we have learnt a great deal from supervising the many M.Sc. students at Birkbeck College who chose to research various aspects of the psychological contract for their dissertations over the past ten years or so.

We also thank Matthew Derbyshire and David Musson at Oxford University Press who have been incredibly patient and supportive.

Neil Conway thanks the Leverhulme Trust, which, through a Special Research Fellowship (SRF/40043), provided support specifically to produce this book. Neil also thanks his partner Gabriele Woelfle and their daughter Giulia, who have shared the many ups and downs encountered along the way.

Lastly, we are hugely indebted to Sarah Owens, whose help was essential during the final stages of the book.

ACKNOWLEDGEMENTS

The authors would like to thank the following publishers and individuals for permission to reproduce material.

'Table 4.2: The content of the psychological contract in the UK' taken from Herriot, Manning and Kidd (1997), 'The Content of the Psychological Contract', *British Journal of Management*, 8: 156. Reproduced with permission. Copyright with Blackwell Publishing Ltd.

'Figure 4.2: Balancing exchange relationships' taken from Shore and Barksdale (1998), 'Examining Degree of Balance and Level of Obligation in the Employment Relationship: A Social Exchange Approach', *Journal of Organizational Behavior*, 17: 734. Reproduced with permission. Copyright with John Wiley & Sons Ltd.

'Box 6.1: A measure of the contents of psychological contracts' taken from Tekleab and Taylor (2003), 'Aren't There Two Parties in an Employment Relationship? Antecedents and Consequences of Organization–Employee Agreement on Contract Obligations and Violations', *Journal of Organizational Behavior*, 24: 607. Reproduced with permission. Copyright with John Wiley & Sons Ltd.

'Box 6.2: A multi-item global measure of psychological contract breach' taken from Robinson and Morrison (2000), 'The Development of Psychological Contract Breach and Violation: A Longitudinal Study', *Journal of Organizational Behavior*, 21: 539. Reproduced with permission. Copyright with John Wiley & Sons Ltd.

'Box 6.3: Example of a scenario methodology' adapted from Rousseau and Anton (1991), 'Fairness and Implied Contract Obligations in Job Terminations: The Role of Contributions, Promises, and Performance', *Journal of Organizational Behavior*, 12: 292. Reproduced with permission. Copyright with John Wiley & Sons Ltd.

'Figure 7.3: Resource exchange configuration' taken from Foa (1971), 'Interpersonal and Economic Resources', *Science*, 171: 347. Reproduced with permission. Copyright with AAAS.

'Figure 8.2: Graphing narratives' taken from Gergen and Gergen (1988), 'Narrative and the Self as Relationship', *Advances in Experimental Social Psychology*, 21: 25–6. Reproduced with permission. Copyright with Elsevier.

'Table 9.1: The effectiveness of human resource management practices in communicating the organization's promises to employees' taken from Guest and Conway (2002), 'Communicating the Psychological Contract: An Employer Perspective', *Human Resource Management Journal*, 12: 30. Reproduced with permission. Copyright with Personnel Publications.

In the Appendix, shortened version of Millward and Hopkins (1998) measure of 'Transactional and relational psychological contracts', taken from Raja, Johns and Ntalianis (2004), 'The Impact of Personality on Psychological Contracts', *Academy of Management Journal*, 47: 367. Reproduced with permission. Copyright with Academy of Management.

Rousseau (2000), 'Psychological contract inventory'. Reproduced with permission. Copyright with Denise M. Rousseau.

Tekleab and Taylor's measures (2003) of 'Employee obligations to the organization', 'Organization obligations to the employee', 'Employee breach of contract to the organization', and 'Organization breach of contract to the employee', taken from Tekleab and Taylor (2003), 'Aren't There Two Parties in an Employment Relationship? Antecedents and Consequences of Organization–Employee Agreement on Contract Obligations and Violations', *Journal of Organizational Behavior*, 24: 607. Reproduced with permission. Copyright with John Wiley & Sons Ltd.

Robinson and Morrison's measure (2000) of 'Psychological contract breach' and 'Psychological contract violation' taken from Robinson and Morrison (2000), 'The Development of Psychological Contract Breach and Violation: A Longitudinal Study', *Journal of Organizational Behavior*, 21: 539. Reproduced with permission. Copyright with John Wiley & Sons Ltd.

Guest and Conway's measure (2002) of 'Organization breach of contract to the employee' taken from Guest and Conway (2002), 'Communicating the Psychological Contract: An Employer Perspective', *Human Resource Management Journal*, 12: 31. Reproduced with permission. Copyright with Personnel Publications.

Kickul, Neuman, Parker and Finkl's measure (2002) of 'Psychological contract breach' taken from Kickul, Neuman, Parker, and Finkl (2002), 'Settling the Score: The Role of Organizational Justice in the Relationship Between Psychological Contract Breach and Anticitizenship Behavior', *Employee Responsibilities and Rights Journal*, 13: 90–1. Reproduced with permission. Copyright with Springer Science and Business Media.

Robinson and Rousseau's measure (1994) of 'Psychological contract breach' taken from Robinson and Rousseau (1994), 'Violating the Psychological Contract: Not the Exception but the Norm', *Journal of Organizational Behavior*, 15: 251. Reproduced with permission. Copyright with John Wiley & Sons Ltd.

▓ CONTENTS

■ LIST OF FIGURES

▓ LIST OF TABLES

▓ LIST OF BOXES

1 | Introduction and Overview

1.1. Ways of understanding behaviour at work: the psychological contract in context

Why do people at work behave the way they do? Answers to such a question are potentially complex and can take many forms. As is evident from any organizational psychology[1] textbook or course outline, a range of theories, models, and constructs are used to understand behaviour at work. Some approaches look to the organizational context or environment to explain behaviour. The job characteristics approach, for example, seeks to identify how particular features of jobs impact on employee behaviour. Other approaches look at the characteristics of individuals rather than the context to find ways of explaining behaviour. For instance, personality researchers focus on individual differences and dispositions as causes of behaviour. A third approach looks at how both the context and the individual interact to affect behaviour. The notion of person-environment fit, for example, explains behaviour through the degree to which the person and the environment are matched or compatible.

In organizational psychology, as in all areas of behavioural and social science, there are, therefore, numerous ways of trying to understand human behaviour. What kind of a theory is the psychological contract? Where can we place it in relation to existing approaches? Put simply, the psychological contract is about the exchange relationship between employee and employer. Employees may do many things for their employer, such as working hard, putting in extra time, working carefully, helping co-workers, staying with their employer, and so on. Likewise employers can do many things for their employees, such as paying them at a good rate, treating them fairly, providing good working conditions, and showing them respect. But what determines what each party of the psychological contract will do? The assumption is that the relationship is based on an exchange in which each party will exchange something they can provide for something the other party can provide.

---

[1] Throughout the book we use the term 'organizational psychology' as a general term to refer to many areas of research and practice concerned with behaviour at work including organizational behaviour, industrial and organizational psychology, work psychology, vocational behaviour, and occupational psychology.

However, what makes the psychological contract a *psychological* as opposed to a *legal* contract is that the nature of this exchange is based on the perceptions of each party rather than what has been written down or explicitly agreed. In other words, while some parts of the exchange between employee and employer are explicit and agreed, much of it is based on an implicit understanding of the sorts of promises each has made to the other.

The psychological contract concept is used to explain behaviour through considering the extent to which the employee believes that the employer has kept the promises the employee perceives were made to them. As in any relationship, if promises are kept, then satisfaction and a desire to stay in the relationship are likely consequences. If, on the other hand, promises are broken, negative emotions and the urge to withdraw may follow.

There are several important and refreshing aspects of the psychological contract concept that do not feature strongly in other ideas used to understand behaviour at work. First, there is a clear focus on the employment *relationship*. To some extent this is neglected in other approaches. Although the relevance of social relationships at work is acknowledged they do not place the relationship between employer and employee centre-stage as is the case with the psychological contract. A second important difference is that this employment relationship is considered in terms of an *exchange* relationship. While other theoretical approaches consider the possible consequences of the exchange in terms of the employee's perception of, say, equity or justice, the nature of the exchange is not explored in any detail. Third, because the psychological contract is about perceptions of a reciprocal exchange relationship it implies that employee behaviour is best understood as a dynamic and ongoing process and one in which employees are active. Other explanations of behaviour at work often seem to look at behaviour in terms of simple cause and effect, rather than processes, and place the employee in a relatively passive role, simply reacting to various features of the context.

The psychological contract is just one of many ways of thinking about behaviour at work. However, as suggested above, it is different in some important ways from many other approaches.

1.2. Why this sort of book and why now?

The three main aims of this book, discussed in more detail below, are to review and then to critically evaluate psychological contract research and theory, and to consider practical applications of the psychological contract. While there has been some attempt to address each of the above aims in previously published work this is, to our knowledge, the only attempt to tackle all three aims together in the comprehensive and detailed manner a book permits. The sort of detailed overview we attempt to provide here is simply not achievable within the scope of a journal article.

One reason for the previous absence of this sort of book may be that the field of psychological contract research has been developing at such a rapid pace that even five years ago it would not have made a great deal of sense to produce a book such as this simply because of the relatively small quantity of published work available for review.

However, the main reason for writing this book is not because it is now possible but rather because we feel it is desirable and necessary. The concept is, just about, still young enough that it sometimes seems that almost any theoretical or empirical contribution is seen as valuable. However, it is also, just about, old enough that we should know better how to discriminate between that which is truly advancing understanding and that which does so to a lesser extent.

The psychological contract concept has a perhaps unusual trajectory. While it is a relatively old concept, which is possible to trace back to just before the 1960s, it was not really until the late 1980s, with the publication of Rousseau's work (1989), that the idea started to take off. Before the late 1980s it is difficult to identify a body of work about the psychological contract, although several writers, often quite independently, do mention the idea. In other words, although the concept had clearly emerged it was largely ignored for several decades and remained undeveloped until more recent times.

Where is the concept heading now? Will it continue in its current upward direction, level off, or even fall back to the low levels of interest it attracted before the late 1980s? This is a difficult question to answer but is one we indirectly address in this book. There is little doubt that the idea is now quite popular amongst practitioners, students and researchers. But what happens next depends a lot on how research and theory develop and how much the psychological contract is seen to provide insights to those seeking to understand behaviour at work.

1.3. Aims of the book

Before discussing the aims it should be made clear that in the main we are approaching the psychological contract from an organizational psychology perspective. This perspective is similar to those found in other disciplines such as organizational behaviour and work psychology. While it would be possible to also take a critical management or organization studies perspective to analysing the psychological contract, these approaches, though certainly valuable and interesting, fall outside the scope of this book.

1.3.1. First aim: to provide a comprehensive review of psychological contract research and theory

As indicated above, the field is now sufficiently developed for such a review to be feasible. What do we really know about what the psychological contract is and how it works?

In making such a review comprehensive it is not our intention to review each and every publication on the psychological contract. Rather our aim is to review significant theoretical and empirical developments within what are easily the two most dominant areas in the field: the contents of the psychological contract, and how the psychological contract affects work behaviour.

The contents of the psychological contract are those things that the employee and employer agree to exchange with one other. Researchers have tended to focus on what those things are and how they can be categorized. Attempts to understand how the psychological contract affects work behaviour have looked mainly to breach (or broken promises) as a way to explain this. If employees feel that implicit promises made to them have been broken, then they are likely to respond in particular ways.

It should be noted that this book, like most research in the field, focuses on the psychological contract from the employee's perspective. This is not because the employer's perspective is unimportant but rather because, as we will discuss later, it has been somewhat overlooked.

1.3.2. Second aim: to critically evaluate psychological contract research and theory and suggest ways in which the field can be further developed

What are the limitations and weaknesses of the field? While there have been a few critiques of some aspects of the psychological contract concept (Arnold 1996; Guest 1998; Meckler, Drake, and Levinson 2003) it has, on the whole, received very little critical attention. Why this should be the case is unclear, particularly given the quite considerable weaknesses and limitations that are readily apparent within both research and theory. One explanation may be that, as already suggested, the field is still emerging and so researchers are more likely to focus on generating new research than criticizing what has already been done.

In critically evaluating the field we will look at problems with existing research and also consider the many gaps in our understanding: those features of psychological contract research and theory that remain under- or just unexplored. In trying to evaluate research it can be just as important to consider what is missing as what is there.

In addition to discussing the strengths and considerable weaknesses of the psychological contract we also wish to identify ways in which the field can be developed further.

1.3.3. Third aim: to consider how the psychological contract can be practically applied in organizational settings

There is little doubt that the psychological contract is popular amongst practitioners, yet there is very little evidence about how and indeed whether the concept is used in organizations. It is not, therefore, possible to provide a review of how the psychological contract *is* used in organizations, but rather we can suggest some ways in which it *could* perhaps be used.

Given the almost complete absence of information we have had to infer possible ways of applying the psychological contract from basic research and theory. We, therefore, regard this as developing some initial thinking about applying the psychological contract, rather than producing a user's manual or definitive practical guide.

While discussions of how the psychological contract can be applied are found, most notably in Rousseau (1995), our approach is somewhat different. This is because we consider ways in which psychological contract theory and research can be applied within the limitations of this research, identified throughout the book.

1.4. Structure and outline of the book

The book is structured such that Chapters 2–5 are concerned mostly with providing an overview of what the field has already achieved. Chapters 6 and 7 provide a critical evaluation of empirical research and identify what we believe to be the major challenges for psychological contract researchers. Chapters 8 and 9 are more speculative and consider how theory might best be developed and ways in which the psychological contract could perhaps be applied. Below is a brief summary of the contents of each chapter.

Chapter 2: The history and development of the psychological contract concept. As mentioned above, the concept has both a long and a short history. Two key historical periods are considered here which can be described as pre- and post-Rousseau. We also consider how the concept is being used currently.

Chapter 3: What is the psychological contract? Defining the concept. Like many concepts, the key components of the psychological contract have been variously and sometimes vaguely defined. This chapter sets out some of the main definitions and considers in detail similarities and differences across accounts and also the meanings of the key terms of most widely used definitions.

Chapter 4: The contents of psychological contracts. Here we consider, first, how the contents have been assessed and categorized. Next, we consider two key questions about contents: how employee perceptions of contents are formed and how the contents affect outcomes.

Chapter 5: How does the psychological contract affect behaviour, attitudes, and emotion? As already mentioned, the psychological contract is just one of a number of ways of explaining behaviour at work. This chapter considers how the idea of breach has been used to understand how the psychological contract affects behaviour. We also consider some weaknesses with the concept of breach and some alternative theoretical approaches.

Chapter 6: Researching the psychological contract. The main purpose of this chapter is to consider in detail exactly how research in this field has been done and its main limitations. We also make some suggestions for other ways of researching the psychological contract that may be more fruitful.

Chapter 7: Challenges for psychological contract researchers. Although there are many such challenges, here we focus on six we believe to be among the most important. Each is concerned in some way with the problems that arise when definitions and theory are insufficiently detailed or specified. We also make some suggestions for ways in which these challenges can be overcome.

Chapter 8: Understanding the psychological contract as a process. In this chapter we argue that one way of developing our understanding of the concept, both theoretically and empirically, is to treat the psychological contract as a process. We then go on to discuss how existing approaches do not adequately consider process and some ways in which this can be done.

Chapter 9: Managing the psychological contract. This chapter starts with a discussion of key issues in managing the psychological contract and then goes on to consider how contents and breach can be managed. As this is done largely from the organization's perspective we then consider how employees can manage their psychological contracts. Some dilemmas which may be encountered in managing the contract are discussed.

Chapter 10: Summary and conclusions: Prospects for psychological contract research and practice. Here we revisit each of the three aims of the book, considering the extent to which each has been met, and then discuss what we believe are some empirical and theoretical priorities for the field.

It is worth noting that understanding how the concept developed and the definitional issues discussed in Chapters 2 and 3 are fundamental to understanding the many weaknesses and limitations of psychological contract research and theory. The themes established here are repeated throughout the remainder of the book and so we would recommend that these be read first.

2 | The History and Development of the Psychological Contract Concept

2.1. Introduction

The psychological contract has achieved considerable prominence in both academic and practitioner discourse over the past fifteen years. One reason for this shift is that it is regarded as a useful way of understanding and perhaps managing apparent changes to employment relationships brought about by new economic and organizational circumstances such as foreign competition, downsizing, increased reliance on temporary workers, and demographic diversity (Arnold 1996; Sparrow 1996; Herriot, Manning, and Kidd 1997). There are many indicators of increasing interest in the psychological contract such as the number of journal special issues on the topic (e.g. *Human Resource Management* 1994; *Human Resource Management Journal* 1994; *European Journal of Work Psychology* 1996; *Journal of Organizational Behavior* 1998, 2003).

While this surge in interest is fairly recent, organizational researchers have in fact known about the psychological contract concept for almost half a century. Argyris first formally used the term 'psychological contract' in 1960, but the idea that relationships may be characterized by implicit exchange can be traced back to Menninger's analysis (1958) of the patient–therapist relationship, the more general ideas of the employer–employee exchange contained in March and Simon's inducement-contribution model (1958), and even earlier to Barnard's equilibrium model (1938) (Roehling 1996).

This chapter provides a context to later chapters by tracing the history and development of the concept. Two major periods are considered. The first is the early history of the psychological contract up to but not including Rousseau's seminal reconceptualization (1989). This period is characterized by rather sporadic theoretical development, the involvement of a number of different disciplines and subdisciplines and limited empirical work. The second or 'modern' period concerns Rousseau's work and developments since that time. This period is somewhat different being characterized by relatively little profound theoretical development, a narrowing of the disciplines involved, and considerable, largely quantitative, empirical work. It is this second period that has produced the vast bulk of the material discussed in this book. The final part of the chapter considers how researchers and practitioners are currently using the concept.

It is worth noting at this point that many of the current debates and confusion in psychological contract theory can be seen, in part, as a consequence of the diverse uses of the psychological contract concept during its historical development.

2.2. Early development of the psychological contract concept

In this section we consider the first period of the history of the concept, covering its origins and early development from 1958 to 1989, up to but not including Rousseau's key reconceptualization (1989) (which will be covered in the next section). As indicated earlier, the initial development of the concept was somewhat patchy. Where development did take place this was not cumulative as researchers tended not to build on or refer to previous research. This development was also slow—which is perhaps surprising given that the idea was introduced and first discussed by quite eminent organizational scholars such as Argyris (1960) and Schein (1965).

As demonstrated by Roehling (1996) in an excellent overview of the origins of the psychological contract the term 'psychological contract' has been used to denote very different phenomena, with researchers often failing to relate their definition of the psychological contract to previous definitions (a full discussion of the definition of the psychological contract will take place in Chapter 3).

The most important early texts in terms of later citations and conceptual contribution were Menninger (1958), Argyris (1960), Levinson et al. (1962) and Schein (1965). Indeed, these publications, with just a few exceptions such as Kotter's empirical study (1973), represent almost all the research conducted on the psychological contract until Rousseau's key contribution (1989). Since then, over 100 journal articles have been published on the topic with most citing Rousseau's paper and drawing on her ideas rather than any of these earlier conceptualizations.

Several other early texts have been thought to influence the development of the psychological contract even though they did not explicitly address the concept. It is with these that we begin our review of the history of the psychological contract.

Attempts to understand the employment relationship as an exchange has a long history in organizational research. Barnard's equilibrium theory (1938) suggests that employees' continued participation depends on adequate rewards from the organization. March and Simon's contribution–inducements model (1958) extended this theory by specifying in more detail the nature of the resources exchanged and arguing that continued participation depends on whether employees perceive the inducements offered by the organization as equal to or exceeding the contributions made by the employee. According to this model, an organization remains solvent, or in equilibrium, through ensuring that the contributions made by employees sufficiently exceed the inducements offered to employees.

The influence of March and Simon's model on shaping psychological contract theory is rarely acknowledged even though there are striking similarities between the two approaches, most notably the idea that the exchange of contributions for inducements is 'defined both explicitly and implicitly by the terms of the employment contract' (March and Simon 1958: 90).

Menninger (1958) is generally credited with first introducing the idea that psychological contracts are involved in a range of interpersonal exchanges in his book *Theory of Psychoanalytic Technique* focusing in particular on the explicit and the unspoken contract between patient and psychotherapist. However, he did not explicitly use the term 'psychological contract' until the reissue of this book in 1970 (Menninger and Holzman 1973). For Menninger this contract and the behaviour of both parties to the contract are influenced, sometimes in contradictory ways, by both unconscious and conscious processes. If both parties feel satisfied with the exchange, the contract will continue although it is not clear from Menninger's writing what 'satisfied' might mean. The continuation of the contract rests on the patient remaining in some way dependent on the therapist's services. Once the patient decides he or she can manage alone, the contract is expected to finish. The crucial distinction between the content of the psychological contract (i.e. what is exchanged?) and the process (how is the exchange regulated?) is evident even in this earliest work.

Argyris (1960) was the first to apply the psychological contract to the workplace. He believed that employees and their organization created psychological contracts that allowed the expression and gratification of each other's needs. In other words, if employees feel that management is respecting their right to develop and grow and use their own initiative then in return employees will also respect the right of the organization to evolve. In his study of a manufacturing plant, Argyris used the term 'psychological work contract' to refer to an implicit agreement between employees and their foreman.

> Since the foremen realize the employees in this system will tend to produce optimally under passive leadership, and since the employees agree, a relationship may be hypothesized to evolve between the employees and the foreman which might be called the 'psychological work contract'. The employee will maintain high production, low grievances, etc., if the foremen guarantee and respect the norms of the employee informal culture (i.e. let the employees alone, make certain they make adequate wages, and have secure jobs). This is precisely what the employees need. (Argyris 1960: 97)

In other words, if employers do not interfere too much with employees, respect their culture or norms of the employee group, and leave them to get on with the job, employees are likely to perform much better.

The employer may not, of course, necessarily approve of the behaviour and cultural norms of the employee group. However, Argyris believed it was not in the employer's interest to challenge such behaviour or norms as it would be likely to cause employees to reduce effort. An interesting observation from this study is that both the employer and employee occasionally chose to overlook the other's unacceptable behaviours in order to maintain a successful ongoing relationship.

As long as employee performance was satisfactory, the organization was largely uninterested in how employees went about their work. Likewise, as long as the employer kept its side of the deal then employees were prepared to work productively. In this sense, the psychological contract was viewed as a simple one but also one which was effective for both parties. While it is clear that Argyris saw the psychological contract as an important concept it was not subjected to detailed analysis or empirical investigation.

A study published in a book entitled *Men, Management and Mental Health* (Levinson et al. 1962) examined how the psychological contract could be used to promote mental health through interviews with 874 employees at a US utility plant. While much contemporary psychological contract research cites early work on the psychological contract, it is perhaps only Levinson et al. that really elaborated the concept. For Argyris and Schein the psychological contract is introduced as simply one of a number of theories that may help explain work experience and little discussion of definitions or psychological theory can be found in their work. In striking contrast, Levinson and colleagues produced a full thesis on the psychological contract, the insights of which can be compared favourably to any contemporary theorizing. Their analysis is remarkably insightful and provides a rich conceptualization of the psychological contract (see, for example, chapters on definition, reciprocation, psychological contract change processes, and links between psychological contracts at work and life outside of work). Many of the insights in this important work remain unexplored and Meckler, Drake, and Levinson (2003) rightfully call for a reappraisal of this work. We briefly cover a number of its key points here including the definition of expectations, the stability of psychological contracts, and the role of needs and reciprocity in forming and maintaining the psychological contract.

Levinson et al. (1962: 21) defined the psychological contract as 'a series of mutual expectations of which the parties to the relationship may not themselves be even dimly aware but which nonetheless govern their relationship to each other'. These expectations are largely unspoken, implicit, and frequently formed before or outside the current employment relationship. The psychological contract is presented as consisting of a specific type of expectations, those having an obligatory quality where one party perceives the other party to be duty-bound to fulfil them. The two parties may not even be 'dimly aware' of these expectations as they are driven by unconscious motives.

The psychological contract is also defined as highly dynamic, subject to the changing circumstances of the parties. Several likely forms of change in the psychological contract are considered including situations where there is increasing separation, joint growth or joint decline between the two parties, where one party is left behind or where the employee is thinking of leaving. We shall return to these ideas as a starting point for our analysis of psychological contract processes in Chapter 8.

The central idea of this work is that individuals have needs that lead them to initiate and develop interdependent relationships where each party behaves in ways that fulfil the other's needs. Expectations arising from this exchange constitute the psychological contract. It is probably the centrality of the concept of needs to early conceptualizations that most differentiate them from contemporary approaches, where psychological contracts are derived to a much greater extent from the behaviour of the parties and driven by conscious expectations. According to the needs approach, if the organization meets employees' needs, the employee feels obliged to reciprocate by trying to fulfil the organization's needs. Hence, needs are very closely related to the obligations that constitute the psychological contract, as Levinson et al. (1962: 36) note: 'It is as if both employees and company are saying to one another, "You *must*, for I require it"', where the employee–employer relationship can be viewed as 'the process of fulfilling a contractual relationship in which both parties seek continuously to meet their respective needs'.

Ongoing reciprocation will continue to the extent that each party's needs are met. According to their approach, the psychological contract is related to a number of mental health outcomes and employee behaviours through the mechanism of reciprocation: where this functions well, favourable outcomes for both employee and organization follow. Reciprocation is defined as the 'total process of fulfilling the psychological contract' (Levinson et al. 1962: 125) and has a number of conditions and features. The felt need to reciprocate provides the motivation to remain a party to the relationship and, when operating well, the organization is seen as becoming personalized in that the individual identifies strongly with the organization's goals and needs. Reciprocation is the mechanism allowing employees access to the things they want from the organization and through renegotiation individuals can work towards their preferred self. From this perspective, therefore, the psychological contract can be related quite directly to psychological well-being and functioning in a way that is not found in contemporary research which is dominated by examining the effects of psychological contract breach, in other words, where reciprocation breaks down. In this respect Levinson's work remains pioneering; Guest and Conway (2004) have recently argued that while breach is useful for understanding negative experiences at work, it is not clear from current research how the psychological contract *violation*

can be used to understand and promote positive well-being. There is currently little understanding of how the psychological contract explains behaviour during those times at which it is *not* being broken—which presumably is most of the time. The idea of reciprocity may be one way of developing such an understanding. This issue will be considered in more detail in Chapter 8.

In addition to discussing what happens when reciprocation functions well, Levinson's work gives some consideration to the consequences of a breakdown in reciprocation. Essentially, employees become frustrated in such a situation due to the loss of gratifications and resist satisfying the needs of the other party by withholding behaviours that would achieve this. Levinson et al. (1962) do not use the contemporary terminology of violation to describe what happens when psychological contracts go wrong, although the idea that such situations will result in anger, withdrawal and hostility is discussed, but rather prefer to consider such situations where employees and organizations have conflicting needs leading to failures in reciprocation.

Levinson et al.'s work appears to come from a humanist perspective where they aim to enhance the experience of work and acknowledge work as playing a crucial role in mental health. (Such an approach would now be regarded as an emphasis on 'positive psychology'; see Wright 2003, for a discussion on positive psychology in organizational behaviour.) Levinson et al. link a theory of work relationships with personal and existential development and organizational functioning in a way that may seem naïve and overambitious by contemporary standards that seek to endlessly respecify and reduce ideas down to small constituent parts. Nevertheless, the work of Levinson et al. is ahead of its time in foreseeing much of the later psychological contract definition and theory development.

The next key work on the psychological contract can be found in Schein's 1965 text *Organizational Psychology*. For Schein, 'the psychological contract implies that the individual has a variety of expectations of the organization and that the organization a variety of expectations of him.... Expectations such as these are not written into any formal agreement between employee and organization, yet they operate powerfully as determinant of behavior' (p. 11). He believed the psychological contract was constantly renegotiated 'unfolding through mutual influence and mutual bargaining to establish a workable psychological contract' (p. 65) and constantly in operation.

Schein (1965) viewed the psychological contract as a key way of analysing the employment relationship. For Schein, the main way in which employees evaluate their psychological contract is through the extent to which there is some correspondence between their own and their organization's expectations:

> By way of conclusion, I would like to underline the importance of the psychological contract as a major variable of analysis. It is my central hypothesis that whether a person is working effectively, whether he generates commitment, loyalty, and enthusiasm for the organization and its goals, and whether he obtains satisfaction from his work, depend to a

large measure on two conditions: 1. The degree to which his own expectations of what the organization will provide him and what he owes the organization *matches* what the organization's expectations are of what it will give and get. 2. Assuming there is agreement on expectations, what actually is to be exchanged—money in exchange for time at work; social-need satisfaction and security in exchange for work and loyalty; opportunities for self-actualization and challenging work in exchange for high productivity, quality work and creative efforts in the service of organizational goals; or various combinations of these and other things.' (Schein 1965: 64–5, italics added)

In spite of the clarity and testability of these propositions, they generated very little research interest. This lack of interest may have been partly due to the psychological contract lacking distinctiveness compared with popular concepts of the period, such as met expectations, social exchange, or organizational culture. For instance, Nicholson and Johns (1985) saw the psychological contract as a set of normative beliefs associated with organizational culture and rewards.

Although Schein's work draws on that of Argyris (1960) and Levinson et al. (1962) he places more emphasis on understanding the relationship from both the employee and the employer's perspective. More detailed consideration is given to the organization's side of the psychological contract and how it can be expressed through organizational culture and at a more micro level through line management. He hypothesizes the likely psychological contracts arising from different types of organizational culture, derived from Etzioni's (1964) typology of coercive, normative and utilitarian cultures, and through people management assumptions, such as Theory X and Theory Y. Considering Theory X assumptions, 'If employees are expected to be indifferent, hostile, motivated only by economic incentives, and the like, the managerial strategies used to deal with them are very likely to train them to behave in precisely this fashion' (Schein 1965: 49). Schein's discussion of Theory X and Theory Y-type psychological contracts mirrors later distinctions between transactional and relational contracts.

Kotter (1973) tested Schein's 'matching' hypothesis in one of the earliest examples of empirical work on the psychological contract. He found that the greater the matching of employee and employer expectations, the more likely employees report job satisfaction, productivity, and reduced turnover. Matching here refers to the similarity of employees' expectations of what they should receive and do for the organization compared with the organization's expectations of what employees should do and what they get in return (i.e. matching at the level of the relationship), rather than an employee's perception of whether he or she thinks a common matching exists between the two parties (i.e. matching as perceived by the individual).

While a few other examples of research on the psychological contract exist (see Roehling 1996, for a review) the above review captures to a large extent the research on the psychological contract up until Rousseau's article (1989).

2.3. Rousseau's seminal reconceptualization

Rousseau's work is widely acknowledged as having had the greatest influence on psychological contract research since the writings of Levinson and Schein. Her article (1989) marked a fundamental shift in understanding the meaning and functioning of the psychological contract and how it could be empirically investigated. As Roehling (1996) notes, this article marked a 'transition' from early to what we understand as contemporary research on the psychological contract and played a central role in the reinvigoration of the field.

Rousseau's reworking of the psychological contract was different from previous research in four key ways. First, in contrast to earlier work that emphasized expectations, she placed greater emphasis on the promissory nature of psychological contracts defining them as 'an individual's beliefs regarding the terms and conditions of a reciprocal exchange agreement between that focal person and another party. Key issues here include the belief that a promise has been made and a consideration offered in exchange for it, binding the parties to some set of reciprocal obligations' (Rousseau 1989: 123). While Levinson et al. (1962) had noted the obligatory quality of psychological contract expectations, Rousseau emphasizes promises rather than expectations although there is still much debate around the definition and meaning of promises and the extent to which they can be separated from the notion of obligations and expectations (this issue is discussed in Chapter 3).

A second important change was a move away from viewing the psychological contract as one involving the perspectives of two interconnected parties towards seeing it as an individual-level subjective phenomenon 'existing in the eye of the beholder' (Rousseau 1989: 123). In other words, earlier approaches emphasized the nature of the agreement between the two parties whereas Rousseau focuses very much on the individual employee's perceptions as the most important influence on feelings, attitudes, and behaviour. Consistent with this view, Rousseau suggested that it was not possible for organizations to have psychological contracts as they can only be held by people and not abstract entities: 'Organizations cannot "perceive", though their individual managers can themselves personally perceive a psychological contract with employees and respond accordingly' (Rousseau 1989: 126).

A third difference can be found by examining accounts of how psychological contracts are formed. Earlier thinking identified basic human needs as the driving force behind the formation of expectations. Rousseau, on the other hand, suggests that psychological contracts are formed by the individual's perceptions of their own and the organization's behaviour in terms of explicit verbal or written promises or implicit promises arising from consistent and repeated patterns of behaviour by parties to the contract. Rather than being formed by some deeper-level motives, such as needs, Rousseau believes that it is primarily an individual's perceptions of observable behaviour that constitute psychological contracts.

Finally, there are differences in the mechanisms used to explain how the psychological contract affects behaviour. Early explanations tended to focus on the extent to which employees perceived a reasonable 'match' between the inducements offered by the organization and their own contributions irrespective of what had been promised. In contrast, Rousseau proposes the idea of 'violation' as the main mechanism linking the psychological contract to various outcomes. Violation is defined as 'failure of organizations or other parties to respond to an employee's contribution in ways the individual believes they are obligated to do so' (Rousseau 1989: 128). It is suggested that violations produce more intense responses than unmet expectations and inequity as they have a 'quasi-irreversible quality where anger lingers and "victims" experience a changed view of the other party and their interrelationship' (Rousseau 1989: 129).

The profound influence of Rousseau's ideas in generating future research and interest in the psychological contract can be accounted for in a number of ways. The most well-documented explanation, mentioned earlier, is that the psychological contract was seen as a way of understanding contemporary changes to the employment relationship during the 1980s and 1990s. A second explanation for its influence is Rousseau's careful demarcation of the psychological contract both from previous conceptualizations and from related ideas, such as equity and met expectations, thus allowing researchers to start investigating what appeared to be a new and exciting idea. Third, compared to previous conceptualizations emphasizing unconscious need-driven expectations, Rousseau's approach to the psychological contract as observable promises made it quantifiable and readily researchable through straightforward and traditional research methods such as questionnaire surveys. Lastly, the key idea of violation provided researchers with a relatively simple mechanism which could be used to help understand and research relationships between the psychological contract and outcomes.

2.4. Contemporary research

Since Rousseau's article (1989), over 100 articles, nearly all empirical, have been published on the psychological contract suggesting that we have now reached a more mature phase in the development of the concept. It has now been linked to many other theories and variables (discussed in later chapters) relevant to the employer–employee relationship and used to explain other kinds of relationships such as wife–husband, doctor–patient, teacher–student, and it has even been suggested that service providers who exceed the customer's psychological contract will produce delight in the customer (Schneider and Bowen 1999). Also, as would be expected in more mature or established research areas several critiques of the psychological contract have also appeared (Arnold 1996; Conway 1996; Guest 1998; Conway and Briner 2004).

While much progress has been made and it is clear that the psychological contract is an important idea, many limitations remain and numerous areas require development. These limitations are serious and require detailed analysis and evaluation, which is the major purpose of this book. Not least are weaknesses and ambiguities around defining and theorizing about the psychological contract such as:

- Do psychological contracts include expectations and/or promises?
- Can organizations have psychological contracts?
- What role do needs play in forming the psychological contract?
- What are the precise linkages between the exchange of employee contributions and organizational inducements?
- How do psychological contracts unfold on a day-to-day basis?
- To what extent is the psychological contract formed by factors unrelated to the employee's current organization (such as influences from outside work and previous relationships)?

The historical review presented in this chapter shows some of the origins of these ambiguities and also how many potentially useful ideas from earlier work have yet to be developed in any meaningful way. For example, while Argyris, Schein and particularly Levinson all discuss the relevance of everyday work experience as the context for the psychological context almost all empirical research fails to take this approach. We believe this idea to be particularly important and will return to it in Chapter 8.

2.5. How is the psychological contract currently used?

This chapter has considered the development of the concept from its earliest emergence to contemporary research. One issue not yet considered is how researchers and practitioners currently use the idea of the psychological contract in their work.

Researchers tend to view the psychological contract as an explanatory framework for the employment relationship (e.g. Shore and Tetrick 1994) using it to predict and understand employee attitudes and behaviours (e.g. Robinson 1996). At a broader level, it is also used, as mentioned earlier, as a way of thinking about the impact on employees of certain kinds of economic and social changes such as foreign competition, downsizing, and demographic diversity (Morrison and Robinson 1997). The focus of much research has been on two main issues: the contents of psychological contracts and their structure; and the effects of violations on employee attitudes and behaviour.

While researchers certainly use the psychological contract concept and it has generated much research activity, it has not been used in a comprehensive way with many features and aspects of the concept remaining underexplored or simply overlooked.

Turning now to practitioners' use of the psychological contract, it must first be noted that we know very little about how or indeed whether practitioners use this concept. Only one study has gathered any data on whether managers use the psychological contract to manage the employment relationship, where a recent survey of 1,300 senior human resources (HR) professionals in the UK found that one-third of organizations report using the psychological contract to manage the employment relationship (Guest and Conway 2002).

There is little information about how practitioners use the concept and even less about what they think about the concept. One, albeit crude, way of doing this is to examine the content of articles about the psychological contract in practitioner publications. In order to do this we have chosen to consider themes appearing in the articles published in the *People Management*, the journal of the Chartered Institute of Personnel and Development (CIPD) which is the main professional body of HR professionals in the UK.

Some twenty articles on the psychological contract have been published in this journal and all were concerned in some way with how different types of 'change' affect the psychological contract. The first theme identified in these articles was the change from the 'old' to the 'new' psychological contract. A second theme was the impact of large-scale organizational changes such as downsizing on the psychological contract. A third theme focused on how changes in government policy would affect the psychological contract. A feature of all these articles is the absence of 'hands-on' advice about how to use the concept to manage people. Rather, the concept is used to help practitioners understand how internal and external economic and other changes are likely to affect employees through changing the psychological contract.

Given the problems researchers have in defining and understanding the psychological contract it is perhaps not surprising that these practitioner articles pay relatively little attention to definitional and conceptual issues. These articles often seem to assume that readers already know the meaning of the concept or, where definitions are offered, they are somewhat vague and occasionally misleading. Only one of these twenty articles addressed the definition of the concept in depth, taking a more critical approach.

These articles give us some indication of how practitioners may use the concept. What they suggest is that it is used in quite a general way to help practitioners get a general feel for how economic and organizational changes may affect the psychological contract and, therefore, employee behaviour and attitudes. What is striking is the absence of more concrete discussion of these possible links and practical guidance about how the concept can be used on a daily basis or strategically to manage people. While the concept does at least appear, from our perspective, to be one which practitioners such as human resource management professionals, industrial and organizational psychologists, and line managers might find useful, this is largely speculation and not supported by the available evidence. We will return to the issue of how the concept could be used practically in Chapter 9.

2.6. Summary and conclusion

The concept of the psychological contract has been written about over forty years. With the exception of some early theoretical developments by Argyris (1960), Levinson et al. (1962) and Schein (1965) there was little interest in the psychological contract until Rousseau's reconceptualization in 1989. Rousseau's interpretation of the psychological contract as consisting of implicit and explicit promises is regarded as highly influential in reinvigorating research on the psychological contract, and her interpretation has been adopted almost exclusively by contemporary psychological contract researchers. Current psychological contract research is mainly concerned with the contents of psychological contracts and their structure and the effects of violations on employee attitudes and behaviour.

In conclusion, the history of the psychological contract concept highlights how the concept has been viewed in significantly different ways by researchers who often fail to acknowledge how their use of the concept relates to previous work (Roehling 1996). In Chapter 3 we attempt to unpack and clarify the meaning of the psychological contract concept.

3 | What Is the Psychological Contract? Defining the Concept

3.1. Introduction

As discussed in the previous chapter, the psychological contract has a long history in organizational research. Argyris first formally used the term 'psychological contract' in 1960, but the idea of an implicit exchange relationship can be traced back to Menninger's analysis (1958) of the patient-therapist relationship, to the more general ideas of the employer-employee exchange of March and Simon's inducement-contribution model (1958), and even earlier to Barnard's (1938) equilibrium model (Roehling 1996).

Chapter 2 revealed that the psychological contract has been viewed and used in different ways by researchers and that the meaning of the psychological contract has changed since the term was first formally introduced forty years ago. There has, however, been little recognition by researchers that the psychological contract has been conceptualized in a number of significantly different ways. Researchers have offered new definitions of their own, or adopted one of the existing definitions, with little or no consideration of alternative views of the construct (Roehling 1996). Thus far no attempt has been made in the literature to spell out systematically how terms central to the definition of the psychological contract have changed over the years. Such an activity seems like an essential starting point for embarking on any programme of empirical research or practical intervention in an organizational setting using the psychological contract concept.

The main aim of this chapter is, therefore, to unpack the definition of the psychological contract through reviewing how it has been defined and identifying variations across definitions offered by researchers. Clearly, many concepts have multiple definitions and are used by researchers in different ways. Sometimes these different uses are broadly similar. In other instances what researchers mean by the supposedly same concept can differ widely. In addition, there are situations in which definitions are so different they can simply confuse. For this reason we will organize our discussion around the key terms and features included in the definition of the psychological contract and discuss key debates.

This section serves to provide a more analytic introduction to the psychological contract and to provide an understanding of the key terms involved in defining the psychological contract.

Such an analysis is important for two main reasons. First, the debates presented here inform many of the later discussions of the strengths and weaknesses of psychological contract research, such as whether studies that claim to be about the psychological contract are actually about the psychological contract or some other related phenomenon. For example, while Kotter's study (1973) of the mutual expectations of new recruits and their employing organization was important in terms of introducing the concept of matching to the psychological contract literature, it is debatable whether this study of general expectations is actually relevant to psychological contracts, which consist of much more specific beliefs. A second important reason for analysing key terms embedded in the definition of the psychological contract is that it helps map out the territory of the psychological contract helping to identify, for example, the kind of cognitions that can be considered as part of or outside of the psychological contract.

It should be noted that this chapter is not about how the psychological contract works in terms of how psychological contracts are developed or how the psychological contract is linked to other attitudes or behaviours (this is discussed in later chapters), it is about what the psychological contract 'is'. In the conclusion to this chapter, we will provide our working definition of the psychological contract.

While this book is restricted to examining the psychological contract between employees and organizations, the idea of a 'psychological contract' as a system of implicit and explicit promises can be applied to almost any interpersonal relationship. This has been noted in a number of areas, where the concept of the psychological contract has been used to help understand relationships between students and teacher, patients and doctor, individuals and the state, and husbands and wives. Hence, some of the key terms in the definition of the psychological contract discussed below can also be understood by considering how they may apply to other sorts of interpersonal relationships.

3.2. What is the psychological contract?

When we want to know what something is we are essentially interested, as a starting point, in how it has been defined. Like many ideas in the social sciences and in organizational psychology there is no agreed definition of the psychological contract. Looking in a standard dictionary is unlikely to help as, unlike some other concepts in organizational psychology such as culture, leadership, stress, and motivation, the psychological contract is not a term that is used in everyday language but rather one constructed by researchers.

For some concepts in organizational psychology there is a single broadly agreed definition which researchers can refer to and also challenge. In the case of the psychological contract, however, there is no one authoritative statement or agreed definition of the psychological contract. As discussed earlier, the term was first introduced by two psychologists, Argyris and Menninger, who were working in different disciplines and were apparently unaware of one another's work. Seen in the context of their other work it was an idea of relatively minor importance, and each used it to explain very different phenomena. The term was subsequently picked up and repeatedly redefined, often for the purposes of explaining yet more different kinds of phenomena.

Given this context, it is perhaps unsurprising that there have been a variety of definitions of the psychological contract since the term was first introduced. Box 3.1 presents a sample of definitions starting first with a definition based on March and Simon's inducement-contribution model (1958) to provide some historical context followed by more formal definitions.

Box 3.1 Definition of the psychological contract

'Those participants in an organization who are called its employees are offered a variety of material and non-material incentives, generally not directly related to the attainment of the organization objective . . . in return for their behaviour during the time of their employment. . . . In joining the organization, he (the employee) accepts an authority relation, i.e. he agrees that within some limits (defined both explicitly and implicitly by the terms of the employment contract) he will accept as the premise of his behaviours orders and instructions supplied by the organizations.' (March and Simon 1958: 90)

'Since the foremen realize the employees in this system will tend to produce optimally under passive leadership, and since the employees agree, a relationship may be hypothesized to evolve between the employees and the foremen which might be called the "psychological work contract".' (Argyris 1960: 97)

'A series of mutual expectations of which the parties to the relationship may not themselves be dimly aware but which nonetheless govern their relationship to each other.' (Levinson et al. 1962: 21)

'An implicit contract between an individual and his organization which specifies what each expect to give and receive from each other in the relationship.' (Kotter 1973: 92)

'The notion of a psychological contract implies that there is an unwritten set of expectations operating at all times between every member of an organization and the various managers and others in that organization.' (Schein 1980: 22)

(continues)

Box 3.1 Definition of the psychological contract (*continued*)

'The term psychological contract refers to an individual's belief regarding the terms and conditions of a reciprocal exchange agreement between the focal person and another party. Key issues here include the belief that a promise has been made and a consideration offered in exchange for it, binding the parties to some set of reciprocal obligations.' (Rousseau 1989: 123)

'In simple terms, the psychological contract encompasses the actions employees believe are expected of them and what response they expect in return from the employer.' (Rousseau and Greller 1994: 386)

'The psychological contract is individual beliefs, shaped by the organization, regarding terms of an exchange agreement between the individual and their organization.' (Rousseau 1995: 9)

'The perceptions of both parties to the employment relationship, organization and individual, of the obligations implied in the relationship.' (Herriot and Pemberton 1997: 45)

'An employee's beliefs about the reciprocal obligations between that employee and his or her organization, where these obligations are based on perceived promises and are not necessarily recognised by agents of the organization.' (Morrison and Robinson 1997: 229)

The above quotations clearly illustrate that, while there are similarities, there is also very marked variation across definitions. There is also little indication of a developing consensus. For example, while Herriot and Pemberton consider the psychological contract to consist of both the employee and the organization's perspective, Rousseau, Morrison, and Robinson believe that it is only employees—not organizations—that can hold psychological contracts.

The following sections present and discuss the key definitional terms and features of the psychological contract found across this diverse range of definitions. Specifically, we include:

- The *beliefs* constituting the psychological contract
- The *implicit* nature of psychological contracts
- The *subjective* nature of the psychological contract
- *Perceived agreement*—not actual agreement—is necessary for psychological contracts
- The psychological contract is about *exchange*
- The psychological contract is the *entire set* of an employee's beliefs regarding the ongoing exchange relationship with his/her employer

- The psychological contract is an *ongoing* exchange between two parties
- The *parties* to the psychological contract
- The psychological contract is *shaped* by the organization

In each section we first explain the meaning of the terms and then describe major debates or differing views about these terms. As we shall see, these debates cannot be dismissed as trivial nit-picking among researchers, but do in fact, as suggested earlier, have very important implications for how the psychological contract should be understood, researched, and applied in a work setting. We hope that a firm foundation for exploring the psychological contract in subsequent chapters is provided by examining the definitions and unpacking the meaning of the psychological contract in this way.

3.2.1. The *beliefs* constituting the psychological contract

Earlier definitions of the psychological contract tend to emphasize beliefs about expectations (e.g. Levinson et al. 1962; Schein 1965; Kotter 1973), whereas later definitions emphasize beliefs about promises and obligations (e.g. Rousseau 1989, 1995; Herriot and Pemberton 1997; Morrison and Robinson 1997) which seem like rather different sorts of belief. In Rousseau's seminal paper (1989) the psychological contract is conceptualized as consisting of promissory-based obligations—far more specific than earlier expectation-focused definitions—which set her conceptualization apart (Roehling 1996).

Since Rousseau's 1989 article, studies of the psychological contract have tended to maintain the promissory focus (e.g. Rousseau and McLean Parks 1993; Guzzo, Noonan, and Elron 1994; McLean Parks and Kidder 1994; Robinson, Kraatz, and Rousseau 1994; Robinson and Rousseau 1994; Robinson 1995, 1996; Morrison and Robinson 1997). Promises have become the preferred term when defining the psychological contract as they are seen as more clearly contractual, whereas expectations and obligations have more general meanings. According to this approach, obligations and expectations are considered part of the psychological contract only if they are based on a perceived promise. Table 3.1 defines and provides examples of promises, obligations and expectations and whether these beliefs need some sort of further specification or qualification before they can be considered to be part of the psychological contract.

We now consider differences between promises and expectations, and between promises and obligations. For Robinson and Rousseau (1994: 246) the psychological contract refers to beliefs which are fundamentally different from beliefs around general expectations:

> Expectations refer simply to what the employee expects to receive from his or her employer (Wanous 1977). The psychological contract, on the other hand, refers to the

Table 3.1 Definitions of psychological contract beliefs and examples

Belief	Definition	Part of psychological contract?	Example
Promise	1. 'a commitment to do (or not do) something' (Rousseau and McLean Parks 1993) 2. 'an assurance that one will or will not undertake a certain action, behaviour' (*Concise Oxford Dictionary*, 1996)	Yes	Your employer has promised that if you work any overtime you can have time off *in lieu* the following day
Obligation	1. 'a feeling of inner compulsion, from whatever source, to act in a certain way towards another, or towards the community; in a narrower sense a feeling arising from benefits received, prompting to service in return; less definite than duty, and not involving, as in the latter, the ability to act in accordance with it.' (Drever, *Dictionary of Psychology*, 1958) 2. 'the constraining power of a law, precept, duty, contract, etc.' (*Concise Oxford Dictionary*, 1996)	Only when accompanied by a belief that a promise has been made	You work overtime today and you feel that your employer is obliged to give you time off tomorrow. (Note: Part of psychological contract only if accompanied by a promise of the type above.) You work overtime today and you feel that your employer is morally obliged to give you time off tomorrow, even though no agreement has been made. (Not part of the psychological contract.)
Expectation	1. 'expectations take many forms from beliefs in the probability of future events to normative beliefs' (Rousseau & McLean Parks 1993) 2. 'the attitude of waiting attentively for something usually to a certain extent defined, however vaguely' (Drever, *Dictionary of Psychology*, 1958) 3. 'the act or an instance of expecting of looking forward; the probability of an event' (*Concise Oxford Dictionary*, 1996)	Only when accompanied by a belief that a promise has been made	You plan to take a morning off next week and expect to have to work overtime the evening before. (Note: Part of psychological contract only if accompanied by a promise of the type above.) You worked overtime a few weeks and expect that it will be permitted for you to take a morning off when you next feel like it. (Not part of the psychological contract.)

perceived mutual obligations that characterize the employee's relationship with his/her employer. The psychological contract, unlike expectations, entails a belief in what the employer is obliged to provide, based on perceived promises of reciprocal exchange.

Promises are regarded as a special case of expectations (Rousseau and McLean Parks 1993). In other words, while all promises involve expectations, expectations do not necessarily involve a promissory element (Rousseau and McLean Parks 1993). For example, expectations may be based on probabilistic beliefs about future events (e.g. 'I'm probably going to get a pay rise at some point') or normative beliefs about what should happen (e.g. 'I think that if employees perform well they should get promoted'). In contrast, promises are grounded in a *contract* and we expect them to be delivered because the other party has communicated or behaved in such a way that leads us to believe a promise has been made. For example, we may believe we will get a pay rise after a certain period of time because we observe others in the organization getting pay rises after particular length of service. Or, we may believe we will get promoted because our line manager told us that we would within the next year. In this sense, promises are much more psychologically engaging than more general expectations (Conway 1996; Guest 1998). Expectations, such as those based on probability or normative beliefs, are a fairly constant and somewhat stable feature of our conscious experience. We just generally expect that some things are more or less likely to happen and that some things should or should not happen. However, once we believe a promise has been made we tend to anticipate the actual delivery of promises, doing things such as checking whether or not the promise has been kept, foregoing possible alternatives, planning what we will do once the promises have been delivered, and making sure we in turn deliver on our side of the bargain. In other words, an expectation is a more general belief about whether something will or should happen or not whereas a promise is a much more specific belief about what will happen, when it will happen, and why it will happen.

We now turn to the somewhat less clear differences between promises and obligations. Only Morrison and Robinson (1997: 228, italics added) have compared the two, stating that: '. . . if a perceived obligation is not accompanied by the belief that a promise has been conveyed (e.g. if the perceived obligation is based *solely* on past experience in other employment relationships), then it falls outside of the psychological contract'. In other words—and in a similar way to expectations—only obligations arising from implicit or explicit promises are part of psychological contracts. Perceived obligations arising from elsewhere, such as relationships pre-dating the current employer, or from an employee's moral values, are not part of the psychological contract. For example, a new employee may believe, based only on their experience of previous jobs, that the organization has an obligation to provide the right tools for the job, or that for moral reasons organizations should guarantee job security; however, if such beliefs have not been promised by the organization, they are not part of the psychological contract.

While the differences between expectations, obligations, and promises are very important, for the sorts of reasons discussed above, they are not clearly elaborated or widely discussed in the literature on psychological contracts, reflecting the field's apparently limited concern for definitional or conceptual clarity and precision. Even in Rousseau's work, which pays particular attention to the promissory focus of psychological contracts, rather general definitions of psychological contracts are presented (see the definitions by Rousseau in Box 3.1) that are only later qualified to reflect the promissory element (Roehling 1996). While efforts to distinguish between promises, obligations, and expectations are important, these distinctions may be hard to identify in practice and further clarification is required. For example, which criteria could be used to compare the three types of beliefs? What is the status of expectations that arise through inferences made by the employee from promises made to them by the organization? In short, although the idea of beliefs is at the heart of most definitions of the psychological contract, and three types of beliefs have been included within these definitions, the meanings of and differences between these definitions are not well-understood. Since Rousseau's article in 1989 researchers tend to define the psychological contract in terms of implicit and explicit promises. Promises offer more conceptual clarity and precision than obligations and expectations and are also more closely aligned with the idea of a contract. For these reasons we will use promises as the main belief constituting psychological contracts. In other words, from hereon we use promises to also refer to obligations and expectations that arise from promises and can thus be seen as part of the psychological contract. We shall use expectations and obligations when other researchers refer specifically to these terms.

3.2.2. The *implicit* nature of psychological contracts

Psychological contracts are usually considered to contain both explicit and implicit promises. Explicit promises arise from verbal or written agreements made by the organization or an agent of the organization. An example of an explicit promise would be a promise, made by a manager to an employee, of promotion to the next grade in return for meeting specific sales targets.

Implicit promises on the other hand arise through 'interpretations of patterns of past exchange, vicarious learning (e.g. witnessing other employees' experiences) as well as through various factors that each party may take for granted (e.g. good faith or fairness)' (Robinson and Rousseau 1994: 246). It is argued that the terms of a psychological contract are implied by the behaviour of the parties to the contract and also by inferences made from existing verbal and written promises. Repeated interactions between the two parties where each observes the other's behaviour and responses create what the employee perceives as an implicit psychological contract that structures their future relationship (Rousseau 1990). For example, an implicit promise may be formed when the organization makes the employee feel valued through extra thanks or recognition on occasions when he or she has made an extra effort on behalf of the organization. Hence, on future occasions when the employee makes an extra effort on behalf of the organization they will come to expect a response from the organization showing that they are valued, because of their psychological contract relating to this particular behaviour.

An important debate concerns just how implicit or unstated promises have to be in order to be included as part of the psychological contract. Clearly, a formal, written contract stating what an employee is expected to do and what the employer will give them in return seems more appropriately labelled as a tangible or legal or employment contract rather than a 'psychological' contract (though tangible employment contracts may shape psychological contracts). The issue, therefore, is the extent to which promises need to be implicit to be considered part of the psychological contract.

Some researchers believe psychological contracts consist largely of implicit promises (Levinson et al. 1962; Schein 1965, 1980; Guest 1998; Meckler, Drake, and Levinson 2003). As Schein (1965: 11) stated, expectations contained in psychological contracts 'are not written into any formal agreement between employer and the organization, yet they operate powerfully as determinants of behaviour'. For these researchers, contracts or promises at the explicit end of the continuum cannot be usefully described as psychological contracts. For other researchers all contracts can be seen as being fundamentally psychological (e.g. Macneil 1985; Rousseau 1995) because even quite explicit promises are open to interpretations of what constitutes sufficient exchange and the timing of the exchange. For example, the relatively explicit promise of a pay rise for perform-ance increases leads to more specific questions and interpretations around the level and timing of the pay rise and also the required performance increase.

The extent to which promises have to be implicit to be included in the psy-chological contract has both research and practical implications. Explicit prom-ises are believed to exert a greater influence over employees' thoughts and behaviours than more subtle implicit promises (Rousseau 1989). This view is supported by social information processing theory (Rousseau 1989) which sug-gests that overt and public commitments exert more influence on cognitions and behaviours than subtle or private ones (Salancik and Pfeffer 1978). Hence, includ-ing more explicit promises in the definition of the psychological contract is likely to make it a more powerful predictor of employee behaviour. From a practical perspective it has been suggested that one way to better manage psychological contracts is to make them more explicit (e.g. Herriot and Pemberton 1995), yet in doing so it is not clear whether we are managing the psychological contract as such or simply moving it from the realms of the psychological or the implicit to the realms of explicit or formal contracts. We will return to this latter issue in later chapters when we consider how the psychological contract can be managed.

While definitions of the psychological contract often cover both explicit and implicit beliefs and promises, there is relatively little agreement about how explicit a promise can be before it stops becoming part of the 'psychological' contract and is better considered simply the legal or employment contract.

3.2.3. The *subjective* nature of the psychological contract

The terms 'subjective' and 'objective' can mean a variety of things. Here we consider two ways in which the idea of 'subjective' has been used in relation to the psychological contract.

First, the subjective-objective distinction can refer to the extent people see things in the same way, where extreme objectivity would mean everyone seeing something in the same way and extreme subjectivity would mean everyone seeing things differently. Most definitions of the psychological contract empha-size that they are held at the individual level and exist in 'the eye of the beholder' (Rousseau and McLean Parks 1993: 18). They are inherently subjective as there are cognitive or information processing limits on the extent to which one party can understand the psychology of the other. In other words, an employee cannot fully understand the intentions and meanings of the behaviour of the organiza-tion, nor can the organization fully understand the employee, and for this reason such interpretations will be incomplete and subjective. In addition, the multiple and sometimes contradictory sources of information which influence the devel-opment and modification of psychological contracts also mean they remain subjective (Shore and Tetrick 1994). In contrast, a more objective psychological contract is where the contract terms are understood in the same way by parties to the contract and by any third party outside the relationship.

A second way of thinking about the subjective-objective distinction relates to the extent to which perceptions can in principle be 'objectively' verified. For example, in the case of the psychological contract, this might mean the extent to which the terms of the contract are explicit or measurable. There is currently little clarity around this issue within the psychological contract literature. Even when items that form part of the exchange appear objective, they remain open to subjective interpretation. Macneil (1985) argues that all contracts, whether writ-ten or unwritten, are fundamentally subjective as contract terms are inevitably open to an individual's subjective interpretation. While it seems reasonable that employees interpret certain psychological contract items or terms more subject-ively than others (a tangible exchange of an amount of money for a number of hours attendance is less subjective than an exchange of employee loyalty in return for respect from management), the extent to which more objective items such as pay are open to subjective interpretation is unclear. Building on this point—that it is impossible to establish the objectivity of any item exchanged and hence every item is inherently subjective—it is also doubtful whether em-ployees would include highly subjective items in their psychological contract (e.g. employee loyalty in return for respect from management) as such terms are so open to interpretation they will have little confidence that their organization could possibly agree to an exchange including such ambiguous terms.

In summary, while psychological contracts are inherently subjective, certain terms of the psychological contract are more open to subjectivity than others. The extent to which items and terms of the psychological contract are subjectively perceived and whether highly subjective terms can form part of psychological contracts is not well understood.

3.2.4. Perceived agreement—not actual agreement—is necessary for psychological contracts

Unlike legal contracts, where 'agreement, or at least the outward appearance of agreement, is an essential ingredient of a contract' (Cheshire, Fifoot, and Furmston 1991: 70), for Rousseau (1990) agreement, or mutuality as it is sometimes referred, is not necessary for psychological contracts. Each party believes that there is agreement on the contract, but there does not have to be actual agreement where both parties have the same understanding of the contract (Robinson and Rousseau 1994). Rousseau (1990: 391) does not see mutuality as important, 'Two parties to a relationship, such as an employee and employer, may each hold different beliefs regarding the existence and terms of a psychological contract. . . . Mutuality is not a requisite condition'.

An important debate concerns whether agreement over psychological contracts should be defined as wholly at the level of an individual's perception or whether some degree of actual agreement between parties is required. In other words, is the psychological contract only the individual employee's beliefs about the exchange relationship or is it where those same beliefs are also held by the organization? Arnold (1996) has drawn attention to the confusion surrounding the meaning of agreement in relation to psychological contracts. A strong sense of agreement would cover both the terms of the contract and what is exchanged for what. Earlier work on the psychological contract (e.g. Levinson et al. 1962; Schein 1965; Kotter 1973) assumed at least a weaker form of agreement, in that both employees and management understood in broad terms what constituted the exchange. In fact, for Argyris agreement was at the heart of the psychological contract between management and workers, as he argued in his case study of a manufacturing plant that managers knowingly overlooked certain 'deviant' behaviours, such as ad hoc tea-breaks, provided employees were broadly compliant with managers' wishes. As noted by Arnold (1996), Rousseau's position implies the psychological contract can be a purely individual interpretation.

The role of mutuality is important because it determines the most appropriate level of analysis. If the psychological contract is predominantly a subjective construct, then analysis at the individual level seems appropriate; if it involves agreement across parties, then analysis at the relational level (i.e. contractual beliefs that are shared by both parties) may be more appropriate.

3.2.5. The psychological contract is about *exchange*

Psychological contracts refer to the perceived exchange agreement between the two parties. In other words, things offered by the organization, or by employees, are conditional on something the other party does in return: 'promises of future behaviour (in this case on the part of the employer) typically are contingent on some reciprocal action by the employee' (Rousseau 1990: 390). The issue of reciprocity is important because, if the assumption of reciprocity is not valid, it then becomes difficult to continue to regard the psychological contract as a 'contract'. Essentially contracts are about 'deals'—something that is exchanged for something else. A one-off gift from one person to another is not a psychological contract as the recipient has not promised to do anything in return. (If upon receipt of the gift the individual feels obliged to reciprocate, then an exchange begins. If the exchange of gifts becomes a consistent and repeated pattern of behaviour between parties, then a psychological contract is formed.)

Figure 3.1 presents an example of a very simple and general psychological contract exchange in which a wide range of organizational inducements are exchanged for a range of employee contributions. Under such a general exchange, exactly how this exchange works or what particular inducement is exchanged for which particular employee contribution is not stated.

While there appears to be agreement that the psychological contract involves exchange, an important debate relates to the specificity of the exchange. In other words, while we may know the list of employee contributions performed in exchange for the list of organization inducements, we do not know the precise ways in which this exchange takes places as described in Figure 3.1. For example, we do not know what specific contributions employees provide in return for, say, pay, promotion, or training.

Rousseau (1990) has called for research into what outcomes the parties to the psychological contract expect from each other in response to their discrete contributions. This is not only an important theoretical and empirical issue: a more precise understanding of the exchange may also have practical importance so that organizations and employees better understand how specific contributions are likely to be exchanged for certain inducements. Returning to the example of pay, a question arises as to how, if at all, employee contributions would

Organization offers		Employee offers
Pay Training Respect Promotion	◄——►	Effort Skills Flexibility Creativity

Figure 3.1 General example of psychological contract exchange

change if pay were increased. Figure 3.2 presents a more specific type of exchange where an employee perceives that their effort and a desire to develop skills is necessary in order to be promoted, whereas, for the receipt of training, only a desire to develop skills is essentially required.

While there is agreement across definitions that the psychological contract is about the 'deal' or the exchange relationship between employer and employee, the nature of this exchange is not always clear. While the exchange is often presented in very general terms—with a range of employer inducements some-how being offered as a 'package' in exchange for a 'package' of employee contri-butions—it seems likely that the exchanges are much more specific.

3.2.6. The psychological contract is the *entire set* of an employee's beliefs regarding the ongoing exchange relationship with his or her employer

There is agreement across definitions that an employee's psychological contract includes his or her beliefs about the entire range of possible exchanges that could take place between themselves and their employer. In other words, it potentially includes beliefs about anything and everything the employee could give to the employer and anything and everything they could receive in return, and the nature of that exchange. The psychological contract does 'not only cover how much work is to be performed for how much pay, but also involves the whole pattern of rights, privileges, and obligations between worker and organization' (Schein 1965: 11). The psychological contract is much broader than a legal or employment contract: 'it may have literally thousands of items... although the employee may consciously think of only a few' (Kotter 1973: 92).

Adopting a definition that sets no limits on the number or nature of the items that can be regarded as part of an employee's psychological contract seems reasonable as it is clearly possible for an employee to perceive a psychological contract in relation to any aspect of their work or working conditions. However, researchers have tended to focus on a set of employer inducements (e.g. pay, training, promotion, respect) and employee contributions (e.g. effort, ability, creativity, honesty) which, it is assumed, lie at the heart of the employment relationship. Within this core set certain elements have been singled-out as

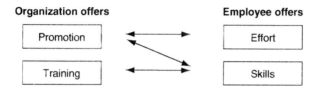

Figure 3.2 More specific example of psychological contract exchange

more important than others, such as psychological contracts around careers (Herriot and Pemberton 1996) and psychological contracts formed during performance appraisals (Stiles et al. 1997). The focus on core items has led to the neglect of the wide and diverse range of possible exchanges in everyday working life.

3.2.7. The psychological contract is an *ongoing* exchange between two parties

Schein (1980) sees the exchange as 'ongoing' in the sense that the psychological contract is in operation at all times and unfolds through mutual bargaining and constant renegotiations, although he does not elaborate on the contents of these negotiations (Rousseau 1989). The 'ongoingness' of the exchange refers to repeated cycles of each party fulfilling their promises to one another.

That psychological contracts are ongoing is a crucial feature of their definition: it is what distinguishes psychological contracts from simpler one-off exchanges. However, definitions of the psychological contract have largely ignored the ongoing aspect of psychological contracts. The meaning of ongoing, unfolding psychological contracts is an issue we discuss at length in Chapter 8.

3.2.8. The *parties* to the psychological contract

Definitions of the psychological contract refer to two parties to the contract: the employee and the organization. The employee, as one of the parties to the contract, is relatively easy to identify, as the psychological contract is, as discussed earlier, viewed as being held at the level of the individual employee. It is generally argued, therefore, that psychological contracts cannot be held by groups, or by third persons.

While the employee as one of the parties to the contract is relatively easy to identify, who, or what, represents the organization or the employer? Is it a specific line manager? The managing director? The human resources department? It has been argued that employees do not perceive any particular person or agent as being the 'organization'. Rather, employees view actions by the organization as an overall view of actions by agents of the organization, such as line managers, and signals from the organization, such as its human resource practices and company documentation. Through actions by the organization's agents, employees ascribe the organization with human qualities capable of reciprocation, a process referred to as anthropomorphizing the organization (Levinson et al. 1962; Schein 1965; Eisenberger et al. 1986; Rousseau 1989; Sims 1994; Morrison and Robinson 1997). For example, an organization becomes capable of being caring, loyal, generous, and so on, as the employee interprets actions by the organization's agents as action by the organization itself.

While most definitions emphasize the individual employee as the main 'holder' of the psychological contract, an area of ongoing debate concerns whether organizations, as the other party to the contract, can and do have psychological contracts. In other words, can organizations have beliefs about the exchange between the organization and its employees in the same or similar ways that employees do? Early conceptualizations (e.g. Argyris 1960; Levinson et al. 1962; Schein 1965, 1980; Kotter 1973) and some more recent definitions (e.g. Herriot and Pemberton 1997; Guest 1998; Coyle-Shapiro and Kessler 1998; Guest and Conway 2002; Tsui and Wang 2002) consider the psychological contract to consist of the beliefs of *both* the employee and the employer. The employer's perspective is held by key agents, such as the line manager or senior manager, or through characteristics of groups or organizations, such as its culture. However, Rousseau and others (e.g. Rousseau and McLean Parks 1993; Morrison and Robinson 1997) argue that the psychological contract is largely concerned with the employee's perspective. According to this view, organizations as abstract entities do not have psychological contracts, although organizational agents such as line managers can have a psychological contract with employees.

> The organization, as the other party in the relationship, provides the context for the creation of a psychological contract, but cannot in turn have a psychological contract with its members. Organizations cannot 'perceive', though their individual managers can themselves personally perceive a psychological contract with employees and respond accordingly. (Rousseau 1989: 126)

On the one hand this position seems reasonable. An organization as an abstract entity cannot have a psychological contract. However, a key problem with Rousseau's position is that, while researchers should not make the mistake of treating the organization as if it can have a psychological contract in the same way that a person can, definitions of the psychological contract state that employees do and indeed must treat the organization in this way if they are to have a psychological contract, as definitions of the psychological contract generally refer to the 'organization' rather than a specific individual, although occasionally definitions refer to individual agents (e.g. the use of 'foreman' by Argyris in Box 3.1).

At present, our understanding of the employer's perspective is at a very early stage. For now it should be noted that, in the main, it is assumed that employees unproblematically treat the organization as if it were a single contract maker as the other party to the psychological contract. To summarize, while there is agreement as to who represents the employee, what constitutes the organization is less clear, and the issue of whether organizations can have psychological contracts remains an area of ongoing controversy.

3.2.9. The psychological contract is *shaped by the organization*

Many definitions consider that the psychological contract consists of those beliefs about the exchange relationship that are shaped or formed by the employees' interaction with and experience with their *current* employing organization. In other words, beliefs that are formed or shaped by factors outside the organization or that have been formed or shaped in previous employment relationships are not necessarily regarded as part of the psychological contract.

However, researchers disagree about the extent to which an employees' psychological contract is shaped by factors external or internal to the organization. Earlier definitions state that the psychological contract is considerably shaped by experiences that pre-date the relationship between the employee and the organization (Levinson et al. 1962; Schein 1980). According to Schein (1980: 24), employees forge their expectations from 'their inner needs, what they have learned from others, traditions and norms which may be operating, their own past experience, and a host of other sources'.

However, more recent conceptualizations from Rousseau and others (e.g. Rousseau and Wade-Benzoni 1994; Rousseau and Greller 1994; Morrison and Robinson 1997) give less emphasis to the influence of experiences pre-dating the current employment relationship in shaping the psychological contract and instead consider the organization to be chiefly responsible for shaping the psychological contract (Roehling 1996). Defining the psychological contract in this way means that even though employees may believe the organization makes promises to them, if these promises do not originate from or are not shaped by the current organization then the beliefs are not part of the psychological contract. For example, employees may believe they will get promoted, as they did in their previous job, for being hard-working. However, if their current organization has not implied or promised this exchange nor shaped this belief in any way then, according to some perspectives, this belief is not part of the psychological contract. Ultimately it is difficult to separate out beliefs that are completely unshaped or uninfluenced by the current organization from beliefs that are in some way, however subtly, shaped by or influenced by the current organization.

These differing positions can perhaps be reconciled by considering that, in theory, as a party to a psychological contract, we would not expect to be judged and held accountable for promises and obligations that the other party may have expected from previous relationships. Nevertheless, it is also likely that each party's view of the relationship and what they want from it is influenced by our previous experience in relationships and our needs. Note that it is earlier writers on the psychological contract that stress the importance of factors outside the relationship on the psychological contract (Levinson et al. 1962; Schein 1965) and this may reflect their more general definition of expectations as constituting the psychological contract. The more recent emphasis on the psychological contract as a legal metaphor and the promissory nature of the psychological contract (Rousseau 1995; Guest 1998) would lend itself to drawing sharper distinctions on who are the parties to the contract and the lines of responsibility. If psychological contracts are about promises, then the role of individual needs becomes less clear. Under this conceptualization, needs are likely to be important in the terms of the types of promises we seek to establish and would like to see fulfilled, but should not be confused with the actual content of the psychological contract. We return to the role of needs in Chapter 4 when we discuss the range of factors that may influence the contents of the psychological contract.

3.3. Summary and conclusion

This chapter has considered various definitions of the psychological contract and the key terms within these definitions. This has revealed that the psychological contract has been defined in very different ways and in some cases referring to quite different phenomena. While many of the disagreements across definitions reflect how the meaning of the psychological contract has changed over time, certain disagreements are the subjects of current debate (see the special edition of *Journal of Organizational Behavior*, 1998; Meckler, Drake, and Levinson 2003).

Currently, the most widely agreed definition of the psychological contract, and the one we will adopt throughout this book, is that put forward by Rousseau, in which the psychological contract is considered to be an employee's subjective understanding of promissory-based reciprocal exchanges between him or herself and the organization. We have chosen this definition for three reasons. First, because it captures the essential features of a contract (i.e. exchange) while acknowledging the employee's individual subjective interpretation of its terms, and thus making it truly psychological, as opposed to a quasi-objective contract over which there is pretty much complete agreement across parties as to its terms. Second, promises are a clearer and more precise construct than obligations and expectations and are also more closely aligned with the idea of a contract. Third, we believe that by focusing on promises this definition is sufficiently conceptually distinct from other related ideas, such as met expectations and fairness perceptions. As stated earlier, we will use promises as the main belief constituting psychological contracts and only refer to expectations and obligations when other researchers use these terms in a specific sense.

Despite definitional ambiguities, research on the psychological contract continues to proliferate. Further, critics of Rousseau's conceptualization of the psychological contract (e.g. Arnold 1996; Guest 1998) do not reject the concept in favour of earlier definitions, but call for further research to clarify certain terms in the definition and to establish whether the psychological contract does explain outcome variables (such as organizational commitment) over and above related constructs, such as met expectations and equity theory.

A final conclusion is that the definitional issues and disagreements discussed in this chapter are fundamental to the whole field of psychological contract research and practice. Rather than being minor problems that can easily be sorted out they represent fundamental confusions in the foundations of the concept. For this reason, many of the issues discussed in this chapter will reappear in various forms throughout the remainder of the book.

4 | The Contents of Psychological Contracts

The contents of psychological contracts refer to the promises an employee believes they have made to their organization and what the employee believes the organization has promised in return. In other words, it is about what is actually in the deal between the employee and their organization—what is exchanged for what, rather than the process of how the psychological contract operates (which is covered in Chapter 5). The contents of psychological contracts are important because forming certain types of deals with different sorts of contents is likely to lead to more or less positive employee and organizational outcomes, such as job satisfaction and job performance. Most of the research in this area attempts to describe the types of deals that lead to desirable outcomes, and the contents of those deals.

This chapter explains what is meant by the contents of the psychological contract, evaluates empirical support for the contents of the psychological contract, considers the factors that form perceptions of promises and obligations, and examines how the contents have been categorized and related to outcomes.

4.1. The contents of the psychological contract

The contents of the psychological contract refer broadly to an employee's perceptions of the contributions they promise to give to their employer and what they believe the organization promises in return. Employee contributions include such things as making sufficient effort, offering skills and knowledge, having a concern for quality, and being flexible. The organization in return provides such things as promotion, training, pay, respect, and feedback. The contents have also been defined as an employee's 'expectations of what the employee feels she or he owes and is owed in turn by the organization' (Rousseau 1990: 393), and as what 'employees expect to give or contribute and what it is that employees expect to receive in return—their entitlements' (Parks, Kidder, and Gallagher 1998: 725). It is important to note that the contents of the psychological contract are not what employees *actually* give and get from their employer, but rather the contents are the *implicit and explicit promises* around this exchange.

As the above definitions suggest, the contents of the psychological contract consist of at least two different types of information. First, the information about *what* is exchanged—the resources each party is prepared to exchange. In other words, what specific things does each party to the psychological contract promise to offer the other? What do they have to give? Second, the information about *how* or the basis on which such exchanges will take place. This addresses the perhaps more complex issue of exactly how the exchange will work: what are the precise linkages between what the employee offers and what the organization offers? Many definitions and discussions of contents tend to emphasize only the first type of information.

A central aspect of the definition is therefore reciprocity, or the idea that the employee makes some form of contribution 'in return' for something back from the organization. This means that items in the employee's psychological contract—both what they promise and what they believe has been promised in return—have to be joined together in a reciprocal manner. In other words, according to these definitions, employee contributions are part of the content of the psychological contract if and only if the employee believes providing the contribution obligates the organization to deliver on a promise it has made. Likewise, organizational inducements and rewards are part of the content of the psychological contract if and only if they are given in return for an employee contribution. As we shall see later in more detail, a major limitation of measures of the contents of the psychological contract is that they assess contributions and inducements as independent entities and do not ask whether or how one is done in return for the other. For example, they may simply ask the employee what they think the organization should provide by way of inducements without asking the employee if they believe these inducements should be provided in return for the contributions the employee makes.

Before reviewing studies of the contents of psychological contracts, you may wish to refer to the Appendix in order to examine and perhaps complete some of the measures typically used in research to assess the content of the psychological contract.

4.2. Assessing the contents of the psychological contract

Even though research on the contents of the psychological contract is probably the second most heavily researched topic after psychological contract breach, relatively few studies have been conducted into this area. In this section we review and evaluate the main studies and how they have assessed the contents of the psychological contract.

The number of items that make up the content is potentially vast as definitions of contents include apparently anything and everything the employee promises to contribute to and anything promised in return from the oganization.

Researchers have, therefore, restricted their investigations of content to a limited subset of employee-perceived promises that are assumed to be the most important.

Rousseau (1990) generated content items by asking managers about promises and commitments they sought from graduate recruits during selection, and promises and commitments made to recruits. Promises sought from recruits included working extra hours, loyalty, volunteering to do non-required tasks on the job, advance notice if taking a job elsewhere, willingness to accept a transfer, refusal to support the employer's competitors, protection of proprietary information, and spending a minimum of two years in the organization. The promises made to recruits included promotion, high pay, pay based on current level of performance, training, long-term job security, career development, and support with personal problems. (This measure has been recently updated by Hui, Lee, and Rousseau 2004, and is presented in full in the Appendix.)

In a survey of expatriate managers, Guzzo, Noonan, and Elron (1994), generated forty-three items based on the human resource practices of the company participating in their study to broadly cover the three areas of financial inducements, general support, and family-orientated support (an abbreviated list of the items is presented in Table 4.1). This measure of content did not ask employees about *promises* made by the organization but rather about what they felt the organization *should* provide. What an organization should do has a broader meaning than what it has promised to do, including such things as, for example, how the organization should morally behave. As noted by Arnold (1996), using the term 'should' is not consistent with the promissory emphasis in most

Table 4.1 Assessing the content of the psychological contract—early studies

Rousseau's study (1990) of MBA graduates		Guzzo, Noonan & Elron's study (1994) of expatriate managers
Employer obligations	Employee obligations	Employer obligations
Promotion	Overtime	Housing allowance
High pay	Loyalty	Household furnishing allowance
Pay based on current level of performance	Volunteering to do non-required tasks on the job	Completion bonus
Training	Advance notice if taking a job elsewhere	Foreign service premium
Long-term job security		Emergency leave
Career development	Willingness to accept a transfer	Language training
Support with personal problems	Refusal to support the employer's competitors	Language training for family
	Protection of proprietary information	Social events
		Career development
	Spending a minimum of two years in the organization	Repatriation planning
		Domestic staff
		Assistance locating schools for children
		Spousal employment in firm

Notes: Indicative items are presented from Guzzo et al.'s study from a list of 43 items.

conceptualizations of the psychological contract. Hence, it is not clear that the Guzzo et al. (1994) measure assesses psychological contract contents as such.

The items included in the studies by Rousseau and Guzzo et al. may appear rather idiosyncratic as they were designed to meet the particular requirements of the research context. For example, one of the items of Guzzo et al. asked employees if they expected language training for their family to be provided by their employer. Clearly not everyone would expect this, but the item makes sense given the sample of expatriate managers.

Probably the most thorough study of the contents of the psychological contract was undertaken by Herriot, Manning, and Kidd (1997) which explored both employee and organization's perspectives (captured through asking managers to give the organization's perspective) using the critical incident technique, asking about occasions where the organization and employee had fallen short of or positively exceeded expectations. The study assumed that for an expectation to be fallen short of or exceeded there must be an underlying promise that constitutes part of the content of psychological contracts. The incidents generated using this technique were subsequently clustered together under themes. The full list of items and the extent to which they were reported by employees and organizations are presented in Table 4.2. For example, 4.2 per cent of employees expected their organization to provide recognition for special contributions, compared with 10.8 per cent of managers answering from an organization's perspective. From the employee's perspective, the most frequently mentioned obligations of the organization were to provide a safe and congenial environment to work in, job security, equitable rates of pay, and procedural fairness in return for employees working their contracted hours, working hard, and being honest; from the organization's perspective the most frequently mentioned obligations expected of employees were to work the contracted hours, to do a good job in terms of quality and quantity, and to be honest and in return they expected to provide humanity, recognition, benefits, and fairness. Herriot, Manning, and Kidd (1997) concluded that employee and organization views differ particularly on the organization's obligations to employees: employees tend to place importance on more basic aspects of work such as pay and fairness whereas organizations emphasize relational aspects of work such as humanity and recognition.

As with the Guzzo et al. (1994) measure it is not clear that the Herriot et al. (1997) approach to assessing the content of the psychological contract is consistent with psychological contract theory and, therefore, whether it is actually assessing the psychological contract. First, the study focused on perceived deviations from *expectations*, yet, as argued by Robinson and Rousseau (1994), expectations are a more general form of belief, not obligations or promises, and not therefore necessarily part of the psychological contract. Second, as the study asked about occasions when organizations fell short of or exceed expectations, it could be argued that the data collected tell us more about the contents of violations and exceeded expectations than the contents of psychological contracts as such.

Table 4.2 The content of the psychological contract in the UK

	% of incidents falling into item category	
What employees can expect from organization	Employee's perspective	Organization's perspective
Providing adequate *training*	9.6	8.3
Fairness in selection, appraisal, promotion, and redundancy procedures	10.8	12.9
Meeting personal and family *needs*	5.7	4.8
Consultation on matters affecting employees	5.3	4.8
Discretion in how employees do their job	5.3	2.0
Humanity, acting in a responsible and supportive way towards employees	7.3	14.3
Recognition for special contributions	4.2	10.8
Safe and congenial *environment*	15.0	8.7
Justice in the application of rules and discipline	5.4	4.2
Pay—equitable with respect to market and across the company	11.9	6.3
Benefits—fairness and consistency of	9.6	16.4
Providing *job security* as much as is possible	9.6	6.3
What organization can expect from employees		
To work contracted *hours*	32.1	28.1
To do a *good job* in terms of quantity and quality	19.4	22.3
To be *honest*	15.2	16.9
Loyalty—staying with the organization and putting its interests first	4.2	11.6
Treating the organization's *property* respectfully	8.4	3.7
Self-presentation—dressing and behaving correctly	10.5	5.8
Flexibility—willing to go beyond job description when required	10.1	11.6

Notes: Adapted from Herriot, Manning, and Kidd (1997), reflecting a representative sample of UK employees (*N*=184) and UK managers (*N*=184).

However, a nationally representative questionnaire study of 1,000 UK workers found broadly similar results (Guest and Conway 1998). Guest and Conway's study was not meant to be a comprehensive examination of the content of psychological contracts, but does reveal the incidence of key promises. In this study, only the employee's perception was sought about promises made to them by the organization. Employees were much more likely to report that their organization had made promises regarding traditional areas of the psychological contract. For instance, 82 per cent believed the organization had promised to ensure fair treatment by managers and supervisors, 76 per cent reported promises of job security, and 72 per cent reported promises of fair pay for work performed. This compares with 60 per cent who believed their organization had promised a career, 55 per cent reported promises of interesting work, and only 36 per cent believed their organization had promised to deal with problems encountered by the employee outside work.

While each of these studies may help shed some light on the contents of the psychological contract, each also has specific methodological limitations that cast doubt on whether what is being assessed is actually the content of the psychological content as described by theory. A general weakness of all of these studies is that they fail to assess the *exchange* aspects of promises. In other words they do not explicitly assess what employees do *in return* for what they get from employers—those behaviours which are performed in exchange for some organizational inducement. As mentioned earlier, the exclusion of the exchange information of contents is also seen in many definitions and discussions of contents. In some cases these studies simply assume that exchange underlies the promises assessed (e.g. Herriot, Manning, and Kidd 1997) and in others exchange is inferred through statistical techniques (e.g. Rousseau 1990). However, to be true to theory, only psychological contract items that are shown to be part of an exchange can be considered as part of the psychological contract.

For example, respondents might be asked to what extent their employer has promised to provide, say, pay, without specifying what pay is conditional upon the employee providing and thus failing to assess the reciprocal arrangement. To be true to the definition of the contents of the psychological contract, this detail is essential. Rousseau and Tijoriwala (1998) give the example that two employees receiving $60,000 annual salaries do not have the same psychological contract if one is paid this amount based on years of service, whereas the other is expected to reach certain performance targets. If this is the case, which seems reasonable, then most attempts to assess content do not accurately capture the psychological contract as they do not gather information about the nature of the exchange.

The only published measure of the contents of the psychological contract that does in part capture exchange is Millward and Hopkin's (1998) Psychological Contract Scale (PCS), used recently in a revised form by Raja, Johns, and Ntalianis (2004; see Appendix for the items used in this measure). Questionnaire items capturing contents were derived from the literature, several of which explicitly tap exchange through making organizational rewards contingent upon employee contributions. Example items include: 'I have a reasonable chance of promotion if I work hard'; 'I am motivated to contribute 100% to this company in return for future employment benefits'. The PCS is a first attempt to capture the exchange between what the organization offers and the employee provides, albeit that the majority of items contained within the measure do not capture exchange and the exchange referred to in the items that do is very broad and rather vague. Furthermore, the PCS does not directly measure psychological contract beliefs of promises, but rather beliefs about the employment relationship more generally.

We have presented a fairly comprehensive review of the empirical evidence about contents. As indicated earlier, although studying contents is probably the second most common type of study published, the number of relevant studies remains very small. In addition, these studies have considerable methodological limitations. What we actually know about the contents of psychological contracts appears to be highly dependent on the method used and, in turn, is therefore limited by the known weaknesses of that method. For instance, questionnaires are largely only able to assess quite general impressions and attitudes and hence our knowledge of the contents of psychological contracts from such studies is restricted to very general descriptions of items, such as 'fair pay', which ultimately reveal little about the nature of the contents.

In spite of the limited quantity and quality of data it is possible to draw some very tentative conclusions as to what we know about the contents of the psychological contract. First, the measurement of contents varies considerably across studies. Second, psychological contracts are much more likely to contain certain promises (e.g. reasonable working conditions) than others (e.g. good pay). Third, perceptions of content differ considerably between employer and employee. As we will go on to discuss later, much empirical and theoretical work remains to be done before we have a stronger grasp of the contents of psychological contracts.

4.3. How have the contents of psychological contracts been categorized?

As indicated earlier, given the definitions of psychological contract contents, the number of items involved could be very large indeed. One means of simplifying and managing such long lists is to categorize items to reflect what are supposed to be particular types or dimensions of psychological contracts. Several typologies have been suggested, such as the extent to which the contract is individualized or standardized (Shore and Tetrick 1994), however another distinction—between transactional and relational contracts—has dominated the research. In this section we discuss transactional and relational psychological contracts and review the evidence for, and usefulness of, such a distinction.

The transactional–relational distinction is based on the work of the legal scholar MacNeil (1974, 1980) and has been adapted for organizational research by Rousseau and others (e.g. Rousseau 1990, 1995; Robinson and Rousseau 1994; Robinson, Kraatz, and Rousseau 1994; Millward and Hopkins 1998; Raja, Johns, and Ntalianis 2004). Turning first to transactional contracts, these involve highly specific exchanges, of narrow scope, which take place over a finite period (Robinson, Rousseau, and Kraatz 1994). The terms and conditions of transactional contracts are likely to be publicly available (e.g. through a written contract) and concerned fundamentally with an economic transaction (e.g. amount of pay for specified level of performance). Negotiation of transactional contracts is likely to be explicit and require formal agreement by both parties.

Relational contracts, in contrast, are broader, more amorphous, open-ended, and subjectively understood by the parties to the exchange. They are concerned with the exchange of personal, socio-emotional, and value-based, as well as economic resources. Relational contracts are characterized by trust and belief in good faith and fairness, and involve exchanges with longer-term time frames such as the exchange of employee commitment for job security (Rousseau 1990).

Table 4.3 Comparing transactional and relational contracts

	Transactional psychological contracts	Relational psychological contracts
Time frame	Short-term, time-bounded promises	Long-term, open-ended promises
Degree of specificity	Highly specified	Loosely specified, amorphous
Resources exchanged	Tangible, having a monetary value	Intangible, likely to be socio-emotional
Explicitness of promises	Explicit	Implicit
Negotiation	Likely to be explicit and require formal agreement by both parties	Implicit and unlikely to involve actual agreement by both parties.
Examples	Pay in exchange for number of hours worked	Job security in exchange for employee loyalty

Negotiation of relational contracts is much more likely to be implicit, occurring through the ongoing evolution of the relationship between employer and employee, and to be the result of, for example, subtle behavioural change by one of the parties without any verbal or written communication between the two parties.

There is sometimes confusion as to whether transactional and relationship contracts are simple opposites, or whether they can coexist so that, in effect, an employee may have both a transactional and a relational contract. Rousseau has argued that rather than two distinct types, transactional and relational contracts are best regarded as the extreme opposite ends of a single continuum underlying contractual arrangements (Rousseau 1990; Rousseau and McLean Parks 1993). In other words, the more relational the contract becomes, the less transactional and vice versa. However, empirical investigations of the two types of contracts conducted by Rousseau and others find that lists of psychological contract content items separate into two independent factors (e.g. Rousseau 1990; Coyle-Shapiro and Kessler 2000), thus supporting the idea that they do not lie on the same single continuum but rather that transactional and relational contracts should be considered as relatively independent dimensions that can vary freely irrespective of one another. While transactional and relational contract may appear opposites (see Table 4.3) the same employee can have both due to the two types of contract including different items (e.g. an employee with a very simple psychological contract including 'pay for hours worked' and 'loyalty in return for security' has both a transactional and relational psychological contract). The evidence for this distinction is discussed in more detail later. However, this position appears to make greater theoretical sense, as it seems likely that an employment relationship could have high or low levels of both transactional and relational elements.

A recent variant of the transactional/relational distinction can be found in the work of Bunderson (2001) who argues that the ideologies around administrative and professional work are sufficiently different that there may also be administrative and professional dimensions of the psychological contract. The administrative psychological contract consists of obligations involving ideas such as the organization operating as an integrated system and system-wide goals. In contrast, the professional psychological contract consists of obligations influenced by an emphasis on encouraging a collegial society organized to achieve excellence, being community oriented, and defending professional autonomy and standards. Bunderson argues that administrative psychological contracts are essentially based on transactional exchanges as they are founded on the impersonal dispatching of duties and assumptions of self-interest and economic rationality, whereas professional psychological contracts are fundamentally relational exchanges, as they emphasize loyalty, expression of identity, and altruism rather than self-interested behaviour.

But how good is the evidence supporting the transactional–relational distinction? Rousseau (1990) conducted a survey of 224 recently employed MBA students who completed questionnaire items describing employee and employer obligations. Rousseau found some empirical support for the distinction between transactional and relational psychological contracts. Associations between items measuring employee obligations and employer obligations showed two significant factors. The first factor contained items relating to employer and employee obligations, which Rousseau interpreted as a transactional contract (high pay, performance-based pay, training and development in exchange for working overtime, engaging in voluntary extra-role activities, give notice before quitting); the items in the second factor were argued to reflect a relational contract (job security in exchange for loyalty, prepared to commit to a minimum stay within the organization, willingness to accept a transfer on behest of the organization). In other words, separate lists of employee and employer obligations were found to correlate with one another in a way that broadly reflects transactional and relational contracts.

This research has since been superseded by an adapted measure, Rousseau's (2000) Psychological Contract Inventory (PCI, see Appendix) that contains revised items based on previous measures to capture the transactional and relational dimensions and new items designed to capture a third type of psychological contract referred to as a 'balanced' contract, containing both transactional and relational elements and combining 'an open-ended relational emphasis with the transactional feature of well-specified performance–reward contingencies' (Hui, Lee, and Rousseau 2004: 312). Factor analysis of data gathered in Singapore, China, and Latin America confirmed the three psychological contract dimensions (Hui et al. 2004).

Millward and Hopkin's PCS (1998) was also designed to measure the transactional–relational distinction and, while their data supports the two dimensions, Raja, Johns, and Ntalianis (2004) did not replicate this result, with some questionnaire items not appearing to measure either a transactional or relational dimension. Raja and colleagues finally used an abbreviated version of the PCS, reducing the original scale down from 33 to 18 items. It is not uncommon for questionnaire scales to require modification before they are regarded as a scientifically valid measure and clearly further replications are required for both the

PCI and PCS before we can be confident that they adequately capture transactional and relational contracts.

In a large-scale survey of a UK local authority, Coyle-Shapiro and Kessler (2000) found that three factors emerged from analysis of their questionnaire items measuring employees' perceived obligations to the organization. These factors broadly indicated a transactional dimension (e.g. fair pay, fair fringe benefits), a relational dimension (e.g. job security, career prospects), and also a third factor they labelled as training obligations (e.g. necessary training to do the job well, support to learn new skills).

In addition to the above findings that show whether questionnaire items separate into different factors, suggesting that transactional and relational contracts represent different dimensions of the psychological contract, there is also further empirical support for this distinction as measures of transactional and relational contracts seem to have different causes and different consequences. Such differences suggest that the distinction between the two dimensions is important, as they relate differently to the same variables. We will review such findings later in this chapter.

While there has been some empirical support for transactional and relational contracts, the distinction between transactional and relational contracts is far from clear-cut for three main reasons. First, there is some evidence that certain items can, depending on the context, be considered to be part of either a transactional or relational contract. As noted by Arnold (1996), the inducement of training is sometimes considered to indicate a transactional contract (e.g. Rousseau 1990), in other cases to indicate a relational contract (e.g. Robinson, Kraatz, and Rousseau 1994), and elsewhere, as we have seen above in the Coyle-Shapiro and Kessler study (2000), it has also been found to be a separate dimension in its own right. Pay, for example, may also be regarded as part of a transactional or relational contract depending on the context. While pay would generally be defined as lying within the domain of transactional contracts, if pay is consistently awarded on a fair basis, and the organization makes efforts to protect and enhance pay over and above such factors as inflation or competitors, then it could well be the case that this item is construed as part of a relational contract, as in the minds of employees it represents considerate treatment by the organization. So, while the distinction between transactional and relational may be a reasonable one, the items that can be found in each may depend strongly on the context.

Second, the distinction between relational and transactional may not be clearcut simply because the exchange may be much messier than is generally suggested, with relational items being exchanged for transactional items. For example, an organization showing concern for its employees' welfare is clearly part of a relational contract, but in return employees may be expected to deliver *both* relational promises (e.g. concern for the organization's image) *and* transactional promises (e.g. delivering acceptable performance). Using a policy-capturing methodology on a sample of 116 evening MBA students in full-time employment, Rousseau and Anton (1991) demonstrated just such an exchange. Participants were asked to consider the role employee contributions (past, present, and future performance; time on job; commitment; and employability) play in instilling an obligation in organizations to retain employees. The results indicated that employees thought that employers should feel more obliged to retain staff when they had contributed good standards of present performance, commitment, and had been in the job for a longer time. However, employability, and past and future performance were not seen as significant contributions. Treating the employer obligation of retaining employees as relational, and the employee obligation of present performance as transactional, these results suggest that relational and transactional items can be exchanged, suggesting that the exchange cannot be easily classified into two mutually exclusive types of contract.

A third way in which the distinction between transactional and relational contracts is not clear-cut is that some studies examining this distinction were not designed primarily with this aim in mind and are not therefore, in this sense, theoretically driven. While such designs can produce interesting findings, they can also lead to inconsistent approaches and results. For example, if we compare two such studies described above, we can see that Rousseau (1990) and Coyle-Shapiro and Kessler (2000) use different sets of items in their studies, use a different statistical method, their dimensions consist of different items, and even different factors.

In summary, while the distinction between transactional and relational contracts seems reasonable and there is some supporting empirical work, there is also evidence that this distinction is suspect. For example, certain content items seem to belong to both transactional and relational contracts, and transactional and relational items can be exchanged for each other. Existing empirical work also tends to be exploratory, relying heavily on *post hoc* rationalization to make sense of findings. It seems quite plausible that there may be many types or dimensions of psychological contracts, though empirical work to date has only just begun to explore this issue.

4.4. What factors shape employee perceptions of the psychological contract?

The previous section considered how the contents of the psychological contract have been categorized. Here, we address the origins of these contents and how they are formed. Or, in other words, where do employee perceptions of their promises to the organization and the organization's reciprocal promises to them come from? Although such questions are of fundamental importance in understanding the psychological contract it should be noted that there are relatively few relevant studies on which to draw.

In a general sense, almost any type of communication or behaviour from the organization or the employee could be interpreted by the other party as information about the nature of the promises that exists between them. For example, an employee may perceive the organization to have made a promise to them to be flexible about working hours as the organization claims to be a 'family-friendly' employer. A manager, for instance, may believe that an employee has promised to take on a particular role as during the interview for their job they indicated they had undertaken such roles before.

This section focuses on factors outside the organization as well as organizational, social and individual factors that may influence the formation of the psychological contract. It also considers organization-employee interactions that have the explicit purpose of shaping psychological contracts through psychological contract breach and what is sometimes referred to as 'psychological contracting'.

4.4.1. Factors outside the organization

As discussed earlier, the contents of the psychological contract refer broadly to the employee's promises to the organization and what the organization promises employees in return. While experiences within the organization and other factors discussed below are likely to be very important it also seems plausible that things that happen outside the employee's employing organization may help shape and form these expectations in several ways.

The first way in which this might happen is through the existing expectations the employee brings to the organization. Even before first employment experiences people have expectations about what employment is about, what their employer is likely to expect of them, and what they can expect of their employer. Such pre-employment expectations are formed by numerous experiences and contexts. For example, an individual's previous history of employment relationships, the employment experiences of other family members, socialization in school and the local community, cultural context, socio-economic status and exposure to mass media will shape what individuals learn about work as they grow up and hence also shape their initial psychological contract. Clearly as we start to experience the employment relationship such initial perceptions of the psychological contract are likely to change. Nonetheless, pre-employment experiences are likely to be important influences on our initial psychological contract and hence shape our psychological contract in later years.

A second way in which factors outside the organization may shape the psychological contract is through personal non-work experiences employees have that inform them about the nature and meaning of mutual promises with their employer. For example, significant personal events such as parenthood, bereavement, or changes in personal relationships may cause employees to reflect on what they expect to get from and contribute to their employer. Also, work experiences of friends and family are likely to exert an influence on an employee's understanding of their psychological contract. For example, through interpersonal comparison with a friend's work situation, an employee may feel they are expecting too little from their employer.

A third category of extra-organizational factors includes broader economic, political, and legal changes that in turn shape perceptions of the psychological contract. There are numerous examples of this. One such is the economic changes discussed earlier that took place in the late 1980s and early 1990s. It was argued that these changes renewed interest in the psychological contract concept because they also brought about changes to the employment relationship. Globalization, greater competition and financial accountability forced organizations to embark on redundancy programmes and restructuring activities to remove managerial levels (Herriot, Manning, and Kidd 1997; Coyle-Shapiro and Kessler 2000) and to seek higher levels of performance and productivity from employees. Ultimately it is difficult to evaluate whether or not there was an actual transition from an 'old' contract to a 'new' contract because no decent historical data with which to test the proposition are available. Accounts of these supposed changes, even if exaggerated at a general level, are probably accurate for certain groups of employees in some situations over this period. However, the assumption made by many researchers that such general shifts in the content of the psychological contract were in fact happening forms an important backdrop and context to research activity. Another example of extra-organizational factors can be found by considering how changes to employment law around, say, hours of work or worker representation will in turn shape the psychological contract.

Clearly there are numerous other ways in which factors outside the organization can shape perceptions of the psychological contract, but how important these are compared to other factors is not known.

4.4.2. Organizational factors

The organization plays a fundamental role in establishing and shaping the psychological contract and, in most cases, initiates part of the content of the psychological contract through offering jobs. Given this, it is remarkable that so few studies have examined this area, though there has been some speculation, most notably by Guest (1998) and Rousseau (1995), about whom within the organization is most likely to make and shape contracts with employees.

Rousseau (1995) makes a distinction between principals and agents who play a role as contract makers. Principals are individuals or organizations that make contracts with others on behalf of themselves whereas agents (e.g. a line manager) are individuals acting on behalf of principals. Organizations also

Table 4.4 How line managers and colleagues communicate the psychological contract

Line manager or co-worker behaviour	Possible promise communicated
Line manager tells Jack that if he continues to perform well he'll get ahead in the organization	Explicit: That advancement is contingent on performance Implicit: the line manager has the authority to make promotions happen and should, in return, be respected by the employee as an influential agent
Since joining, Jane has consistently worked overtime at the company and her line manager invites her for the first time to attend a meeting with senior managers	Implicit: Jane believes that to be promoted to higher levels of the organization you have to demonstrate your commitment
Colleagues who work late are not treated with any more respect than others who do not	Implicit: Rewards are contingent on how much you produce, rather than how long it takes you to do it
A colleague constructively criticizes the work methods of his line manager and is subsequently publicly humiliated	Explicit: Employee dissent will be punished by management Implicit: The organization does not support constructive feedback and hence is not supportive and should not receive employee loyalty

communicate promises to employees in other ways, such as through human resource and personnel practices. Rousseau draws a further distinction between human (e.g. recruiters, managers, co-workers, mentors) and structural contract makers (e.g. the range of human resource practices, such as compensation, benefits, career prospects, training). These contract makers communicate promises to employees in both explicit and implicit ways. Explicit ways of communicating the contents of the psychological contract include written communications, emails, statements, announcements, and so on. Implicit forms of communication are complex and subtle but may be just as powerful. For example, the ways in which contract makers respond to particular employee behaviours is likely to be important in shaping the content of the contract. A new employee may learn a great deal about the mutual promises and obligations through observing the behaviours and responses of other employees and contract makers such as line managers.

Human contract makers play a vital role in communicating to employees what they are expected to do and what they will get in return from the organization. A particularly important agent of the organization in communicating promises is likely to be the line manager given the potential influence they have over those they manage (Guest and Conway 2000). Line managers have been found to exaggerate the extent of provision and quality of human resource practices during communications, especially during periods of organizational change, leading to inflated employee expectations which are later not met (Grant 1999; Greene, Ackers, and Black 2001). However, there is little evidence about what it is that line and other managers actually do to shape the contents of the psychological contract (we provide some examples in Table 4.4). A number of types of management behaviour, such as providing support (Eisenberger et al. 1986) and attempting to inspire employees (Podsakoff et al. 1990) are likely to play a part in forming the contents of psychological contracts.

A small number of studies, however, have considered the effects of structural rather than human psychological contract makers by focusing on the influence of human resource policies and practices in shaping psychological contracts. Rousseau (1995) has speculated how a range of individual human resource practices—recruitment, performance review, compensation, training, personnel manuals and benefits—communicate future promises and performance expectations. The relationship between psychological contracts and human resource practices was examined in a nationally representative survey of 1,000 UK employees (Guest and Conway 1998). Employees reporting their organization as having such practices were also much more likely to report promises as having been made to them by their organization (see also Westwood, Sparrow, and Leung's study of Hong Kong managers, 2001). A later study of 1,300 senior managers' perceptions of the promises made to employees found similar results in that managers in organizations with more human resource practices also tended to report that more promises had been made (Guest and Conway 2002).

Given the rapid growth in studies aiming to understand the links between human resource practices and employee attitudes and behaviours (e.g. Applebaum et al. 2000), we are likely to see more studies addressing how these practices shape the psychological contract, as one way of thinking about how structural features of organizations, such as human resource practices, impact on employee attitudes such as job satisfaction and organizational commitment is through the impact of such practices on the psychological contract (Guest 1998). In other words, it may be the case that human resource practices affect employee behaviour and attitudes through changing the psychological contract.

4.4.3. Individual and social factors

By definition, the psychological contract is subjectively understood. Even if an organization attempted to offer the 'same' deal to everyone the psychological contract would still vary widely across employees. Individual and group differences that shape perception such as personality, ideology, and self-serving biases will have a considerable impact on how employees make sense of their work environments and, more specifically, the promises they believe their organization has made to them, what their obligations are in return, and the extent to which these promises are kept. In this section we consider individual and social factors including the role of personality, exchange ideologies, cognitive biases, social information processing, and socialization.

Most research into individual factors that shape the psychological contract has focused on occupational and exchange ideologies. As mentioned above, Bunderson (2001) found support for the idea that administrative and professional occupational ideologies influence the nature of the psychological contracts held by doctors. Coyle-Shapiro and Neuman (2004) examined the influence of exchange and creditor ideologies on psychological contracts. These ideologies are thought of as dispositional orientations similar to personality in that they are stable and fundamental to the way people behave.

Exchange ideology refers to the extent to which employees believe that the way they are treated by the organization should reflect the effort they put into the job. Some employees ('entitleds') are comfortable with being overrewarded given the effort they put into the job, some employees ('equity sensitives') are keen to strive for a fair or equitable return on their efforts, and finally other employees tolerate being underrewarded for their efforts ('benevolents').

Creditor ideology refers to an orientation to give more than you receive. Individuals who hold such orientations feel uncomfortable about being indebted to others and would prefer for others to be indebted to them. Coyle-Shapiro and Neuman (2004) found that employees who score low on exchange ideology (i.e. benevolents) and high on creditor ideology feel more obligated to the organization and more receptive to responding to inducements from the organization than employees who are not. These studies suggest that an individual's ideology influences what they feel predisposed to give to the organization and also affects how much they feel under an obligation to reciprocate following organizational inducements.

One of the main explanations for the idiosyncratic nature of psychological contracts is likely to be an employee's personality. This occurs through three processes: personality influences employees' *choice* of job and task; how they *construe* the terms of the contract; and how employees *enact* contractual behaviour (Raja, Johns, and Ntalianis 2004). In a survey of employees in Pakistan across a range of companies, Raja, Johns, and Ntalianis (2004) found personality traits differentially predicted psychological contract type, with neuroticism and equity sensitivity related to transactional contracts and employees with high self-esteem and conscientiousness more likely to have relational contracts. Taking the relationship between neuroticism and transactional contracts to illustrate how personality may affect psychological contracts, neuroticism is related to emotional instability and a lack of trust and anxiety, hence those with higher levels of neuroticism will tend not to engage in relationships requiring trust, long-term commitments, confidence in another person and delayed gratification.

Cognitive biases are another individual factor that may shape both the making and the interpretation of promises (Rousseau 2001). For example, when making promises, people tend to be overoptimistic and promise too much. Cognitive biases can also be self-serving, for instance, when people are more likely to attribute their success to personal, internal characteristics, such as how hard they worked or to their abilities, and attribute failures to situational, external causes, such as the difficulty of the task or a lack of support from the organization. Robinson, Kraatz, and Rousseau (1994) argue that these self-serving biases make individuals overestimate their own contributions and underestimate the costs to the organization of the inducements they receive. In other words, employees who have such biases may, for example, perceive that the efforts they make are considerable and what they get back in return is of little value. Clearly, the more that employee perceptions are affected by this self-serving bias, the more they will feel entitled to any inducements received and the less they will feel obliged to reciprocate. These arguments seem plausible, but have yet to be empirically examined.

The final type of individual and social factors that shape the psychological contract considered here are social cues and workplace socialization. The most frequently cited way by which social cues affect the formation of the psychological contract is through social information processing. Social information processing is the process whereby employees pick up and internalize the attitudes and behaviours of others around them through social cues (Salancik and Pfeffer 1978). These social cues are gathered during interactions with and observations of others such as co-workers, supervisors, friends at work, and customers. For example, an employee may enter a new job feeling highly motivated and committed, only to find that co-workers look bored with their work and grumble about how they are treated by managers, with the effect that the newcomer reappraises their own attitudes towards the job. Social cues include such things as utterances by colleagues and perceptions of other employees' moods and behaviours; however, overt and public communications and behaviours will exert more influence on cognitions and behaviours than subtle or private ones (Salancik and Pfeffer 1978).

Turning now to socialization, while it has been conceptualized in many ways, it can broadly be regarded as the processes through which an employee's attitudes and behaviours are influenced by their early experiences in the organization in ways that make them more similar to those of existing members of the organization. A study by Thomas and Anderson (1998) explored the effects of certain aspects of socialization on the content of the psychological contract in British Army recruits. They found that a more active approach to seeking information about one's role, interpersonal support, organizational practices, and social relationships resulted in the development of stronger expectations of what should be received from the army. They also found that newcomers' expectations were similar to those of experienced soldiers. These results highlight that while the psychological contract is understood subjectively and is therefore likely to vary greatly between employees, other influences operate to make employees' psychological contracts more similar.

4.4.4. Psychological contract breach and 'psychological contracting'

Two key influences on the contents of psychological contracts are concepts specifically developed from psychological contract theory, namely, psychological contract breach and 'psychological contracting'. While these concepts could have been discussed under social factors above they are presented separately here as they are unique to psychological contract literature and illustrate how key constructs within psychological contract theory interact.

Dealing first with the relationship between psychological contract breach and contents, studies provide strong evidence that changes in obligations over time—in other words changes in the content—are due to psychological contract breach events (i.e. occasions where employees perceive their organization to have broken promises made to them). A number of longitudinal studies have found that perceived organizational breach leads to a lowering of employee's transactional and relational obligations (Robinson, Kraatz, and Rousseau 1994; Coyle-Shapiro and Kessler 2002a). Occasions when employees breach their obligations also lead to employers reducing their obligations to the employee (Coyle-Shapiro and Kessler 2002b).

The final set of antecedents to changes in the content we consider here are those surrounding negotiation encounters between the two parties, sometimes referred to as 'psychological contracting' (Herriot and Pemberton 1997). Herriot and Pemberton propose a four-stage model of psychological contracting:

1. *Informing*: Each party informs the other of their needs and what they are prepared to offer.
2. *Negotiating*: The employee and the organization negotiate and agree what they are prepared to do for one another.
3. *Monitoring*: The parties to the contract monitor one another to ensure the contract is being kept and remains fair.
4. *Renegotiating and exiting*: Successful renegotiations occur on an ongoing basis, or one of the parties decides to exit the relationship.

Herriot and Pemberton argue that although their model may be a description of how psychological contracting works in practice it is better considered as a model prescribing how psychological contracting should in principle be done. They argue that negotiating psychological contracts in this manner is likely to lead to a more explicit contract. They go on to argue that explicit contracts build trust in the relationship as parties can more clearly monitor delivery. Furthermore, they suggest that explicit contracts are likely to increase the match between employee and organizational expectations making breach less likely to occur. We will consider in more detail how the psychological contract can be managed in Chapter 9.

This particular model, and other ways of thinking about how negotiations of the psychological contract take place, have received virtually no empirical examination. A study of implicit and explicit negotiations in a sample of nannies and their employers (i.e. the child's parents) found it was implicit rather than explicit negotiation at the point of hire that was a more important positive influence on perceptions of trust following the selection interview (Millward, Purvis, and

Cropley 2003). The explanation offered was that implicitly defined contracts present a framework of interdependence between parties and also one which also allows both parties flexibility and room to manoeuvre, allowing the relationship to be fine-tuned over time, in contrast to explicit contracts where behaviour is precisely specified and any deviation from delivery will be instantly detected.

Clearly this area, like most of the other types of factors influencing the psychological contract concept thus far discussed, requires further conceptual development and empirical investigation. It raises a number of fundamental questions about the nature and stability of psychological contracts, such as the extent to which they are episodically versus continuously renegotiated, what both parties need to bring to the table (e.g. needs, wants, expectations) in order to negotiate long-term stability, and what the conditions are under which it is preferable to keep the contents explicit or implicit.

While it is clear that the contents of the psychological contract are subject to change and many factors may influence such changes, we know little about what factors are most important and how this diverse range of potential influences work together to shape and change the contents of psychological contracts.

4.5. How the content of psychological contracts affects outcomes

The main way in which the content of the psychological contract matters is when it has important outcomes for employees and organizations. In other words, if the contents of different employees' psychological contracts are different and if there are changes to the contents does this lead to different or changing kinds of outcomes? For example, do employees who hold transactional contracts report higher levels of satisfaction, commitment and performance than those who hold relational contracts?

Before we can address this issue we need to consider how the contents of the psychological contract may in principle affect such outcomes. Outcomes typically researched include job satisfaction, organizational commitment, job performance, and an employee's intentions and behaviours in relation to quitting. In general, the relationship between the contents and outcomes has not been clearly articulated in the literature even though one of the key claims of psychological contract theory is that the contents do influence important outcomes. Empirical studies into this issue have only begun to emerge (Rousseau 2001; Hui, Lee, and Rousseau 2004; Raja, Johns, and Ntalianis 2004).

There are, however, a number of explanations or frameworks for relating psychological contract contents to outcomes and three are discussed here. The first of these is the idea that the contents of psychological contracts provide *goal structures* and it is such goal structures that affect employee behaviour. The second approach uses *social exchange theory* to help explain why specific kinds of contents affect outcomes. The third explanation considers the extent of *balance* between employer and employee obligations. Clearly, all three explanations may apply at the same time and in practice it may be difficult to separate the utility of one framework ahead of another in terms of explaining outcomes.

4.5.1. Psychological contracts providing goal structures

According to this approach, the psychological contract affects outcomes because the simple existence of a psychological contract promotes work attitudes and job performance through operating as a framework for structuring goals. One of the main things employees want from organizations is rewards and organizations want performance from employees; a basic function of the psychological contract is to specify required performance levels in return for rewards and hence, as we explain below, establishes both short and long-term goal structures.

Dealing first with short-term goals, it is argued that promises operate as goals or standards against which employees can compare their behaviour, similar to the way in which goals regulate behaviour more generally in goal-setting theory, control theory, and other self-regulation theories of motivation (Shore and Tetrick 1991; Rousseau 2001). In other words, when employees believe they are not behaving in a way which is fulfilling a promise they have made to the organization, they will alter their behaviour so as to reduce the discrepancy. Reciprocal promises constitute a very effective goal or standard to achieve, as they are goals that individuals accept, that they associate with particular rewards, and are partly controlled by the desire to avoid the negative consequences of failing to keep promises such as being viewed as untrustworthy (Rousseau 1995).

Turning to longer-term goals, when psychological contracts contain terms and exchanges relevant to an employee's long-term goals, such as career development, they can provide employees with a feeling that they can influence their own destinies within the organization (Shore and Tetrick 1991), as they are party to a contract that can be renegotiated and understand the behaviours required in order to achieve long-term rewards such as promotion. The perceptions of predictability and control that result from a sense of knowing how to achieve goals are likely to enhance motivation.

4.5.2. Social exchange theory

Social exchange theory posits that all social relationships essentially consist of exchanges of both economic (e.g. money, materials) and social resources (e.g. respect, love, support) (Blau 1964). Individuals seek out and remain in social exchanges for many reasons, not least because of the incentives available for doing so. However, the most important reason in the context of understanding the psychological contract is that when individuals receive benefits they feel indebted and obliged to reciprocate. The idea that individuals feel obliged to reciprocate if they receive something is central to social exchange theory and is based on Gouldner's idea (1960: 171) that a social norm for reciprocity exists such that '(1) people should help those who have helped them and, (2) people should not injure those who have helped them'. While such a norm seems plausible, its nature and prevalence remain largely unexplored (Coyle-Shapiro and Conway 2003). The reciprocity norm also includes the idea that what is given in return should be roughly similar to that which has been received. The reciprocity norm is so crucial to social exchange as it perpetuates the ongoing fulfilment of obligations and thus the relationship itself.

Social exchange theory predicts that what an employee receives from the organization will be returned in kind. Hence, if an organization attempts to change its psychological contract with an employee from, say, a transactional to a relational one, it is expected that the employee's behaviour and attitudes will move in this direction as well. In other words, if the reciprocity norm holds, we would expect an increase in long-term commitments and trust by the organization to be followed by a similar shift in the type of promises made by the employee.

As suggested by the above example, social exchange predictions relating the contents of psychological contracts to attitudinal and behavioural outcomes involve four main stages and assumptions: (*a*) employer promises lead to employer behaviour (e.g. providing rewards); (*b*) because of the norm of reciprocity, employer behaviour leads to employee promises; (*c*) employee promises lead to employee attitudes (e.g. increased commitment) and behaviour (e.g. working harder, producing more); (*d*) employee behaviour, again as a consequence of the norm of reciprocity, feeds back to influence employer promises. One simple way of summarizing such a social exchange is presented in Figure 4.1.

What empirical evidence is there for the links presented in Figure 4.1? Empirical studies tend to focus only on the relationships between two of the four stages rather than considering the whole process, thus omitting the discussion or testing of the intervening stages (e.g. Hui, Lee, and Rousseau 2004; Raja, Johns, and Ntalianis 2004).

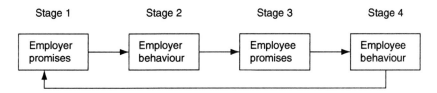

Figure 4.1 Linking the contents of psychological contracts with employee behaviour

The first set of empirical studies we review relating to the model explore whether promises made by the organization to the employees instil obligations in employees (stages 1 and 3 in Figure 4.1). The evidence from these studies is mixed. A longitudinal survey within the public sector found perceptions of employer promises combining both transactional and relational items was not directly related to employee promises (Coyle-Shapiro and Kessler 2002c), although there was an indirect link where perceived employer promises related to employee obligations only in cases where the organization had fulfilled its promises. Rousseau's cross-sectional study (1990) of US MBA students found employee perceptions of the organization's transactional promises were correlated with transactional employee promises and the organization's relational promises were correlated with relational employee promises; there were no associations between transactional and relational promises (Rousseau 1990). From these studies we may conclude that the extent to which an organization's promises to employees result in reciprocal employee promises rests critically on whether the organization fulfils its promises. However, the size of the associations between employer and employee promises (as indicated by the size of the correlation coefficients) are small; while this implies some degree of reciprocity, it does not approach the type of full reciprocity in kind predicted by social exchange theory.

The second set of studies examine whether employee perceptions of employer promises predict employee attitudes and behaviour (stages 1 and 4 in Figure 4.1). Again, the evidence is contradictory. Coyle-Shapiro and Kessler (2000) found public sector employee perceptions of their employer's relational, training, and transactional promises were unassociated with employee job satisfaction, organizational citizenship behaviour, and organizational commitment, with the exception of a small correlation between training promises and OCBs; however, a second study produced contrary results where employee perceptions of employer promises were positively related to employee citizenship behaviour in the form of encouraging innovative participation from other employees, helping employees experiencing difficulties, and making efforts to exceed performance expectations (Coyle-Shapiro and Kessler 2002a). In a study of a steel conglomerate in China, employee perceptions of their organization's relational and transactional promises had small positive associations across a range of organizational citizenship behaviours (Hui, Lee, and Rousseau 2004). Finally, in a study conducted in Pakistan of mainly professional workers, perceptions of their organization's relational promises were positively associated with job satisfaction, affective organizational commitment, and intentions to quit, whereas transactional promises were negatively associated with the same outcomes (Raja, Johns, and Ntalianis 2004).

The third set of studies, which examines the links between employee promises and their attitudes and behaviour (stages 3 and 4 in Figure 4.1) appears more consistent. Flood et al. (2001) found employees that felt obliged to contribute were more likely to be committed to the organization, and Rousseau (1990) found that tenure related to employees' relational promises, but not to the perception of employer's relational promises.

In summary, there is preliminary evidence that employee promises relate to work behaviours. Empirical support for the relationship between employer promises and employee behaviour and employer promises and employee promises are somewhat contradictory and appear dependent upon context and type of contract. Integrating these findings, however, lends some support to the social exchange process presented in Figure 4.1, where employees perceive employers to have certain obligations and when these are fulfilled they feel obliged to reciprocate in some way, for example, through actual behaviour. Even so, the full model is yet to be fully elaborated in theory and empirical work.

4.5.3. Level of balance between employee and organization obligations

As discussed in the previous section, social exchange theory posits that the efforts and contributions made by one party in a relationship will be broadly reciprocated in kind by the other party. Shore and Barksdale (1998) build on social exchange by considering the exchange in terms of the extent of balance or imbalance and level of obligations between the employee and the employer, as seen by the employee, and derive a two-by-two typology of exchange relationships (Figure 4.2).

In a balanced relationship, the employee and the employer hold similar levels of obligations to one another. In an unbalanced relationship, one of the parties is perceived as being significantly more or less obligated than the other party. For example, an employee may feel that they owe the organization relatively little but that the organization owes them quite a lot (employee under obligation).

The important concept here is the suggestion that it is the extent of balance or imbalance between employee and employer obligations that matters more

		Employer obligations	
		High	Moderate to low
Employee obligations	High	Mutual high obligations	Employee over-obligation
	Moderate to low	Employee under-obligation	Mutual low obligations

Figure 4.2 Balancing exchange relationships
Note: Reproduced from Shore and Barksdale (1998).

than specific content. Shore and Barksdale (1998) argue that employee responses can be predicted from the typology. When there are balanced mutual high obligations between the parties, this is referred to as a 'strong social exchange' with both parties feeling highly obligated to provide a wide range of contract items. They argue that mutual high obligations will result in greater levels of employee contributions, such as organizational commitment. Because of the reciprocity norm, where balance does not exist, parties are likely to seek to achieve balance over time through either implicit or explicit negotiation, or through more covert means of cognitively and or behaviourally adjusting their contributions. For example, if employees feel under-obligated they can try to increase their contributions by working harder. If balance is not achievable in the longer term, Shore and Barksdale (1998) argue that one or both of the parties will seek to terminate the relationship. For example, if employees feel over-obligated to their employers and believe their employers are not prepared to reciprocate their efforts, they will choose to end the relationship.

Shore and Barksdale (1998) in a study of MBA students found that, in line with the norm of reciprocity, the most common types of reported relationships were mutual high (46 per cent) and mutual low (38 per cent). Only 12 per cent of employees reported feeling over-obligated and just 3 per cent under-obligated. The incidence of any kind of reported imbalance is therefore relatively low.

When Shore and Barksdale examined the associations between the four types of balance and attitudes and behaviours, the mutual high obligations group had the most positive work attitudes in terms higher of levels of perceived organizational support, organizational commitment, and lower levels of turnover intentions. The group of employees feeling under-obligated had the least positive attitudes. There were few differences between the over-obligated group and the mutually low obligations group in terms of employee attitudes. The negative attitude of under-obligated employees was due to perceiving the organization to be failing to fulfil its promises and seeking ways to restore balance.

The concept of balance is a valuable attempt to understand how the psychological contract relates to work attitudes and behaviours. There is, however, a major concern that the typology is nothing more than a proxy for psychological contract breach, with mutual high obligations reflecting a relationship with long-term psychological contract fulfilment, employee over or under-obligation reflecting where either the organization or employee has breached, and mutual low obligations reflect relationships characterized by breach by both parties. Indeed, Shore and Barksdale (1998) repeatedly draw on the notion of psychological contract breach when explaining the effects of balance on outcomes. Further research should examine whether imbalance extends our understanding beyond psychological contract breach.

4.6. Summary and conclusion

This chapter set out to explore various aspects of the psychological contract contents including what those contents are, how they are assessed and categorized, factors that change the contents, and ways of understanding how contents relate to outcomes. We have also noted that the content of the psychological contract operates in conjunction with other aspects of psychological contract theory, most notably the concept of breach/fulfilment. Without question, breach is *the* big idea within psychological contract theory and the main subject of Chapter 5.

As we have discussed, research on the contents of the psychological contract has largely been concerned with describing dimensions of the psychological contract, rather than explaining what causes or shapes the content or how it affects outcomes. This neglect is a serious omission and there is considerable scope and need for future research and development in this area (Rousseau 2001).

In part, these gaps in our knowledge are because the widespread use of survey methods means it is not possible to adequately capture the fundamental exchange-based nature of psychological contracts. Furthermore, attempts to fit what are, by definition, idiosyncratic reciprocal promises into content types, such as the transactional–relational distinction, are somewhat logically and empirically questionable.

In conclusion, while researchers have viewed the content as having a number of causes and effects, the psychological contract is an ongoing dynamic exchange process where the causes and effects of the content cannot be viewed statically. Outcomes of the exchange at one point in time become a cause of the next cycle of the exchange. Currently, the ongoing reciprocal nature of the contents of the psychological contract is insufficiently conceptualized.

5 How Does the Psychological Contract Affect Behaviour, Attitudes, and Emotion? The Importance of Psychological Contract Breach

5.1. Introduction

Breach is probably the most important idea in psychological contract theory as it is the main way of understanding how the psychological contract affects the feelings, attitudes, and behaviours of employees. The power and flexibility of the breach concept are also demonstrated by the way in which it can be used to explain other concepts within psychological contract theory (recall Section 4.5, how the typology of 'balancing obligations' could be viewed as little more than a proxy for psychological contract breach). Furthermore, psychological contract breach is seen as occurring relatively frequently at work because of the many factors that can affect the employment relationship. Given its importance it is not surprising that most psychological contract research has focused on breach, with the vast majority of studies considering the employees' perspective, when employees perceive their organization to have broken a promise made to them. (To help explain the idea of breach more clearly and describe how it has been assessed, various questionnaire items used in research to measure breach have been included in Appendix; it may be useful to look at these now.)

We first define psychological contract breach and distinguish it from psychological contract violation. Next we discuss how often psychological contracts are breached and consider the few studies examining the antecedents to breach. We then consider the consequences of breach—the topic that has attracted the most empirical attention within breach research—and whether breach always leads to negative outcomes or if the consequences of breach depend on other factors. As will become apparent, there are several unresolved conceptual issues around the breach idea, such as the extent to which it is distinct from other concepts such as justice, and these are discussed. Finally, we consider alternative mechanisms linking psychological contract to outcomes.

5.2. Defining breach and violation

The idea of a breach of the psychological contract is a metaphor taken from legal contracts where a breach is taken to be a less than perfect performance by one of the parties regarding contract terms (Cheshire, Fifoot, and Furmston 1989). A breach of the psychological contract occurs similarly 'when one party in a relationship perceives another to have failed to fulfil promised obligation(s)' (Robinson and Rousseau 1994: 247). As the definition suggests, the opposite of breach is fulfilment, and so it is commonplace for researchers to use the term fulfilment in this way to mean the opposite of breach. Breach, like the concept of the psychological contract itself, is subjective and based on a perceived rather than an actual agreement, and can occur in relation to any explicit or implicit promise.

Researchers used the terms 'breach' and 'violation' interchangeably until Morrison and Robinson (1997) made a key distinction that is now accepted by most working in the field. They describe breach as a cognitive comparison of what has been received and what was promised and violation as the extreme affective or emotional reactions that may accompany breaches. In other words, breaches are perceived discrepancies between what has been promised and what is delivered, whereas violation is the emotional reaction that may also be experienced when such discrepancies are perceived. They suggest that such a distinction is consistent with previous theory describing violations as deeply distressing emotional experiences (e.g. Rousseau 1989).

There are both advantages and disadvantages in making such a distinction. The main advantage is that by separating the cognition of breach from its possible affective reaction (i.e. violation), we avoid the problems that can occur when the phenomena are defined in ways that include and potentially confound cause and effect. In other words, it is helpful to make a distinction between perceived breaches and the reactions to those breaches. A second advantage of this distinction is that other sorts of responses to breach, apart from extreme emotional ones, can also be considered. It seems likely that a wide range of responses is possible. These may be less intense, perhaps involving mixed emotions, and have more subtle impacts on feelings and behaviours. For example, an employee may feel on one particular day that his or her organization has broken promises in relation to a particular work assignment, but this may not provoke the intense negative emotions necessary in order for a reaction to be classified as a violation, even though the perceived breach may still explain the employee's feelings of mild disappointment and their withdrawal of effort on that day.

The main disadvantage of making this distinction is that the meaning of breach, in some senses, becomes, paradoxically, less clear. The distinction means that breach now refers to any sort of perceived discrepancy, from very small breaches of subtle implicit promises (e.g. your boss normally greets you with a smile and says 'hello' in the mornings, but today his greeting is not quite as hearty as normal) to very major breaches of explicit promises (e.g. having had written reassurances that your job was secure, you arrive at work to be told by your manager to clear your desk as you have been made redundant for no apparent reason). Making this distinction means that breach refers to a very wide range of perceptual phenomena, from the slightest sense of a tiny discrepancy between what was promised and what was delivered to a clear and firm perception that a highly significant promise has been broken. So, on the one hand, defining breach (the cause) in terms of its effects (strong negative emotions) confounds cause and effect. On the other hand, making the distinction means that breach now refers to any sort of perceived discrepancy—many of which may not conceptually or empirically have much relevance.

Since Morrison and Robinson (1997) made the distinction between breach and violation, it is notable that, while breach remains a very active area of empirical research, interest in the concept of violation has not really developed. Overall, however, the advantages of distinction between breach and violation appear to outweigh the disadvantages and we adopt the distinction between breach and violation for the remainder of the text.

5.3. How often are psychological contracts breached?

An important initial question is how often does breach occur? One reason for the interest in breach, as already indicated, is that it is believed to have a strong impact on employee attitudes and behaviours. However, we actually know very little about how often psychological contracts are breached and studies find contrasting results. In a survey of recently employed MBA graduates (Robinson and Rousseau 1994), 55 per cent reported that their organization had at some point broken promises during the first two years of employment. These broken promises were most likely to be related to the provision of training, levels of compensation, and opportunities for promotion. When psychological contract breach was examined using a daily diary method (Conway and Briner 2002a), employees reported organizations breaking promises on a weekly rather than annual basis, with 69 per cent of respondents reporting at least one broken promise during the 10 working day diary collection period.

The discrepancy in the incidence rates across the two studies is likely to be explained by the different time frames respondents were asked to consider. The daily diary required respondents to recall events happening at the end of a working day and, therefore, was likely to capture both minor and major breach events, whereas the survey required respondents to recall events during the past year and, as a result, respondents may have had difficulty remembering minor breaches.

How often breach is perceived to happen will depend on whose viewpoint is considered. For instance, an employee's perceptions of how often the organization breaks its promises toward them are likely to differ from their manager's perceptions of how often the organization breaks promises towards employees under their management. Lester et al. (2002) compared employees' and their managers' perceptions and found that employees are more likely than their supervisors to believe that the organization breaks promises towards employees on the issues of pay, advancement opportunities, and a good employment relationship; however, no differences were found for promises around benefits, the work itself, or resource support.

Differences in manager and employee perceptions of psychological contract breach are probably due to a number of factors, such as variations in information employees receive from different psychological contract makers (e.g. line manager, HR department, senior management), and the likelihood that employees tend to view inducements offered by the organization less favourably than do organizational representatives (Lester et al. 2002).

5.4. Antecedents of breach

Antecedents of breach are those factors that are thought to cause breach. Only a few studies have examined the antecedents of psychological contract breach. This is surprising from both a practical and research perspective. It would be useful for organizations to know about antecedents in order to prevent breach. Understanding the causes of breach would, in research terms, tell us much about many other aspects of the psychological contract.

The limited number of studies means that we do not know much about what causes breach or how breach develops. The empirical studies that have been conducted suggest that the causes of breach can be viewed in terms of the inadequate provision of human resource management practices, a lack of organizational and supervisor support, events happening outside of the organization, and when employees compare their deal, unfavourably, with other employees. These different types of causes are discussed in turn and then the section ends with a discussion of chains of causal factors leading up to breach. Note that while studies tend to discuss the relationship between the psychological contract and other concepts using language that suggests causality—for instance, in this section we discuss factors that are the *antecedents* of or *causes* of breach—causality is often assumed rather than tested empirically. This is because most empirical studies of the psychological contract use cross-sectional designs (i.e. collecting all their data at one point in time) and can, therefore, not test causality, which is obviously a major limitation of research in this field. This issue is discussed in more detail in Chapter 6.

The first possible cause of breach is inadequate human resource management practices. Two streams of empirical studies are relevant here. The first are studies that consistently find employees are more likely to report psychological contract fulfilment if they perceive that their organization adopts human resource management practices (Guest and Conway 1997, 1998, 1999, 2000, 2001, 2002*a*, 2004). This finding also receives some support from research looking at the employers' perspective. Senior HR managers from different companies are more likely to report that their organization keeps its promises if the organization has also adopted human resource practices (Guest and Conway 2002*b*). The second stream of studies suggests that it is not only the provision of human resource management practices that cause psychological contract fulfilment, but it is also important that the human resource management organizations provide lives up to management communications about what the human resource management practices are and should deliver. Several case studies show that employees perceive psychological contract breach when there is a mismatch between management communications about human resource management practices and what employees actually experience (Grant 1999; Greene, Ackers, and Black 2001).

A second cause of breach is when employees feel unsupported by either the organization (Tekleab, Takeuchi, and Taylor 2005) or their supervisors (Sutton and Griffin 2004). In a longitudinal study, Tekleab, Takeuchi, and Taylor (2005) found that perceived organizational support predicts psychological contract fulfilment. In other words, where employees believe that their organization is supportive—by doing such things as showing concern for their employees' well-being and offering help to employees when they need it—they are more likely to believe that the organization has fulfilled its promises. A likely explanation is that organizational support predisposes employees to overlook small breaches or forgive more serious breaches as one-off events. Explanations for why supervisor support leads employees to overlook breach are similar to those explanations linking organizational support and breach. Organizational support is also likely to be an important moderator of how employees react to breach, in line with other research that shows how support moderates affective reactions to distressing events.

The third type of cause of employee breach is events happening outside the organization or before the employee became a member of the organization. Robinson and Morrison (2000) found that employees are more likely to perceive breach by their current employer where, first, they have experienced breach by former employers and, second, where employees perceive themselves to have many employment alternatives. Employees with a history of perceiving breach in past employment relationships will be less trusting and hence more likely to monitor their current organization more vigilantly to make sure it fulfils promises. Such a heightened vigilance increases the likelihood of detecting breach. Where employees have few other job options, because of external economic conditions such as high unemployment, they are less inclined to be vigilant as they are powerless to do anything about breach in terms of seeking alternative employment. In contrast, in situations where employees do have employment alternatives they are likely to monitor more actively whether their organization fulfils its promises—as they can readily seek a better deal elsewhere if their organization fails to deliver—and hence are more likely to detect breach.

In a theoretical paper Ho (2005) suggests that a fourth way in which breach can be caused is when employees compare their deals unfavourably with other employees and perceive inequity. For example, if an employee compares their psychological contract to that of another employee and concludes they are getting a worse deal, then they are more likely to perceive breach of their own psychological contract. In contrast, if such a comparison leads the employee to view their deal more favourably, they are more likely to perceive a fulfilled psychological contract. There are no empirical studies directly testing the impact of social comparisons on psychological contract breach; however, support can be inferred from studies comparing employees doing the same job but employed on different working schedules (i.e. employed on either a part-time or full-time basis). These studies consistently find that part-time employees report different levels of psychological contract breach to that of full-time counterparts, where researchers explain differences by the social comparisons that part-time and full-time employees make between themselves (Millward and Hopkins 1998; Conway and Briner 2002b; Gakovic and Tetrick 2003). For example, part-timers report a more fulfilled psychological contract compared with full-timers, as they perceive the overall exchange of what they do for the organization and what they get back in return as more favourable than their full-time counterparts (Conway and Briner 2004).

Finally, Robinson and Morrison (2000) present a theoretical model proposing two pathways through which breach can occur. The first is where poor overall performance by the organization relative to its goals and objectives leads it to deliberately break promises, referred to as *reneging*, which causes employees to perceive psychological contract breach. Using a longitudinal survey, Robinson and Morrison (2000) found that poor organizational performance predicts employee perceptions of breach. The authors did not, however, measure whether the breach was due to the organization deliberately reneging (presumably organizations do not intentionally underperform), or due to factors outside the organizations control. The second path to breach is where insufficient organizational socialization and misleading pre-hire interaction causes misunderstandings between employees and organizations, referred to as *incongruence*, which in turn leads employees to perceive breach (Morrison and Robinson 1997). Socialization processes, in the form of training and induction, and the number of interactions with organizational representatives prior to being hired were found to significantly reduce the extent to which employees perceive breach; however, the extent to which this was due to fewer misunderstandings was not tested.

The chain of causal factors leading up to breach also appears to be moderated by a number of other variables (Morrison and Robinson 1997; Edwards et al. 2003). (Please note that here we are discussing factors that moderate the relationship between a potential cause of breach and breach—we discuss factors that moderate the consequences of breach later in this chapter.) Certain ideologies, for example, have been found to moderate the extent to which organizational changes, as potential causes of breach, do actually lead to psychological contract breach. Edwards et al. (2003) examine the ideology of employee self-reliance, which refers to an employee's belief that he or she should depend on the employer as little as possible and take responsibility for his or her own employability. In an imaginative study combining the results from experiments and questionnaire surveys, Edwards et al. (2003) found that the ideology of employee self-reliance reduces the extent to which employees perceive redundancy programmes as psychological contract breach. This relationship was found both for employees who have experienced being laid-off and for employees observing lay-offs happening to others. An ideology of employee self-reliance makes employees less likely to see their organization as being responsible for job security and thus any failure by the organization to deliver job security is less likely to be perceived as breach.

To conclude, research has identified several important antecedents to breach but clearly much more theoretical and empirical research is needed to gain a better understanding of the factors leading up to breach and how these factors causally interrelate and interact.

5.5. The consequences of breach

In general, researchers believe that psychological contract breach has serious consequences for employees and organizations, viewing breach as the most important way employees evaluate the state of their psychological contract and as the main way of explaining how the psychological contract affects outcomes. Reflecting this importance, most empirical studies of the psychological contract have investigated the consequences of breach. Empirical studies have found breach to be related to lower employee well-being, negative attitudes towards the job and the organization, such as job dissatisfaction and low organizational commitment, lower job performance, reduced levels of organizational

Table 5.1 The consequences of breach: things a person might feel, think, and do following psychological contract breach

Feel	Think	Do
• Anger • Violation • Upset • Dissatisfied • Betrayal • Sadness	• 'How can I trust this organization anymore?' • 'I'm not going to put myself out again for this organization.' • 'What's the point in being loyal to this organization when they behave in this way?' • 'How dare they treat me like that?'	• Put in less effort • Not prepared to go the extra mile for the organization • Refuse to work beyond their contract • Retaliate – through turning up late, leaving early, taking days off, using company equipment for purposes unrelated to work

citizenship behaviour, and increased withdrawal behaviours such as leaving the organization. While many outcomes have been considered, the basic explanation behind the findings of these empirical studies is very simple. When employees perceive the organization to have breached the psychological contract they view their relationship with the organization more negatively and are less likely to do things for the organization. General examples of this reasoning are shown in Table 5.1.

This section begins by explaining why breach affects outcomes and then reviews empirical studies examining the relationship between breach and outcomes. As with our earlier discussion of antecedents, it should be noted that while researchers often describe the relationship between psychological contract breach and variables such as affect, attitudes, and behaviours using the language of causality—such as *consequences* and *outcomes*—this only reflects researchers' theoretical beliefs rather than the evidence; about 90 per cent of the empirical studies examining the consequences of breach use cross-sectional designs and, therefore, cannot determine causality. Again this is a serious limitation of research addressing the consequences of breach.

Why should breach lead to such consequences? At present we do not know the answer to this question; however, researchers suggest several explanations that apply generally across outcomes, whether such outcomes are affective, attitudinal, or behavioural.

The first explanation is that, because promises imply expectations, breach will imply unmet expectations, where unmet expectations are known to affect job satisfaction and performance (Wanous et al. 1992). The second explanation is that breach decreases trust which in turn affects outcomes (Robinson and Rousseau 1994). Contracts require parties to have a certain amount of confidence that the other party to the contract will deliver. When employees perceive breach their trust in the organization declines and so employees consequently feel less inclined to invest emotionally or behaviourally in the relationship with the employer, as they feel less confident that the organization will reciprocate in the future, and also doubt the organization's past integrity (Rousseau 1989). In extreme cases, employees feel betrayed due to being misled and deceived, which can result in vengeful behaviour. The third explanation for the effects of breach involves the perceived inequity that follows when the organization fails to deliver on their side of the deal (Robinson, Kraatz, and Rousseau 1994). Employees consequently try to rebalance the deal by reducing their contributions to the employer, for example, through adjusting the quantity or quality of their work performance. Fourth, breach deprives employees of inducements at work that are important sources of work satisfaction and motivation (Robinson and Rousseau 1994). For example, where employees believe the organization has broken a promise about a pay rise, it is not just the fact that a promise has been broken that may affect their job satisfaction, but also that employees will be deprived of extra pay. Last, breach is likely to impede an employee's progress towards important goals (Conway and Briner 2002a), such as gaining promotion, and this will lead to goal frustration which has well-documented relationships with affect (e.g. Weiss and Cropanzano 1996). In summary, the main reasons why breach leads to outcomes are that breach involves unmet expectations, a breakdown of trust, a loss of inducements, feelings of inequity, and an impediment to goal progression. It is worth noting here that having multiple explanations for why breach affects outcomes also has its limitations, which we discuss later in Section 5.7.

While the previous paragraph dealt with explanations of the effects of breach, researchers also speculate that breach is a more intense experience with more profound effects than any of the experiences, such as a loss of inducements, described in each of the explanations. Because breach can potentially trigger all these experiences—unmet expectations, inequity, mistrust, a loss of inducements, and the thwarting of goals—it is both a more intense experience and distinct in its effects from any of the individual experiences (Robinson and Rousseau 1994). For example, inequity need not involve broken promises and, therefore, can be remedied by restoring the balance between contributions and inducements. In contrast, the damage caused by breach goes beyond inequity by leading to mistrust and feelings of betrayal and inspiring retaliatory behaviours (Robinson, Kraatz, and Rousseau 1994). Restoring trust is more difficult than restoring inequity because employees will be suspicious of any future actions taken by the organization, as they believe the organization has deceived them in the past. Similarly, in the case of unmet expectations, responses to breach are 'likely to be more intense than in the case of unfulfilled expectations. The intensity of the reaction is attributable not only to unmet expectations of specific rewards or benefits, but also to more general beliefs about respect for persons, codes of conduct, and other patterns of behaviour associated with relationships' (Robinson and Rousseau 1994: 247). However, at present there is insufficient evidence that breach affects outcomes beyond inequity and unmet expectations.

So what do researchers find when they investigate the consequences of psychological contract breach? Employee reactions to breach include:

- decreased levels of trust in the organization (e.g. Robinson 1996)
- cynical attitudes towards the organization (e.g. Johnson and O'Leary-Kelly 2003)
- thinking about, and in some cases actually leaving, the organization (e.g. Robinson and Rousseau 1994; Robinson 1995; Robinson 1996; Turnley and Feldman 1999; Tekleab and Taylor 2003)
- reduced psychological well-being (Conway and Briner 2002*a*)
- specific moods and emotions such as feeling anxious, violated, depressed and hurt (Conway and Briner 2002*b*)
- job dissatisfaction (e.g. Tekleab and Taylor 2003)
- reduced organizational commitment (e.g. Lester et al. 2002; Turnley and Feldman 1999)
- lowering their obligations towards the organization (e.g. Robinson, Kraatz, and Rousseau 1994; Coyle-Shapiro and Kessler 2002*c*)
- decreased levels of performance, including self-reported in-role performance (e.g. Robinson 1996; Turnley and Feldman 1999, 2000), supervisor-rated in-role performance (e.g. Lester et al. 2002), and various organizational citizenship or extra-role behaviours (e.g. Robinson and Morrison 1995; Robinson 1996; Turnley and Feldman 2000).

Rather than individually discussing each of the above outcomes we now select outcomes that have been investigated in five or more studies in order to provide a summary of the strength of associations between psychological contract breach and outcomes. The outcomes we discuss, therefore, include attitudes (job satisfaction, organizational commitment, and the intention to quit) and workplace behaviour (actual quitting, organizational citizenship behaviour, and job performance). (Note that while there are only three studies examining breach and actual quitting, we include these viewing quitting as the behavioural counterpart of the intention to quit.) Tables 5.2–5.5 summarize studies examining these relationships.

Some important points should be noted before we interpret the tables. First, the extent to which breach affects outcomes is indicated by the correlation coefficient *r*. The correlation coefficient is a statistical index for assessing the extent to which two variables are associated and can assume any value between -1 through to 0 through to $+1$; 0 indicates no association, -1 indicates a perfect negative association and $+1$ indicates a perfect positive association. The correlation coefficient is considered the standard indicator of effect size. Second, as already stated, researchers mainly use cross-sectional rather than longitudinal designs when examining the consequences of breach and so do not examine causality. Results of these studies do allow us to examine associations between variables but do not allow us to infer causality. Third, each construct has been measured in various ways across these studies. For example, measures of breach vary considerably in terms of the number of items, and whether respondents are required to

Table 5.2 The effects of psychological contract breach on job satisfaction, organizational commitment, and the intention to quit

Authors	Year	Sample size	Job satisfaction	Organizational commitment	Intention to quit
			Correlation coefficient between breach and outcome		
Cross-sectional studies					
Tekleab, Takeuchi, and Taylor	2005	200	−0.37		0.14
Sutton and Griffin	2004	235	−0.57		0.32
Raja, Johns, and Ntalianis	2004	197	−0.30	−0.49	0.48
Johnson and O'Leary-Kelly	2003	103	−0.59	−0.52	
Lo and Aryee	2003	152			0.48
Tekleab and Taylor	2003	130	−0.34		0.23
Conway and Briner	2002	1608	−0.57	−0.41	0.42
Conway and Briner	2002	366	−0.57	−0.39	0.41
Kickul, Lester, and Finkl	2002	246	−0.36 (extrinsic) −0.53 (intrinsic)		0.16 (extrinsic) 0.38 (intrinsic)
Lester et al.	2002	134		−0.25	
Bunderson	2001	283	0.04 (administrative) −0.36 (professional)	0.17 (administrative) −0.50 (professional)	0.02 (administrative) 0.34 (professional)
Flood, Turner, Ramamoorthy, and Pearson	2001	402		−0.42	0.47
Turnley and Feldman	2000	804	−0.56		0.48
Coyle-Shapiro and Kessler	2000	6953	−0.38 (transactional) −0.46 (training) −0.46 (relational)	−0.30 (transactional) −0.27 (training) −0.23 (relational)	
Turnley and Feldman	1999	804			0.38
Cavanaugh and Noe	1999	136	−0.72		0.25
Guzzo, Noonan, and Elron	1994	148		−0.27	0.16
Robinson and Rousseau	1994	128	−0.76		0.42
Average correlation			***−0.46***	***−0.32***	***0.33***
Longitudinal studies					
Bunderson	2001	167	−0.12 (administrative) −0.28 (professional)	0.10 (administrative) −0.47 (professional)	0.19 (administrative) 0.29 (professional)

Notes for Tables 5.2 to 5.5:
1. We use a policy of one row entry per data-set. This means that Conway and Briner's study has two rows as it includes samples drawn from two independent organizations. It also means that where a single data-set forms the basis of several empirical papers, and where the same finding is reported across two or more articles, we include the correlation only once. For example, Robinson (1996) and Robinson and Morrison (1995) report correlations from the same data-set, so only one of the papers is included in Table 5.4.
2. Terms in brackets following correlation coefficients indicate where a specific dimension of breach was measured (e.g. 'transactional' refers to a measure of transactional contract breach). The average correlation includes correlations between outcomes and dimensions of breach.

rate discrete psychological contract items—such as pay, training, promotion opportunities—or provide global evaluations of their psychological contract (Chapter 6 extensively discusses measures of breach). Measures of performance also vary widely in terms of what aspect of work performance is considered

Table 5.3 The effects of psychological contract breach on employee turnover

Authors	Year	Sample size	Employees actually quitting (correlation r)
Tekleab, Takeuchi, and Taylor	2005	191	−0.02
Bunderson	2001	283	0.17 (administrative)
			0.09 (professional)
Robinson	1996	126	0.20
Average correlation			*0.11*

Table 5.4 The effects of psychological contract breach on organizational citizenship behaviour

Authors	Year	Sample size	OCB measure	Correlation r
Cross-sectional studies				
Coyle-Shapiro and Kessler	2000	6953	General measure, self-report	−0.02 (transactional)
				−0.22 (training)
				−0.16 (relational)
Turnley and Feldman	2000	804	General measure, self-report	−0.46
Conway and Briner	2002a	1608	General measure, self-report	−0.14
Conway and Briner	2002b	366	General measure, self-report	−0.15
Kickul, Lester, and Finkl	2002	246	OCBIs, self-report	−0.01 (extrinsic PCB)
				−0.07 (intrinsic PCB)
			OCBOs, self-report	−0.05 (extrinsic PCB)
				−0.05 (intrinsic PCB)
Turnley and Feldman	1999	804	Loyalty subscale, self-report	−0.45
Lo and Aryee	2003	152	Civic virtue (a dimension of OCB), self-report	−0.31
Turnley et al.	2003	134	OCBIs, supervisor-rated	−0.11 (pay)
				−0.30 (relationship)
			OCBOs, supervisor-rated	−0.31 (pay)
				−0.45 (relationship)
Kickul, Lester, and Finkl	2002	322	Anti-citizenship behaviour, supervisor-rated	−0.33 (reversed)
Tekleab and Taylor	2003	130	OCB, supervisor-rated	−0.16
Johnson and O'Leary-Kelly	2003	103	Helping behaviours, rated by colleagues	−0.07
Average effect size				*−0.20*
Longitudinal studies				
Robinson	1996	125	Civic virtue, self-report	−0.25

Note: OCB refers to general measures of organizational citizenship behaviour; OCBI refers to organizational citizenship behaviours towards other individuals (e.g. helping a colleague); OCBO refers to organizational citizenship behaviours towards the organization (e.g. upholding the organization's reputation outside work).

(overall performance, in-role performance) and where the performance rating comes from (Do employees rate their own performance? Is their performance rated by their supervisor? Is employee performance taken from more objective sources such as organizational records?). In contrast, measures of organizational commitment, for example, vary in relatively minor ways. However, when interpreting the findings, and in order to summarize across studies, we assume that variation in correlations across studies reflect variation in the association between the two underlying constructs rather than how they are measured. Finally,

Table 5.5 The effects of breach on performance

Authors	Year	Sample size	Performance measure	Correlation r
Cross-sectional studies				
Tekleab and Taylor	2003	130	Overall performance, supervisor rated	−0.14
Johnson and O'Leary-Kelly	2003	103	In-role performance, supervisor rated	−0.33
Turnley et al.	2003	134	In-role, supervisor rated	−0.20 (pay)
				−0.41 (relationship)
Kickul, Lester, and Finkl	2002	246	In-role performance, self-report	−0.05 (intrinsic breach)
				−0.08 (extrinsic breach)
Lester et al.	2002	134	Overall job performance, self-rated	0.07
			Overall job performance, supervisor-rated	−0.37
Average effect size				***−0.19***
Longitudinal studies				
Bunderson	2001	123	Objective job performance derived from organizational records	0.13 (administrative)
				−0.21 (professional)
Robinson	1996	126	Overall job performance, self-report	−0.18
Average effect size				***−0.09***

nearly all measures of breach do not ask about breach directly but instead ask about the extent to which the employees believe their psychological contract has been fulfilled—researchers interpret totally or largely fulfilled as not experiencing breach whereas totally or largely *un*fulfilled is taken to mean that the employee has experienced breach. Where studies report fulfilment rather than breach, correlation coefficients have been reversed in the tables.

What do the findings presented in the tables tell us about the consequences of breach? We focus on three areas. First, how important is the concept of breach as a predictor of work attitudes and behaviour? Results from cross-sectional studies show that breach is a reasonably strong predictor of work attitudes, but has much weaker relationships with work behaviour. Breach is strongly related to job satisfaction (average correlation = −0.46) and moderately related to organizational commitment (average correlation = −0.32), and the intention to quit (average correlation = 0.33). However, breach is only weakly related to organizational citizenship behaviours, job performance, and actual turnover (average correlations = −0.20, −0.19, and 0.11 respectively). The weak relationships between breach and behavioural outcomes suggest that breach may not be a particularly useful concept for understanding work behaviour. There are at the present too few longitudinal studies to conclude whether better quality evidence would find the same pattern of results.

A second and related issue is the importance of the concept of breach relative to other frameworks for understanding employee attitudes and behaviour. Recall that one of the main reasons for researchers' interest in breach is that it predicts outcomes over and above other well-established concepts, such as justice perceptions and met expectations. Here, we compare psychological contract breach with just one of these areas, perceived organizational justice. Research on workplace justice, rather like the psychological contract, began in the 1960s and has grown considerably in the last fifteen years.

Cohen-Charash and Spector's recent (2001) meta-analysis of workplace justice found that distributive justice and procedural justice both have moderately large correlations with job satisfaction (respectively, $r = 0.47$ across 23 studies and 0.43 across 36 studies), and with affective organizational commitment (respectively, $r = 0.47$ across 27 studies and 0.50 across 52 studies), and with the intention to quit (respectively, $r = -0.40$ across 8 studies and -0.40 across 18 studies). For workplace behaviours, distributive justice and procedural justice both have fairly small correlations with organizational citizenship behaviour (respectively, $r = 0.25$ across 7 studies and 0.23 across 8 studies), whereas distributive justice and procedural justice correlations with performance differ markedly, with distributive justice having a small correlation with job performance ($r = 0.13$ across 6 studies), while procedural justice has a large correlation with performance ($r = 0.45$ across 11 studies).

Comparing the findings from justice studies with psychological contract breach studies, we can see that the pattern of findings between justice and outcomes and breach and outcomes are remarkably similar, with the slight suggestion that justice has marginally stronger associations with outcomes. Hence we can conclude that breach is as important as justice in terms of predicting attitudes and behaviour at work. One important conceptual and empirical issue discussed later, in Section 5.7, is whether justice and breach are sufficiently distinct.

A third issue is whether the dimensions of psychological contract breach (e.g. transactional-relational, administrative-professional) relate differently to outcomes? For example, do employees react more strongly to breach of relational promises than to breach of transactional promises? It is unclear from the studies reported here whether dimensions of breach differentially affect outcomes. More research is needed here to examine whether it is appropriate to treat organizational breach as a single construct or whether such treatment is likely to mask important distinctions and thus mask significant relationships between dimensions of breach and outcomes.

In summary, empirical studies find many consequences of psychological contract breach. Researchers explain the effects of breach in several ways, although these explanations have so far been insufficiently tested. Breach has much stronger effects on attitudes than behaviours. The effects of breach on outcomes are similar in magnitude to perceived injustice; indeed, breach and injustice are likely to occur simultaneously. Finally, the lack of longitudinal studies restricts making confident claims about causality. It seems to be the case that after forty years of psychological contract research we cannot draw any firm causal conclusions about the consequences of breach.

5.6. Moderators of the effects of breach on outcomes

Whether breach leads to the kinds of outcomes presented in Section 5.5 is likely to depend on a number of factors. Section 5.6 reviews factors that moderate the effects of breach on outcomes, which include the perceived importance of the broken promise, employee attributions for the cause of breach, justice perceptions, and employees' ideological views.

A likely and somewhat obvious moderator of the effects of breach is the perceived importance of the broken promise. In other words, the more important the promise, the stronger the reactions are likely to be if it is broken. Although relatively few studies have examined this, there is empirical support for the moderating effects of the perceived importance of the promise (e.g. Conway and Briner 2002a).

Another factor determining how employees react to breach is employees' beliefs about or attributions of the causes of the breach. For example, an employee is likely to react differently to a promise they believe that the organization deliberately broke than a broken promise they believe came about by accident or through a misunderstanding.

Researchers have generally only considered the effects of one type of attribution—whether the employee believes the cause of the breach was within or outside the control of the organization. In the former case the breach would be viewed as deliberate reneging, whereas in the latter case the breach would be viewed as being caused by factors the organization could not control, such as economic conditions. The few studies conducted in this area find only weak support for the moderating role of attributions. The extent to which employees attribute breach to deliberate reneging by the organization has been found to affect the relationship between breach and feelings of betrayal (Conway and Briner 2002a), intention to quit (Turnley and Feldman 1999) and organizational citizenship behaviour (Turnley et al. 2003), where employees respond more negatively in each case where they believe the organization has intentionally reneged. However, the extent to which employees attribute breach to deliberate reneging by the organization has not been found to affect the relationship between breach and violation (Robinson and Morrison 2000), feeling hurt or measures of daily mood (Conway and Briner 2002a), voice, loyalty or neglectful behaviours (Turnley and Feldman 1999), or in-role behaviours (Turnley et al. 2003).

It is, therefore, difficult to draw any firm conclusions about the role of attributions in moderating employees' reactions to breach, partly because attributions have been measured in somewhat different ways across studies and the outcomes measured likewise vary considerably across studies. Overall, the limited evidence available suggests that employees tend to react badly to breach regardless of whether or not they believe the organization has intentionally reneged on its promises.

We would also expect that employees' perceptions of fairness would moderate reactions to breach. Three types of fairness have been considered: distributive fairness, referring to whether employees believe they receive fair rewards for efforts and contributions made; procedural fairness, referring to whether employees believe that the procedures allocating rewards are fair (e.g. are procedures sufficiently transparent, applied consistently, etc.); and interactional fairness, referring to the interpersonal treatment employees receive during their contact with decision-makers. Two studies have explored whether general perceptions of justice (or fairness, as the two terms are often used interchangeably) moderate reactions to breach, and two studies have explored whether fairness perceptions specific to organizational breach moderate reactions to breach. We would expect that in each case fair treatment following breach reduces any negative consequences. However, there is little empirical support for fairness moderating the relationship between overall perceptions of breach and outcomes, whether researchers use general or specific measures of fairness. Studies that use general measures of justice find procedural justice moderates the relationship between breach and turnover intentions, but not between breach and employee voice, loyalty to the organization, or withdrawal behaviours (Turnley and Feldman 1999); and neither procedural justice nor interactional justice moderate the relationship between breach and anti-citizenship behaviour (Kickul et al. 2001). Studies that consider justice measures specific to breach find interactional justice does not moderate the relationship between breach and trust, withdrawal behaviours, civic virtue, turnover intentions (Lo and Aryee 2003) or feelings of violation (Robinson and Morrison 2000).

However, treating employees justly does appear to reduce negative reactions to breach when the content of the broken promise is matched with an appropriate type of justice. Kickul, Lester, and Finkl (2002) examined employees whose organizations had undergone large-scale change programmes and found that procedural justice moderated employee reactions to broken promises about items which organizations allocate through formal rules and procedures, such as pay, whereas interactional justice moderated employee reactions to broken promises about items requiring interpersonal treatment, such as respect and participation. In summary, researchers find very little support for justice as a moderator of the effects of breach on outcomes, except in cases where the type of justice is appropriately matched with the content of the broken promise.

Finally, personal ideologies may shape how employees view their psychological contract and also affect their response to breach. Bunderson (2001) examined the psychological contracts of doctors and found that they respond differently to breach depending on whether the breach conflicts with administrative or professional ideologies. Breach of administrative promises (such as the organization's failure to operate consistently across employees) predicted job satisfaction, the intention to quit, and actually quitting the job. However, breach of professional promises (such as the organization's failure to support high quality health care) predicted organizational commitment and job performance, where Bunderson argues breach leads employees to question whether the organization respects their professional needs and hence, following breach, doctors are more likely to withhold contributions of loyalty and performance.

To conclude, while there is likely to be a great number of potential factors moderating employees' reactions to breach, only a few have been examined. It is somewhat difficult to integrate the findings from these studies because of the wide range of outcomes considered and because factors that moderate the effects of breach on some outcomes, such as immediate emotional reactions, do not moderate effects on other outcomes. Given the weak support for any of these moderators, it appears that employees generally react negatively to breach. Factors are more likely to moderate reactions to breach when they fit the specific context, for example, when the type of justice matches the type of broken promise.

5.7. Examining breach: unresolved issues

This section considers several unresolved issues relating to breach. The first concerns which of the two components of breach, what is promised or what is delivered, is more important in terms of explaining outcomes—promises made, actual rewards, or the discrepancy between the two (i.e. breach)? The second issue is about whether breach is sufficiently distinct from two closely related concepts—inequity and unmet expectations. The third is whether it is possible to identify different types of breach. Finally, we consider the different effects of breach and fulfilment on outcomes.

5.7.1. Breach combines two concepts—promises and rewards

Recall that researchers define breach as the perceived discrepancy between what is promised and what is actually received. Breach, therefore, combines the two components of promises and delivered rewards. However, a serious concern is that, because both promises and rewards have independent effects on outcomes, any relationship found between breach and outcomes is not in fact due to perceived breach itself but, instead, due to either the effects of promises or rewards on the outcome (Arnold 1996). In other words, which concept really matters in terms of explaining outcomes—promises made, actual rewards, or the discrepancy between the two (i.e. breach)?

There is, therefore, an urgent need to disentangle the components of breach in order to discover the unique or independent contribution each makes to explaining outcomes over and above the influence of the others (Arnold 1996). Only one study has so far attempted to unpack the components of breach and the findings reveal that the components, particularly the actual rewards received, are more important predictors of organizational citizenship behaviour and feeling valued by the organization than psychological contract breach (Coyle-Shapiro and Conway 2005).

Clearly further studies are required to establish the unique impact of breach. At the same time, however, the findings by Coyle-Shapiro and Conway (2005) challenge the utility of the breach idea by suggesting that it is what is actually received that really affects employees rather than what was promised. As Arnold (1996) observes, if reward is the most important component researchers then practitioners should adopt a behaviourist perspective and concentrate only on the level of reinforcement employees receive, rather than whether or not promises of such rewards are broken or fulfilled.

5.7.2. The relationship between the breach concept and inequity and unmet expectations

As breach is clearly quite closely associated with other concepts, such as inequity, unmet expectations, and distrust, there is a concern that, where breach does seem to explain outcomes, is it actually these other related concepts rather than breach that are having an effect. For example, when employees perceive breach they are also very likely—perhaps inevitably—going to feel unfairly treated. Will their reaction be determined more by feelings of breach or unfairness? This is an important issue because, like the previous one, it raises the problem that breach may be a redundant idea for explaining employee attitudes and behaviours as it adds little if any value beyond these other concepts. Because they have received more attention, we focus here on the conceptual and empirical overlaps between breach and unmet expectations and breach and inequity (Robinson and Rousseau 1994).

The conceptual overlap between breach and unmet expectations and breach and inequity appear considerable. Recall from earlier discussion that the concepts of inequity, reduced trust, a loss of inducements, impeded goal progression, and unmet expectations are possible explanations for the effects of breach on outcomes. Hence, as breach may itself be explained by these concepts, this also questions just how different breach is from these concepts. In the case of the relationship between breach and inequity and unmet expectations, researchers go further, suggesting that every breach event will also involve employees perceiving unmet expectations and inequity (Rousseau 1989; Robinson and Rousseau 1994). In other words, from a theoretical perspective, these other concepts are seen to either explain breach or be part of the process of breach.

Turning to the empirical overlap, our above analysis of empirical findings from a number of studies into the consequences of breach shows a remarkably similar pattern to meta-analytic findings about the consequences of justice (Cohen-Charash and Spector 2001) and met expectations (e.g. Wanous et al. 1992).

While several attempts have been made to compare breach and unmet expectations within the same study (e.g. Robinson 1996; Turnley and Feldman 2000), the extent to which the two concepts are empirically distinct remains unclear because researchers have used measures of breach and unmet expectations that do not allow for effective comparison. For example, Robinson contrasts a two-item measure of global unmet expectations with a seven-item measure of breach concerned with specific aspects of work. Clearly, given the very different nature of the questionnaire items, any differences found across these two measures in explaining outcomes cannot be confidently attributed to the fact that one measure asks about promises and the other about expectations. What would ideally be required to make such a comparison, for instance, is for a measure of breach specific to the contract item (such as pay) to be compared with the extent to which there were unmet expectations for the same contract item. The same problem of not being able to precisely compare measures of breach and injustice also means that hereto we are unable to assess the degree of conceptual overlap or otherwise. For example, we would ideally like to compare a measure of breach of a pay promise, say, with a measure of perceived distributive, procedural, and interactional justice relating specifically to the breached pay promise.

In summary, the overlap between the concept of breach and the concepts of inequity and unmet expectations raises concerns about which concept really matters in terms of explaining outcomes and, therefore, the extent to which the breach concept is contributing anything new to our understanding.

5.7.3. Breach as an umbrella term for many different types of breach

As discussed earlier, definitions of breach are somewhat general and refer to any sort of broken promise. Very little attention is paid to the nature of the broken promise or, more specifically, to the *way* in which it is broken. Thinking about the experience of broken promises in everyday life, it is clear that when someone breaks a promise made to us this can happen in different ways. For example, if we believe that a friend has promised to meet us on their own at a particular time and place in order to have dinner they may break this promise in several ways. They may turn up late, not arrive at all, go to the wrong place, turn up and decide they would rather go to the cinema than have dinner, or arrive with a bunch of friends. In other words, not all broken promises are equal in kind and, therefore, are unlikely to be equal in their effects.

In a study by Cassar and Briner (2005), employees were asked whether certain promises they believed the organization had made to them were unfulfilled and, if so, to talk about exactly how the promise had been unfulfilled or breached. The results suggested that five components of breach could be identified and these are described as follows:

1. *Delay* refers to where the fulfilment of the promise occurs later than expected. For example, where an employee gets the promotion they were promised, but it happens at a point in time much after they were led to believe it would happen.
2. *Magnitude* is a breach that occurs because what is delivered is less than what was promised. So, for example, an employee might be promised a certain level of pay rise but get less than what was promised.
3. *Different type or form of reward* refers to a situation in which what is delivered is of a different form from what has been promised. An employee might have been promised additional training in, say, computer skills but instead is sent on a personal development programme.
4. *Inequity* is a component of breach where the employee believes that what they are receiving is less than or different from what others in similar positions are getting in terms of rewards. For example, an employee may experience this component of breach in a situation where they discover that others in the same position in another part of the organization have far superior physical working conditions.
5. *Reciprocal imbalance* refers to a situation where the employee perceives that they are giving far more to the organization than they are getting back in return. Employees may, for instance, feel that if they put in a lot of extra hours then this should be rewarded with being allowed more flexibility in terms of when and where they work.

It should be noted that these are not types of breach but rather possible forms of breach or ways in which employees may perceive breach to have occurred. The essential point here, as mentioned above, is that there is more than one way in which a promise can be broken. In addition there is some evidence that these different component forms of breach may be related in different ways to attitudes (Cassar 2004). In other words, employees may, for example, respond differently to a breach characterized by delay (too late) than to a breach characterized by lesser magnitude (too little).

While there is very little empirical or theoretical work on forms, types or components of breach it seems likely that breaches can occur or be characterized in very specific ways, which may be highly related to the outcomes of breaches.

5.7.4. The differential effects of breach and fulfilment on outcomes

The traditional view of psychological contract researchers is that contract fulfilment is a single continuum running from breach through to fulfilment through to overfulfilment, and that contract fulfilment has linear effects on outcomes (Lambert, Edwards, and Cable 2003). In other words, the association between breach–fulfilment and outcomes can be represented by a straight line where breach is associated with negative consequences, say job dissatisfaction, and as fulfilment increases there are proportionate increases in job satisfaction, through to overfulfilment being associated with further proportionate increases in job satisfaction.

However, studies that examine the separate effects of breach and fulfilment do not support this view. Conway and Briner (2002a) measured broken and exceeded promises separately thus allowing for an examination of their independent effects. Their findings suggest that broken promises have a greater effect on the outcome of daily mood than exceeded promises, which contradicts the idea of a linear relationship, where we would expect broken and exceeded promises to have proportionately the same effects on outcomes. In a second study, promises exceeded on certain items (e.g. pay) were associated with job satisfaction, however, promises exceeded on other items (e.g. task variety) were associated with job dissatisfaction (Lambert, Edwards, and Cable 2003); this again contradicts the idea of a linear relationship between breach–fulfilment and outcomes, as we would expect exceeded promises to have consistently positive effects on outcomes.

If broken promises do have differential effects on outcomes compared with exceeded promises, then there are important theoretical implications for research on contract fulfilment. There are at least three possible types of relationship between contract fulfilment and outcomes described in Figure 5.1 using the example of job satisfaction as the outcome. The first possibility is that there is a non-linear relationship between contract fulfilment and outcomes. For example, there may be a linear relationship between contract fulfilment and outcomes as breach–fulfilment varies from broken to kept promises, but then the relationship levels off as contract fulfilment goes beyond 'metness'; that is, when the organization exceeds its promises in a positive sense. Beyond metness and through increasing stages of contract fulfilment there is no, or minimal, changes in the outcome.

The second possibility is that within breached contracts and within exceeded contracts there are a number of different relationships depending on which promise is being considered, which is supported by the findings of Lambert,

Non-linear relationship between breach–fulfilment and job satisfaction

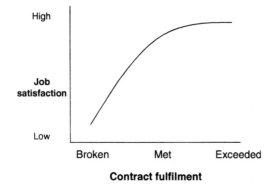

Contract fulfilment

Multiple dimensions within broken and exceeded contracts (figure presents exceeded contracts)

Exceeding promises on pay   **Exceeding promises on task variety**

Breaking and fulfilling promises are independent dimensions for same contract item

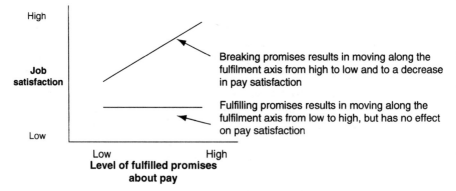

Figure 5.1 Alternative relationships between breach–fulfilment and the outcome of job satisfaction

Edwards, and Cable (2003). For example, exceeding promises in relation to pay may increase job satisfaction, whereas exceeding promises on task variety may decrease job satisfaction, as it means having too many tasks to perform.

The third possibility is that breaking promises and fulfilling promises for the same contract item are not on the same continuum but rather are relatively independent dimensions, in a similar way to Herzberg's classic distinction between hygiene and motivator factors (Herzberg, Mausner, and Snyderman 1959). Regardless of the level of contract fulfilment, while broken promises about pay may decrease job satisfaction, pay increases may not result in corresponding increases in job satisfaction. This is also similar to the 'Vitamin Model' developed by Warr (1987) to explain the non-linear relationships between job characteristics and outcomes.

In short, these three possibilities present a considerably more complicated relationship between breach–fulfilment and outcomes (for an extended discussion of the first two possibilities see Lambert, Edwards, and Cable 2003). While other ways of construing breach and fulfilment and the relation between the two are possible, it is clear that the traditional view of breach and fulfilment as lying on a single continuum and having a linear relationship with outcomes is too simple and requires considerable elaboration.

5.8. An alternative approach to breach linking psychological contract to outcomes—a 'features-based' analysis

Given the many limitations of most existing approaches to understanding the effects of breach, discussed above, this section considers a recent 'features-based' approach that might increase our understanding of how the psychological contract affects attitudes and behaviour. Features-based approaches consider various dimensions, referred to as features, along which psychological contracts can vary, such as stability, scope, tangibility, focus, time frame, and volition (Rousseau and McLean Parks 1993; McLean Parks, Kidder, and Gallagher 1998; Sels, Janssens, and Van Den Brande 2004). Advocates of the approach argue that the standard way of comparing different employment groups by comparing the contents of their psychological contracts is often inappropriate as too often content items apply strongly to certain groups of workers but not at all for others. In other words, a contract item concerning, for example, career development or long-term job security, may simply not be relevant in an organization where most employees have taken the job as a temporary stop-gap. Hence, as some content items are just not applicable to some contexts, there may be need for overarching dimensions based on features of the contract rather than items. The contents of employees' psychological contracts are, by definition, too idiosyncratic, dynamic, and evolving, to make it possible to develop a single measure of contents that will be appropriate to a wide range of different jobs.

Furthermore, McLean Parks, Kidder, and Gallagher (1998) propose that the features-based approach complements and goes beyond our understanding of psychological contract fulfilment. While contracts change and are breached, we also need to better understand how contract differences affect the occurrence of and reactions to breach, and also what makes for a better or worse psychological contract during psychological contract stability (i.e. when promises are being kept).

Building on an earlier analysis by Rousseau and McLean-Parks (1993), McLean Parks, Kidder, and Gallagher (1998) describe a number of psychological contract features including the following:

1. *Focus* refers to 'the relative emphasis of the psychological contract on socio-emotional versus economic concerns'. For example, does the employee place more importance on transactional aspects of the work, such as pay, or more importance on relational aspects such as respect?

2. *Time frame* refers to the length of the contract and is subdivided into the two components of *precision* and *duration*. Duration refers to the expected length of the psychological contract (e.g. short- versus long-term), precision refers to whether the duration of the contract is known or undefined.

3. *Stability* refers to the extent to which the terms of the psychological contract can change outside of an explicit or implicit renegotiation of the contract. In other words, an unstable psychological contract implies that either party can make unilateral changes to the terms of the psychological contract without consulting the other party.

4. *Scope* refers to whether clear boundaries and limits can be placed upon the breadth of the contract. A psychological contract with a narrow scope consists of a set of narrow clearly defined promises (e.g. a person employed solely to answer the phone); a psychological contract with a wide scope implies that the terms of the contract can spill over and pervade any aspect of the individual's life, either inside or outside work.

5. *Tangibility* refers to the terms of the contract being explicit and clearly observable to third parties and, therefore, not open to disagreement between the two parties due to subjective interpretation.

6. *Particularism* refers to the 'degree to which the employee perceives the resources exchanged within the contract as unique and non-substitutable'. For example, a psychological contract high on particularism may be where an employee has an inimitable set of skills, knowledge and abilities that the organization could not find elsewhere.

These features of psychological contracts will differentially influence attitudes and behaviours. For example, employees with highly tangible psychological contracts will be less likely to perform spontaneous or innovative behaviours as these behaviours are not expected and may detract from employees meeting their explicit promises.

Although there have been some recent advances in developing a features-based approach to psychological contracts (see Sels, Janssens, and Van Den Brande 2004) it remains underdeveloped. Some limitations of this approach have already been identified. For example, the list of features appears to be intuitive rather than theoretically derived (Guest 1998). However, given the potential of the approach for comparing different types of psychological contracts and employment relationships it clearly warrants further investigation. It is also one of the only attempts by researchers to consider how psychological contracts are regulated during psychological contract stability (also see Rousseau's discussion (2001) of mutuality).

5.9. Summary and conclusion

Most empirical studies focus on the consequences of breach, where it is found that breach has much stronger effects on attitudes than behaviours. However, the lack of longitudinal studies prevents the making of confident claims about causality. We know surprisingly little about other aspects of breach, including the answers to basic questions such as how often it happens, why it happens, and what factors moderate employees' reactions to breach. There are also concerns about whether breach contributes significantly to our understanding of the employment relationship beyond closely related concepts. Alternative mechanisms linking psychological contracts to outcomes are beginning to emerge, but are conceptually underdeveloped, and have yet to be researched in any detail.

A key conclusion is that—given the centrality of the breach idea to the psychological contract—researchers have made very little progress in understanding breach or researching the causes and effects of breach using appropriate methods. One possible explanation is that, at its core, the breach idea is about an *event*: a specific and particular thing that happens at a point in time. The approaches taken to explaining the effects of breach, such as fairness or unmet expectations, are not conceptualized or researched in terms of events. Rather, they are construed, like many constructs in organizational psychology, as perceptions or attitudes, held more or less strongly, varying in strength between individuals. These approaches do little to help us understand how events such as breach occur and the likely effects of such events. Furthermore, events can probably best be understood in the context of ongoing processes, which is also at odds with most approaches within organizational psychology. It seems to be the case that the idea of breach as an event-based phenomenon has presented researchers with problems that are simply not solvable using traditional research ideas and methods. This is why, as we shall discuss further in Chapter 8, taking a process approach to breach, and to the psychological contract in general, is perhaps the main way in which advances in understanding the psychological contract can be made.

6 | Researching the Psychological Contract

6.1. Introduction

Understanding the strengths and weaknesses of the methods and designs used to research the psychological contract is important, as their quality determines the reliability and validity of data gathered using the methods and, hence, also the validity of claims made about the psychological contract on the basis of these data. In other words, if the methods used to research the psychological contract have serious weaknesses then it is simply not possible to be confident about assertions made on the basis of this research. All research methods and designs have strengths and limitations. Here, however, we consider those strengths and limitations as they apply specifically to the methods used to research the psychological contract.

While a number of different research methods and designs have been used to investigate the psychological contract the field is dominated by one sort of study—the cross-sectional questionnaire survey. The dominance of this method has led some researchers to observe that psychological contract research has fallen into a 'methodological rut' (Taylor and Tekleab 2002: 279). For instance, out of the fifty-six empirical studies examining either the contents or breach of psychological contracts included in our review, about 70 per cent were based on cross-sectional questionnaire studies, 20 per cent were based on longitudinal questionnaire surveys, and 10 per cent were based on qualitative data from participant interviews. So, although we will discuss a range of methods, and a number of criticisms and limitations of research in this field, most of our observations will inevitably focus on what is the typical or most common type of research.

This chapter begins by describing the main methods used to research the psychological contract and briefly considers their strengths and weaknesses. We then go into more detail to consider the weaknesses of the most widely-used method, the questionnaire survey, along with other methodological and design limitations of typical studies in the field. The daily diary methodology is then described and evaluated, as one example of an alternative approach that can be used to overcome many of the limitations of currently used methods. We then consider a number of important areas of the psychological contract that have received relatively little research attention.

It is important throughout this chapter to bear in mind that one of the major ways in which any method can be judged as having strengths and limitations is in relation to the definition of the phenomena under investigation, the theoretical assumptions that are made about the nature of those phenomena, and the extent to which the methodology used can, in principle, get at those phenomena. While, as discussed in Chapter 3, the psychological contract has been variously defined, it refers, at its core, to the employee's beliefs about and understandings of promissory-based reciprocal exchanges between themselves and their employer. In addition to the contents and the nature of the exchange, the other main psychological contract phenomenon that has been widely discussed and researched is breach.

6.2. How has the psychological contract been researched?

The psychological contract has been researched using six different types of methods: questionnaire surveys; scenario methodologies; critical incident techniques; interviews; diary studies; and, case studies. This section describes studies that use these methods and briefly considers their strengths and weaknesses. A more detailed discussion of the weaknesses of the most typical kind of psychological contract study—the cross-sectional survey—will take place in the next section.

6.2.1. Questionnaire surveys

As mentioned earlier, questionnaire surveys are by far the most commonly used method in psychological contract research and we estimate that some 90 per cent of all empirical studies are of this type. For this reason we will discuss studies that use these methods in more detail than studies that use other methods. We will also focus on the measures that researchers have developed to study psychological contract contents and breach.

Survey approaches to researching the psychological contract follow the well-established conventions of survey methods found in other areas of organizational research. The surveys typically consist of large samples (200 or more employees), most often drawn from a single organization, and use self-report questionnaires to measure variables such as content, breach and outcomes. The majority of psychological contract measures are framed in terms of promises and obligations and are completed from an employee's perspective, reflecting Rousseau's more recent and commonly accepted definition of the psychological contract. About eight out of ten psychological contract studies survey participants on just one occasion (referred to as a cross-sectional study), whereas about two out of ten studies gather data from participants on several occasions (referred to as a longitudinal study). Relationships between variables are quantified and their statistical significance is assessed using techniques such as multiple regression and correlation.

The general advantages and disadvantages of questionnaire survey methods are well documented (e.g. Vaus 2001) and in the next section of this chapter we will discuss some of the more important limitations of using surveys for examining psychological contracts. Here, however, we will focus on describing the measures most commonly used to assess contents and breach of psychological contracts, consider how outcomes have been measured, and briefly evaluate the strengths and limitations of the measures. A selection of measures used to assess content and breach are presented in the Appendix. See Rousseau and Tijoriwala (1998) for an extensive discussion of the alternative ways of measuring psychological contracts.

Measures of contents

Most measures of psychological contract contents are multi-item measures in which employees make ratings about promises that may be exchanged between employees and organizations. The measures aim to gather employee perceptions of the terms of the deal, in other words, the employee perceptions of the specific promises their organization has made to them and the promises the employee has made to the organization. Researchers then create an overall score for each employee by calculating an average for the set of items. Box 6.1 reproduces an example of a measure of psychological contract contents taken from a recent study by Tekleab and Taylor (1998).

Of the twenty-five studies on the contents of psychological contracts included in our review, about 70 per cent (seventeen studies) used a measure similar in design to that in Box 6.1. Within these seventeen studies, measures varied in terms of the belief specified (where most studies asked participants to report on obligations, but other measures requested employee perceptions of promises, or commitments, or expectations) and the number of items included.

Some advantages of this type of measure, which asks respondents to comment on a list of terms, are that researchers can specify what they believe to be the main items of importance, and that such measures are easy to administer and relatively straightforward to answer. Some disadvantages are that items important to the participant may not be included, that the items do not capture exchange (as discussed in Chapter 3), and that the list of items chosen can appear to be somewhat arbitrary, varying considerably across studies. These limitations are a reflection of the weak theoretical understanding of how employees make sense of the contents of their psychological contracts.

Measures of breach

Three types of scale have been used for measuring breach. The first presents respondents with a list of specific contract items and asks about the extent to

---

Box 6.1 A measure of the contents of psychological contracts

Organization obligations to the employee

To what extent is the (company) obligated to provide each of the following to you:

(i) An attractive benefits package.
(ii) Fair treatment.
(iii) A relatively secure job.
(iv) Feedback on my performance.
(v) Training.
(vi) Leadership.

Employee obligations to the organization

To what extent do you feel you are obligated to provide each of the following to the (company):

(i) Volunteer to do tasks that fall outside my job description.
(ii) Develop new skills as needed.
(iii) Perform my job in a reliable manner.
(iv) Deal honestly with the (company).
(v) Work extra hours if needed to get the job done.
(vi) Follow the (company) policies and procedures.

Rated on a 5-point scale: 1 = not at all; 5 = very highly

Source: Tekleab and Taylor (1998).

---

which promises made in relation to those items have been fulfilled. The second type of scale uses several general questions that ask about the extent to which promises made have been fulfilled. The third uses a single general question that asks about the extent to which promises have been fulfilled (see Appendix). Here we will discuss the first two types as only two studies have used the third type (Robinson and Rousseau 1994; Robinson, Kraatz, and Rousseau 1994).

Most measures of breach are of the first type that focuses on whether employees perceive that their employer has kept their side of the deal through asking employees about the extent to which their employer has fulfilled specific promises made to them. Researchers then create an overall breach score for each employee by calculating an average for the set of items. The items in Box 6.1 listed under the heading 'organizations' obligations to the employee' can be used to assess breach by asking employees the extent to which their organization has fulfilled their promises in relation to each of the items. For example, Kickul, Lester, and Finkl (2002) presented employees with a set of 26 items such as competitive salary, meaningful work, retirement benefits, participation in decision-making, continued professional development and a reasonable workload and asked employees to rate the extent to which promises made about each item had been fulfilled using a 5-point Likert scale (1 = not at all fulfilled; 5 = very fulfilled).

Of the twenty-six questionnaire survey studies of psychological contract breach included in our review, about 62 per cent (sixteen studies) used multi-item measures similar to Kickul et al. (2002, see Appendix). Within these sixteen studies, measures vary in terms of the belief specified (most studies asked participants to report on fulfilled promises, but others requested employee perceptions of obligations, or commitments, or expectations) and the number of items included.

About 15 per cent of psychological contract breach studies use the second type of measure—a multi-item global measure of psychological contract breach. An example of such a measure is presented in Box 6.2. These measures ask employees several general questions about whether overall their psychological contract has been fulfilled, rather than asking about the extent to which specific promises have been fulfilment.

One of the first things to note is that almost all measures of breach do not ask about breach directly but rather ask about the extent to which the respondent feels their psychological contract has been fulfilled. Where respondents believe their contract has been totally or largely fulfilled this is taken to mean that the respondent has not experienced breach. On the other hand, where respondents believe their contract has been totally or largely *un*fulfilled this is taken to mean that the respondent has experienced breach. In general then, breach and fulfilment are seen as two ends of a single continuum. Only two studies examine this issue, where both Conway and Briner (2002) and Lambert et al. (2003) find support for treating breach and fulfilment as separate, rather than bipolar constructs. Hence, these studies suggest that it is not necessarily valid to measure breach by asking questions about fulfilment.

Box 6.2 A multi-item global measure of psychological contract breach

Almost all the promises made by my employer during recruitment have been kept so far (reversed)

I feel that my employer has come through in fulfilling the promises made to me when I was hired (reversed)

So far my employer has done an excellent job of fulfilling his promises to me (reversed)

I have not received everything promised to me in exchange for my contributions

My employer has broken many of his promises to me even though I've upheld my side of the deal

Rated on a 5-point scale: 1 = not at all; 5 = very highly

Source: Robinson and Morrison (2000).

It is not clear and somewhat curious why researchers ask about fulfilment when they actually wish to measure breach. One possible reason may be that asking directly about breach might seem negative and unacceptable to organizations hosting the research, hence researchers try to frame the questionnaire items more positively.

Specific and global measures make different theoretical assumptions about how employees evaluate their psychological contract. Specific item measures assume that individuals judge breach on a promise-by-promise, item-by-item basis whereas global measures assume individuals evaluate the extent to which promises have been kept on a general or overall basis. The main advantage of a specific item measure over a global evaluation is that it can identify which items are being fulfilled and which are not; the main disadvantages of specific item measures is that important psychological contract items may be omitted from the set of promises, and that the method of aggregating the items into a composite score by taking a simple average is unlikely to reflect how an employee psychologically aggregates experiences.

Measures of outcomes

Many presumed outcomes and consequences of the psychological contract have been investigated, largely in studies of psychological contract breach. These outcomes can be broadly classified as attitudes (e.g. job satisfaction, organizational commitment), feelings (e.g. moods), or behaviour (e.g. organizational citizenship behaviour, employee performance, absenteeism, turnover). In most cases, reasonably well-validated outcome measures are used. The major limitation of the outcome measures is that they are almost exclusively employee self-report, which presents particular problems for the measurement of behaviours.

To summarize, questionnaire surveys are by far the most commonly used method to examine the psychological contract. There are a variety of measures for assessing both breach and the contents of psychological contracts, showing there is no single, agreed upon measure of either of these constructs. Outcome measures used tend to be well-validated, but are largely self-report, and present particular problems in assessing behaviours. Problems with questionnaire surveys, as they are the most commonly used method, will be discussed in more detail in Section 6.3.

6.2.2. Scenario methodologies

This method presents participants with a number of passages of text that describe similar scenarios or stories but ones that vary in a systematic way across different passages. So, for example, one passage may suggest that a character in the scenario is quite young while another that the character is quite mature. In this way the researcher designs the scenarios so that the independent variables (predictors) are manipulated across different scenarios to see if they affect the way the person makes a judgement about the person or situation. Scenario methods are commonly used in conjunction with questionnaires that include measures of the study's dependent or outcome variables. Two psychological contract studies have used the scenario method. Rousseau and Anton (1991) examined whether the level of employee contributions affected third-party judgements of termination fairness, and Edwards et al. (2003) examined whether employees that believe in the ideology of self-reliance are less likely to perceive layoffs as a breach of psychological contracts.

We illustrate this method in Box 6.3 using two scenarios from Rousseau and Anton's study (1991). The independent variables described in these scenarios are, in order, present performance, how long the person has been in the job, job security according to the company when hired, past job performance, skills useful to the company, and employability. These variables are all described at a low level in the first scenario and a high level in the second scenario in Box 6.3. So, for example, in the first scenario performance is described as low while in the second scenario performance is described as high. The study also included twenty-five other scenarios where the number of independent variables specified at either high or low levels were systematically varied. Immediately after reading a scenario, respondents completed questionnaire items judging the fairness of the termination that, in this case, was the outcome or dependent variable.

A major advantage of scenario methods is the controlled manipulation of independent variables. Key disadvantages of the method are its low ecological

---

Box 6.3 Example of a scenario methodology

Independent variables all set at low

Jane Janis is being terminated by Acumen Inc. Jane's present job performance is below average. Jane was employed by Acumen Inc. for two years. When hired, Jane was told that the company could not guarantee long-term employment. Jane's past job performance was below average. Jane has few skills likely to be useful to the firm in the future. It will be very difficult for Jane to get another job.

Independent variables all set at high

Chris Steward is being terminated by Acumen Inc. Chris's present job performance is above average. Chris was employed by Acumen Inc. for 14 years. When hired, Chris was told that the prospects for long-term employment were good. Chris's past job performance was above average. Chris has many skills likely to be useful to the firm in the future. It will be fairly easy for Chris to get another job.

Source: Rousseau and Anton (1991).

validity (i.e. the scenario is not representative of the participant's everyday working environment) and that the method is potentially tedious for participants as it requires rating numerous scenarios in order to generate sufficient data for meaningful statistical analysis (e.g. Rousseau and Anton's participants were presented with twenty-seven scenarios to rate).

6.2.3. Critical incident techniques

Only one study of the psychological contract, by Herriot, Manning, and Kidd (1997) has used a critical incident technique to examine the content of psychological contracts (this study is reviewed in Chapter 4). In critical incident techniques participants are asked to recall an event that was particularly salient or important in a specific way and are then asked a series of questions about the incident. In this study, participants were asked to recall an incident at work where the organization had either fallen short of or exceeded expectations.

Critical incident techniques are well suited to capturing employee recollections of vivid experiences and as such are a potentially useful method for gathering data for psychological contract breach. However, a major limitation of this method is that the accuracy of any recollections is substantially distorted by the various limitations of memory (see Section 6.3). A further limitation is that critical incident techniques may overlook and not assess the more mundane day-to-day operation of the psychological contract when it is being maintained fairly well though with no salient or important incidents relating to broken or exceeded promises.

6.2.4. Diary studies

Recording activities and behaviours repeatedly over relatively short periods of time, as you may do in a diary, has a long history in organizational research dating back to Taylor (1911) and his time and motion studies. In the 1950s and 1960s organizational researchers used diaries to study managers' typical working days by asking them to keep daily records of their activities (e.g. Carlson 1951; Stewart 1967). In organizational psychology, diaries are currently most likely to be used to examine stressful events (Symon 1998). Diaries have also featured in other areas of psychology, for example in the study of work motivation (e.g. Csikszentmihalyi and Csikszentmihalyi 1988; Csikszentmihalyi and LeFever 1989), personal relationships (e.g. Drigotas, Whitney, and Rusbult 1995), health and illness behaviour (e.g. Roghman and Haggerty 1972), and personality (e.g. Cantor et al. 1991). This very brief review may give the impression that diary methods have been commonly adopted, however, diaries remain a relatively rare and novel method.

Given the suitability of diaries for capturing everyday events and experiences, it is surprising that only one study by Conway and Briner (2002*a*) has examined the psychological contract using a diary study. We believe the psychological contract—with its emphasis on events happening over time at the within-person level—is ideally suited to study through diary methods which are capable of capturing events, behaviour, experiences, and feelings close to when they actually occur and in a relatively unobtrusive manner. In particular, such a method seems particularly well suited to exploring experiences of and reactions to breach. Later in this chapter we argue for using diary studies ahead of existing methods and describe this methodology and its strengths and limitations in more detail.

6.2.5. Interviews

Studies using interviews to assess the psychological contract have ranged from asking respondents a few simple questions through to in-depth interviews. Interviews have often been combined with other methods, such as questionnaires. Early empirical studies of the psychological contract by Argyris (1960) and Levinson et al. (1962) were based on interviews with employees, combined with the researchers' observations of employees and managers at the workplace.

Using in-depth interviews produces data of idiosyncratic experiences and interpretations of the psychological contract, grounded in the language of employees and organizational context. Such accounts are consistent with the psychological contract as a highly individualized subjective construct (Rousseau and Tijoriwala 1998), and are vital for elaborating our understanding of how employees understand and describe key aspects of the psychological contract; however, this method is not designed to examine causal relationships or to generalize findings across cases.

6.2.6. Case studies

A small number of studies utilize a case study approach by collecting data from multiple sources using multiple methods with the aim of providing rich descriptions of the psychological contract between employees and their employers in a single organizational setting (e.g. Argyris 1960; Grant 1999; Green, Ackers, and Black 2001). For example, Grant's case study of a Japanese-owned 'greenfield' site in England collected quantitative and qualitative data from employees, management, and union officials using questionnaires, interviews, and researchers' observations of employees and managers at the workplace. The limitations of a case study approach will obviously depend on the limitations of the various methods used as part of the case study, although the limitations of some methods may be offset by the strengths of another method.

6.2.7. Summary

While a number of different methods have been used to examine the psychological contract, by far the most common is the questionnaire survey. Furthermore, alternatives to surveys often still use questionnaire type methods (e.g. scenario methods, case studies, diary studies) as part of their design. While several measures of the contents and breach of psychological contracts are available, and certain measures are more commonly used than others, there is no widely acknowledged, rigorously tested measure of either construct at present.

6.3. A critique of designs and methods most commonly used to research the psychological contract

From Section 6.2 we can see that most research on the psychological contract has two methodological and design characteristics. First, it uses self-report questionnaire survey measures of psychological contract breach and contents and outcomes. Second, it uses cross-sectional designs, or occasionally longitudinal designs conducted across very few time points. In this section we critically evaluate these two main features of designs and explain why such designs are limited for researching psychological contracts.

6.3.1. Problems with using self-report questionnaire survey measures of breach and contents and outcomes of the psychological contract

We briefly described the strengths and weaknesses of self-report questionnaire survey measures of breach, contents and outcomes in Section 6.2.1 above, and also discussed a range of specific limitations of these measures. Here we consider in more detail the weaknesses of such methods.

We have organized our concerns about the use of these types of measures within three main areas: first, the limitations of using questionnaires to ask respondents to recall, select, and summarize events from the past; second, the limitations of the wording of individual questionnaires items used to measure psychological contract contents and breach; and third, the limitations of using employee self-reports to measure behavioural consequences or outcomes of the psychological contract.

Problems associated with the selection, recall, and aggregation of information

Reis and Wheeler (1991) present a powerful critique of self-report questionnaires, noting the problems relating to the selection, recall, and aggregation of information when using questionnaires to collect data. The critique is based around recalling previous events taking place during social interaction and so is particularly relevant to assessing social exchange relationships such as psychological contracts. However, the critique also applies to reporting past behaviour and is thus relevant to measuring behavioural outcomes using self-report questionnaires.

Self-report questionnaires do provide very general and overall perceptions of social activity, but are best regarded as 'personalized impressions' that have been 'percolated, construed, and reframed through various perceptual, cognitive, and motivational processes' (Reis and Wheeler 1991: 271). Drawing mainly from the literature on social cognition, Reis and Wheeler's criticisms demonstrate how the reporting of events is substantially distorted through relying on standard self-report questionnaires. The criticisms are organized according to the *selection* of representative events, *recalling* the characteristics of those events, and *aggregating* information across multiple events and situations.

Self-report questionnaires are likely to distort how participants *select* events. First, the domain of events the questionnaire item refers to is often imprecisely stated or even absent due to the requirement of questionnaire items to be as short and simple as possible. For example, when asked the question 'how often has your organization kept its promises to you?' it is not clear what period of time to consider, or to what events at work the item refers. Second, selection bias arises through, for example, selecting more memorable or recent events, as it is more difficult recalling information about events that happened several months or a year ago. Third, selecting events is prone to mood-congruent effects at the time of retrieval. In other words, how respondents feel momentarily while completing the questionnaire will affect their responses. For example, if we are feeling very happy when completing a questionnaire we tend to judge parties more favourably, whereas if we are feeling angry then we might answer much less favourably. When these factors affecting selection are taken together the level of distortion can be considerable. Conrath, Higgins, and McClean (1983) for instance, found that when employees recall their interactions with significant others, only 27 per cent of interactions are recalled by both partners. Questionnaires measuring psychological contract contents and breach are likely to be influenced by all these types of biases.

Biases affect participants' accuracy of *recalling* social interactions, where accuracy decreases as the length of time between the event and the point of recall increases (Reis and Wheeler 1991). Biases include failings of memory such as forgetting and others based on motivational factors, such as defence mechanisms, that may distort recall. Furthermore, the longer the time interval between the event and recall, the more likely it is that these processes will be reiterated to further obscure the 'reality' of the actual situation. Questionnaire items measuring the psychological contract do not typically limit how far back a respondent is expected to recall so we have to assume that respondents potentially recall any event since the beginning of their employment.

Finally, it is poorly understood how people *aggregate* multiple events to arrive at a single impression. There are many possible ways to aggregate multiple events, such as deriving a simple average, a weighted average (e.g. by emotional significance), or prioritizing by availability or atypical events. These aggregations are unlikely to be applied systematically or precisely either across employees or by the same employee over time. Because of such factors, aggregations are not good indicators of events that actually took place at the time (Reis and Wheeler 1991). Applying this to measures of the psychological contract and selecting as an example the item 'Overall, how well has your employer fulfilled the promised obligations that they owed you?' we do not know how or indeed if employees aggregate the multiple discrete events of broken, kept, and exceeded promises across all the items that may be exchanged when attempting to answer such a question. While such measurement techniques certainly generate data, the meaning of those data is difficult to establish.

Obviously, factors affecting selection, recall and aggregation apply equally well to longitudinal questionnaire surveys whenever there is a substantial elapse of time between measurements, and would certainly apply to all longitudinal studies that have examined the psychological contract.

These criticisms of self-report questionnaires are, as Reis and Wheeler (1991) also make clear, not intended in any way to diminish the importance of an individual's views of their previous experiences. Such impressions are clearly important in terms of making sense of the past and anticipating the future. They are, however, arrived at through numerous reinterpretations over time and will represent a different phenomenon to what was experienced at the time of the event. Retrospective reports of breach will compound many events and experiences subsequent to the initial breach and are, therefore, not only capturing the breach event but subsequent experiences as well. The great majority of psychological contract research ignores this simple observation.

The biases described here in relation to the selection, recall, and aggregation of information gathered in self-report questionnaires apply to many contexts in which such questionnaires are used. However, they are particularly problematic in contexts such as this where respondents are being asked to give answers to questions which require them to think back over long time periods about possibly very large numbers of events in order to construct an answer.

Limitations of questionnaire items measuring breach and contents

This section focuses on the wording of questionnaire items. We illustrate our observations using the following example of a questionnaire item measuring breach: 'How well, overall, has your employer fulfilled the promised obligations that they owed you' (Robinson and Rousseau 1994). Please note that the points made later apply equally well to other measures of breach and the first five points also apply to measures of content. A summary of the issues is presented in Figure 6.1.

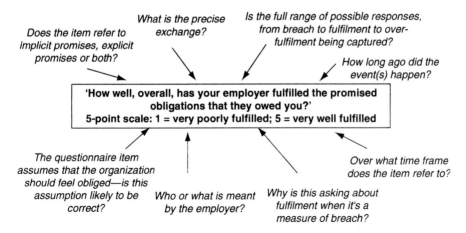

Figure 6.1 Key issues when measuring the psychological contract

1. The measures do not ask respondents to specify when the breach occurred (or when the promise was made in the case of measuring the contents of psychological contracts), it may have happened yesterday or ten years ago. It seems likely that the timing of the breach or the making of the promise will affect any impact on attitudes and behaviours.

2. The measures do not assess breach events as they happen or even recent breach events, such as within the last day, but instead ask employees to reflect back over an unspecified time period and recall whether or not a breach has taken place (or whether a promise has been made in the case of measuring the contents of psychological contracts). We have already discussed general problems associated with recall, selection, and aggregation earlier; here we consider the specific example of hindsight bias. Hindsight bias refers to the tendency of individuals to exaggerate the discrepancy between what they expected and what they actually got when recalling events from their past, especially when they are disappointed with the outcome (Schkade and Kilbourne 1991). Applying hindsight bias to psychological contract breach suggests that individuals may exaggerate, or even invent, the extent to which a breach took place after the event as a way of making sense of previous disappointments.

3. Most measures of breach and contents make no distinction between explicit and implicit promises. While the explicit/implicit promise distinction is theoretically important—for example, the reactions to broken explicit promises are believed to exceed those to implicit promises—the distinction is rarely investigated.

4. The measures of breach and contents do not specify in any detail who or what the 'employer' (or 'organization', if that term is used) means and it is, therefore, not possible to determine how people combine data from multiple

interactions, and whether employees do this in systematic ways. Rather than considering the organization as a single monolithic entity it is arguably more appropriate to view an organization in terms of its various constituencies, coalitions, groups, and contract makers, such as top management, supervisors, departments, teams, and customers (Reichers 1985). An important implication for psychological contract research is that questionnaire items need to specify the agent of the organization much more precisely.

5. Specific item measures of breach/fulfilment and measures of the contents of psychological contracts do not assess exchange and, therefore, neglect a defining feature of psychological contracts. If we consider as an example the item 'How well has your organization kept its promises to you regarding pay', 'pay', in the wording of this item, is not made conditional on anything the employee is expected to do in return, such as working hard. Measuring the exchange is important not only because it is fundamental to the definition of a psychological contract, but also because without knowing what pay is exchanged for, there is no way of knowing whether employee reactions (e.g. withholding citizenship behaviours) following breach of a pay promise go beyond the prior pay-for-contributions exchange.

6. Measures of contract fulfilment often do not assess the full range of the breach—fulfilment scale. The majority of studies measure the extent to which the psychological contract has been fulfilled, but do not consider occasions when the organization may have over-fulfilled its promises, and are thus only capturing half of this scale.

7. Measures of breach, such as that presented in Figure 6.1, assume that the organization is obliged to fulfil the promises it has made; however, if the employee has not fulfilled his or her side of the bargain, then the organization is no longer obliged to keep its promises. The assumption that employees have kept their side of the deal is not considered sufficiently by measures of organizational breach.

8. As discussed in more detail in the previous section, almost all items specify the extent to which promises have been fulfilled rather than the extent to which they have been breached. There are no strong reasons to assume that breach and fulfilment are at two ends of a single dimension, hence it seems possible that such measures are not measuring breach as such.

The limitations of using employee self-reports to measure behavioural outcomes

Behavioural outcomes—such as job performance, absenteeism, turnover, and organizational citizenship behaviours—tend to be measured using self-reports. In other words, researchers ask employees to report on their own behaviours, or how they intend to behave, rather than asking relevant others, such as their supervisor about the employee's behaviour, or attempting to collect more objective data, such as actual productivity, or whether employees actually quit their job or not. In our review we found twenty questionnaire survey studies of psychological contract breach that collected data on employee behaviours, 65 per cent of these rely on employee self-reports to measure behaviours, 25 per cent use supervisor ratings of employee behaviours, and 20 per cent use more objective measures of employee behaviour taken from organizational records (percentages total exceeds 100 per cent as some studies gather performance ratings from several sources).

While there are very few studies examining the validity of employee self-reports for capturing actual employee behaviour, it is likely to be low. For instance, the single psychological contract study to match employee self-reports of their work performance with supervisor evaluations of employee work performance found no significant relationship between employee ratings of their own performance and supervisor ratings of employee performance (Lester et al. 2002).

One of the main reasons why self-report measures of behaviour are of questionable validity is because they are subject to a number of biases, such as employees wishing to present their behaviour in a more socially desirable way, or where employees incorrectly attribute good performance to their own efforts rather than, say, other work colleagues (Schmitt 1994).

6.3.2. The limitations of cross-sectional designs, or longitudinal designs conducted across very few time points

As mentioned earlier, 70 per cent of psychological contract studies use cross-sectional designs, which refer to when researchers survey participants on just one occasion. Longitudinal designs survey participants on several occasions and are used in about 20 per cent of psychological contract studies. In this section we begin by presenting two limitations of using cross-sectional designs for examining psychological contracts, namely that cross-sectional designs cannot adequately test cause-and-effect relationships and cannot examine how psychological contracts are enacted over time. We end this section by discussing longitudinal designs, which could potentially address these limitations, but in practice do not, due to the design features of existing longitudinal psychological contract studies.

The first limitation is that, while most studies seek to examine how the psychological contract is causally related to other variables, cross-sectional designs can only show associations between variables and cannot verify cause-and-effect relationships. This is because cross-sectional designs collect data at one point in time and, therefore, it is impossible to determine whether a proposed causal variable precedes in time the variable it is supposed to effect, where the correct temporal ordering of variables is a key criterion for establishing causality. If we take one of our own studies as an example, we proposed that psychological contract fulfilment would have a positive effect on employee well-being (Conway and Briner 2002). This was tested using a cross-sectional survey and we found the two variables to be positively correlated. Because these variables were measured at the same time, we cannot be sure whether psychological contract fulfilment precedes and causes employee well-being or whether employee well-being precedes and causes psychological contract fulfilment or the perception of psychological contract fulfilment. It seems entirely plausible that happy and content employees may be less likely to monitor their psychological contract and, therefore, to detect breach or that happy and content employees are less likely to recall and, therefore, report breach. Even though the major aim of many psychological contract studies is to examine causality, most of these studies use a design that cannot do this. Cross-sectional surveys provide a snapshot of the variables measured and may find interesting patterns of associations between variables, but cannot establish causality.

The second limitation of cross-sectional designs is that they cannot examine a defining feature of the psychological contract: that it is an ongoing exchange process. We discuss the psychological contract as a process in detail in Chapter 8, so here we shall just give one very simple example of the relationship between psychological contract breach and organizational citizenship behaviour. When an employee perceives a breach they are unlikely to immediately and permanently withhold citizenship behaviours. Rather, they are likely to respond to some extent and then observe the reactions of the employer or line manager. For instance, employees may first investigate to establish the nature of the breach, then change their behaviour in some way, which may in turn be noticed by their employer who reacts in some way, which is then responded to by the employee, and so on. Clearly, understanding how this exchange process works and evolves over time cannot be captured using cross-sectional methods that collect data at one point in time.

A further limitation of neglecting to study the exchange-process over time is that we cannot examine psychological contracts at the within-person level. Within-person level analyses refer to studying how an employee's perception of their psychological contract changes over time, and how such changes influence their behaviour. Such an analysis requires a method that collects data from the employee across multiple time points. Cross-sectional designs collect data at the between-person level where snapshots of employee perceptions of their psychological contract and other variables are gathered across employees and compared. The distinction between within-person and between-person analysis is fundamentally important as the psychological contract is conceptualized as a within-person construct, where employees evaluate promises relative to their own previous experiences and relationship histories and react accordingly. For example, how an employee reacts when he or she perceives a breach will be influenced by factors such as how often the event has happened in the past and how they have responded previously.

Longitudinal designs taking repeated measurements could potentially overcome the above limitations and are better suited to examining reciprocal relationships (Williams and Podsakoff 1989). While some studies of the psychological contract do collect longitudinal data they have done so in a limited way, primarily by taking too few repeated measurements and, hence, providing little insight into psychological contract processes. For instance, longitudinal studies have only measured outcomes on at most two time points (e.g. Robinson 1995) and have tended to measure breach at one time point only, thereby making it impossible to track variation over time or to assess reciprocity.

Furthermore, the length of time between survey waves has almost always been very long (e.g. twelve months) compared with how often psychological contracts seem likely to change. The time lag between surveys appears to be chosen on the basis of convenience rather than theory, as is the case in other research on reciprocal relationships in organizational psychology (see Williams and Podsakoff 1989, for a review). While there is currently no theory specifying what would be an appropriate time lag or how it should be identified, it seems that long time intervals are inappropriate. After all, breaches of psychological contracts are events that are likely to involve immediate emotional and behavioural reactions and, therefore, studies need to make assessments quite frequently in order to capture important points in the processes involved in breach and responses to breach.

6.3.3. Summary

This section has documented a number of limitations that apply to the designs of most psychological contract studies. As a result of these limitations, findings from most empirical studies of the psychological contract are likely to be inaccurate and neglect fundamentally important features of the psychological contract. The use of cross-sectional self-report questionnaires means that there is a mismatch between our theoretical understanding of the psychological contract and the methodologies with which it is usually investigated.

6.4. An example of an alternative methodology— daily diaries

There are many other methodologies in addition to the typical cross-sectional questionnaire survey that could usefully and more appropriately be used to study the psychological contract. While some of these were mentioned earlier there are so few studies that do use such methods it is not possible to provide a review of these studies.

Instead we will provide an example of an alternative methodology, daily diaries, by discussing one particular study we conducted some years ago (Conway and

Briner 2002). It should be noted that we have not chosen one of our own studies because we believe it is particularly good but simply because it is one of the few examples we can provide and it has the additional advantage of being an example of a study with which we are very familiar.

In this study we focused on perceived breach and occasions when organizations go above and beyond their psychological contract with employees at the day-to-day level. This study attempted to answer questions that could not be addressed using a cross-sectional questionnaire methodology, such as examining immediate emotional responses following transgressed psychological contracts. The results were reported earlier, and unpublished data from this research will be presented in a later chapter in an attempt to better understand psychological contract processes. In this section we propose daily diaries as a method we believe addresses many of the limitations presented under Section 6.3. We briefly present the main design elements of the diary method and discuss the advantages and disadvantages of this method in contrast to questionnaire surveys. The diary instrument used by Conway and Briner (2002) is presented in the Appendix.

Diaries can collect quantitative, qualitative, or both types of data. Quantitative diaries very often consist of repeated measures, such as daily mood ratings, where the content of the diary is pre-specified by the researcher. In qualitative diaries, respondents recount feelings about personally meaningful events as they happen, or shortly afterwards (Symon 1998). The duration specified by researchers for participants to keep diaries varies considerably, although the average period is around two weeks (DeLongis, Hemphill, and Lehman 1992).

Generally, three procedures are used for recording daily phenomena (Reis and Wheeler 1991; Parkinson, Totterdell, Briner, and Reynolds 1996). First researchers use an *interval-contingent* recording procedure, where participants report their experience at regular and predetermined intervals (e.g. each day; every two hours). For example, participants may be asked to report how they feel at that precise moment (e.g. 'How do you feel right now?'), or their experiences during the interval (e.g. 'How have you felt today?'). There is a strong argument for keeping the intervals short, as longer time intervals involve retrospective biases that will distort the accurate reporting of events. Second, researchers use a *signal-contingent* recording procedure, where participants report their experiences whenever they are prompted to do so by a signal of some kind, such as a bleeper or a telephone call. Finally, an *event-contingent* procedure can be used, requiring respondents to record experiences of particular events, pre-defined by the researcher, every time they occur. The method is most suitable when the researcher is interested in only one, or very few, clearly defined events (Parkinson, Totterdell, Briner, and Reynolds 1996).

Daily diaries have a number of benefits over cross-sectional methods. One of the most important is the ability of diaries to capture events (such as the making or breaking of promises) close to when they actually happen. Many of the limitations presented earlier associated with the selection, recall, and aggregation of information using questionnaire surveys are greatly reduced through using a diary methodology.

DeLongis, Hemphill, and Lehman (1992) state three further benefits of the diary study approach. First, diary methods are capable of studying processes over time. Clearly, theories that describe processes, such as the psychological contract, require a method suited for examining processes. Second, diaries are capable of assessing day-to-day experiences. Small events at work which may have little impact on an employee's overall attitude towards his job may be of considerable importance in determining mood, emotions, and behaviour on a daily basis. Additionally, major work life events, for instance, organizational changes such as downsizing or mergers, are likely to have their effect on well-being and behaviour through changing daily experiences. It is difficult to ascertain the factors affecting behaviour and well-being using research methods that take assessments separated by long periods of time. Third, findings from daily diaries are likely to be more valid and reliable than survey methods, as daily diaries enable repeated measurement allowing aggregation during analysis across multiple time points. Clearly, taking an average from ten episodes of an employee's response to breach will give a better indication of their typical behaviour than just using one episode. The final advantage to be discussed, and regarded as one of the most significant, is the ability of daily diaries to study the effects of phenomena at the within-person level over time (Bolger et al. 1989). Between-person analyses assume individuals respond in the same way; however, it is likely that one employee's reaction to a breach will differ to another and, therefore, within-person analysis is required.

Diary methods also have disadvantages, one of the most obvious being that diaries are time consuming and burdensome to both participants, due to the demanding nature of participation, and to researchers, due to involving more complex analyses. A related disadvantage is participants' high refusal and drop-out rates and, therefore, gaining participants for a diary study can be a difficult task (Symon 1998). The commitment required from participants to complete a dairy raises some doubts about whether findings would generalize to wider populations (Tennen, Suls, and Affleck 1991).

A more subtle criticism is that the self-reporting of daily experiences may alter participants' impressions of their experiences. Participants can become more sensitized, introspective, and self-conscious about the phenomena under study, which they may have never thought much about before, and this may influence their attitudes and behaviours (Wheeler and Reis 1991; DeLongis, Hemphill, and Lehman 1992). Diary participation does lead to a heightened awareness of the phenomena under study that tends to increase the reporting of the phenomena over time (DeLongis, Hemphill, and Lehman 1992). This is partly inevitable as one of the reasons for using diaries is to chart processes over time, and the interim reporting may interrupt the process, or change the way we think about it. The heightened awareness due to diary participation is particularly relevant to psychological contract breach, which is believed to increase employee monitoring and vigilance (Rousseau 1995).

In summary, diaries permit access to ongoing everyday experiences and behaviour in a relatively unobtrusive manner. Despite limitations, they appear to provide a potentially more valid means of researching psychological contracts, getting closer to the realities of everyday unfolding experience than methods traditionally used to study psychological contracts (e.g. questionnaire surveys).

We finish this section by briefly discussing what it is that methods and designs should be capable of achieving if they are to be useful in researching psychological contracts. Clearly how useful any method may be depends on the extent to which it is appropriate to the theoretical assumptions made about the phenomenon under investigation and appropriate to the specific research questions being addressed. As we argue later in detail in Chapter 8, we believe that the psychological contract is best understood in terms of an ongoing process. Appropriate methods are, therefore, those that can in some way get at processes. This would clearly involve looking at changes over time and identifying key events or stages in a process.

Given the wide range of qualitative and quantitative methods that can be used to get at processes, it is in many ways easier to identify inappropriate methods and designs, such as cross-sectional questionnaire surveys. There are some signs that psychological contract research is using more sophisticated research designs, such as diaries (Conway and Briner 2002), experiments (Edwards et al. 2003), and in-depth qualitative case studies (Greene, Ackers, and Black 2001; Nadin 2005); however, such studies are rare. We will return to the issue of the sorts of methods that could be used in future studies in Chapter 10.

6.5. What has been researched and what else should be?

As indicated previously, the only two issues that have thus far really caught the attention of psychological contract researchers are breach and contents. While these are certainly important research topics, they represent just two of a much wider range that could be researched. Thus far this chapter has focused on the limitations of existing research focusing largely on these two issues and how research into these two particular aspects of the psychological contract could be improved. Here we briefly consider what other aspects of the psychological contract merit research attention.

Given the numerous limitations of and gaps in psychological contract theory it can sometimes appear that researching any other topic apart from breach and violation would make an important contribution. However, we will identify what we believe to be a number of key research areas that deserve more attention.

The first of these is the nature of the exchange. Or, to put it simply, research that addresses the question of what is exchanged for what? As suggested in many places in this book, we know very little indeed about how exchanges actually work. Second, and linked to the first point, is the nature of the cognitive representation of the exchange. It seems likely that employees have dynamic mental models of the exchange that help guide behaviour and focus attention on whether the organization is delivering on particular promises.

A third important area, given the dynamic nature of the psychological contract, is understanding how and in what circumstances the psychological contract actually changes. Such changes might be quite small and subtle or quite dramatic, and may be influenced by numerous processes. Whatever the size and nature of these changes, understanding how they come about seems fundamental to understanding the psychological contract.

6.6. Summary and conclusion

The most common method for researching the psychological contract is the cross-sectional questionnaire survey. This method is designed to detect associations between attitudes at a very general level and will be of little use in studying the occurrence, experience, consequence, and evolution of psychological contract content and breach. We presented a number of specific methodological criticisms and followed this with presenting an example of an alternative methodology—daily diaries—that we believe addresses a number of these criticisms.

In conclusion, the near exclusive use of the survey method has no doubt hampered conceptual, theoretical, and empirical advance in this area. There is, therefore, an urgent need to use more appropriate means—a diary method being one example—of examining the psychological contract as an event-based social process.

7 | Challenges for Psychological Contract Researchers

7.1. Introduction

Most concepts and theories are likely to present considerable challenges to those who use them. The weaknesses and limitations of ideas are often discovered through the process of researching a theory or trying to use it in a practical context. Common weaknesses of theories include, for example, ideas within the theory which are inconsistent with one another, key concepts which are not specified or insufficiently defined, or explanations which are insufficiently detailed, unclear, or unconvincing. In spite of its almost fifty-year history and many fairly obvious weaknesses and limitations the psychological contract has thus far received surprisingly limited critical attention (for exceptions see Arnold 1996; Guest 1998).

Broadly speaking there are two ways to develop theory. One is through empirical investigation where data are gathered in order to test, explore, or examine the phenomena or processes explained by the theory. Another way to develop theory is rational or theoretical. Rather than using data this approach draws on logic, argument, and other theories in order to unpack, examine, evaluate, and elaborate the theory.

This chapter takes the latter route by presenting a number of key challenges facing psychological contract researchers that need to be addressed to strengthen psychological contract theory and make it more useful to practitioners. We have already described, in various chapters, a number of challenges for psychological contract researchers, which we summarize in Table 7.1. This summary clearly shows that these challenges cover a wide range of areas, including the definition of the psychological contract, psychological contract theory, and appropriate ways of researching the psychological contract.

In Chapter 3 we showed that key terms in the definition of the psychological contract are often insufficiently defined or not defined at all. Here we consider in more detail some of the definitional issues raised earlier, the conceptual problems they raise, and suggest ways in which aspects of the psychological contract concept can be clarified and developed. While there are certainly challenges to

Table 7.1 Challenges for psychological contract researchers

Chapter	Challenge
Chapter 3: Psychological contract definition	• Which types of beliefs does the psychological contract consist of—promises, obligations, or expectations? • What are the distinctions between promises, obligations, and expectations? • What is the status of expectations that arise from emplyee inferences made from promises made to them by the organization? • How implicit do psychological contracts have to be in order to be considered psychological contracts? • Do psychological contracts require any level of actual, as opposed to perceived, agreement? • What is the specific nature of the exchange between employee obligations and employer obligations? • Who or what represents the organization? • To what extent is the psychological contract shaped by factors outside the organization?
Chapter 4: Contents of psychological contracts	• Research on the contents of psychological contracts has largely ignored the fact that the psychological contract is an exchange. • There is insufficient support for the distinction between transactional and relational contracts. • Does it make sense to try to fit what is by definition idiosyncratic reciprocal expectations into content types, such as the transactional–relational distinction? • Research on the contents of psychological contracts has largely concentrated on explicit promises; we know very little about the contents of implicit psychological contracts. • How do pre-employment experiences shape the contents of psychological contracts? • How do experiences outside of the organization (such as family circumstances) shape the contents of psychological contracts? • What is the relative importance of organizational, extra-organizational, and pre-organizational factors in terms of shaping the contents of psychological contracts? • How do line managers shape the contents of employees' psychological contracts? • When and how are the contents of psychological contracts negotiated? • Little is known about how individual differences (such as personality) or social factors (such as working in teams) affect the contents of psychological contracts. • Does the contents of psychological contracts affect outcomes (such as job satisfaction) and, if so, how can we explain any relationship? • Most research on the contents of the psychological contract uses questionnaire surveys—what other research designs may be more appropriate for examining the contents of psychological contracts? • What are the relationships between the contents and breach of psychological contracts?
Chapter 5: Psychological contract breach	• How often does breach happen? • Can we make distinctions between breaches that happen on daily, monthly, or yearly basis? • What factors lead up to breach? • Are certain individuals more likely to report breach than others? • Are certain organizational contexts more likely to breach psychological contracts than others? • How is breach similar and how does it differ to similar constructs, such as fairness and unmet expectations? • To what extent—and if so why—does breach explain outcomes over and above similar constructs?

- Which concept really matters in terms of explaining outcomes—promises made, actual rewards, or the discrepancy between the two (i.e. breach)?
- There is an urgent need for more rigorous methods to examine the consequences of breach—after nearly forty years of research we know very little about the effects of breach due to the dominance of cross-sectional methods.
- Why is breach of limited success in explaining behaviour at work?
- How do breaches of different types of psychological contracts (e.g. transactional versus relational) affect outcomes?
- How are the outcomes to breach affected by the way promises are broken (e.g. delay, magnitude, reciprocal imbalance)?
- Do breached and fulfilled psychological contracts differentially affect outcomes?
- What alternative mechanisms are there for linking the psychological contract and outcomes?
- How do breaches unfold? When and why do they escalate out of control?
- Psychological contract research is often conducted at an inappropriate level of analysis.
- How would findings from questionnaire measures differ if they actually assessed breach by asking about broken as opposed to fulfilled promises?
- Most survey research on the psychological contract uses self-report questionnaires—there is a need to examine actual behaviours rather than self-reported behaviours.
- Existing designs are not equipped to examine fundamental definitional features of the psychological contract, such as the psychological contract as an unfolding process.
- Can questionnaire items reflect more closely how researchers actually define the psychological contract?

Chapter 6: Researching the psychological contract

---

other aspects of the psychological contract, such as contents and breach, as illustrated in Table 7.1, these have been discussed in earlier chapters. We do make clear, however, where problems relating to the definition of the psychological contract impact on these other areas of psychological contract theory.

The key six challenges we consider are:

1. What are the differences between expectations, obligations, and promises?
2. What is meant by implicit promises?
3. Are psychological contract beliefs only those shaped by the employee's current organization?
4. What are the precise specific links in the reciprocal exchange between the employer and the employee?
5. Who, or what, do employees perceive to be the organization?
6. How do employees anthropomorphize the organization?

Note that the issues presented here represent just a small proportion of the challenges facing psychological contract researchers. We believe these six represent fundamental challenges researchers need to prioritize, as they relate directly to how the psychological contract is defined and, as we shall demonstrate, impact significantly on other areas of psychological contract theory.

7.2. Challenges for psychological contract researchers

7.2.1. Challenge 1: What are the differences between expectations, obligations, and promises?

In Chapter 3 we showed how distinctions between expectations, obligations, and promises are not clearly elaborated in the psychological contract literature. The terms are used loosely, with some researchers defining the psychological contract in terms of promises, while on other occasions defining the psychological contract in terms of expectations. For example, Rousseau (1989: 123) defines the psychological contract in terms of promises where the 'psychological contract refers to an individual's belief regarding the terms and conditions of a reciprocal exchange agreement between the focal person and another party. Key issues here include the belief that a promise has been made and a consideration offered in exchange for it'. Rousseau and Greller (1994: 386) define the psychological contract in terms of expectations: 'In simple terms, the psychological contract encompasses the actions employees believe are expected of them and what response they expect in return from the employer.' Sometimes the terms are used in conjunction with another as in the following definition of the psychological contract: 'An employee's beliefs about the reciprocal obligations between that employee and his or her organization, where these obligations are based on perceived promises and are not necessarily recognized by agents of the organization' (Morrison and Robinson 1997: 229).

The lack of clarity or consistency in specifying the types of belief that constitute the psychological contract raises two problems. First, if we do not know what exactly the psychological contract refers to, it becomes difficult to clearly interpret or make sense of theoretical statements made about the psychological contract. For example, a breach could mean a broken promise, an unfulfilled obligation, or an unmet expectation. Second, if the psychological contract is defined quite loosely so that it includes a wide range of beliefs about the exchange then it means that almost any workplace perception could be thought of as part of the psychological contract. At present the psychological contract includes a wide range of beliefs from explicit promises to subtle, possibly unconsciously held, expectations. If any sort of belief can be part of the psychological contract then the concept is weakened as an analytic or explanatory tool.

In order to consider the three types of beliefs more closely, we begin by presenting definitions of these in Table 7.2 (reproducing the column of definitions from Table 3.2), along with some examples of how each type of belief is formed. From Table 7.2 we can see that the differences between promises, obligations, and expectations are considerable and so should be treated as distinct types of belief.

The challenge for researchers is to clarify which types of belief—promises, obligations, expectations—are most appropriate to the psychological contract

Table 7.2 Three types of beliefs: promises, obligations, and expectations

Definitions of beliefs	Examples of how each belief is formed
Promise:	
1. 'a commitment to do (or not do) something' (Rousseau and McLean Parks 1993).	• Explicit promises that arise out of verbal or written statements.
2. 'an assurance that one will or will not undertake a certain action, behaviour' (*Concise Oxford Dictionary* 1996).	• Implicit promises that arise out of observing behaviour.
	• Based on reward (things you must do)/ punishment (things you must not do).
Obligation:	
1. 'a feeling of inner compulsion, from whatever source, to act in a certain way towards another, or towards the community; in a narrower sense a feeling arising from benefits received, prompting to service in return; less definite than duty, and not involving, as in the latter, the ability to act in accordance with it'. (Drever, *Dictionary of Psychology*, 1958)	• Obligations that arise out of promises made.
	• Obligations that arise out of the receipt of a benefit (akin to indebtedness).
	• Obligations arising from a sense of moral duty.
2. 'the constraining power of a law, precept, duty, contract, etc.' (*Concise Oxford Dictionary* 1996).	
Expectation:	
1. 'expectations take many forms from beliefs in the probability of future events to normative beliefs' (Rousseau and McLean Parks 1993).	• Expectations that arise out of promises or obligations made.
2. 'the attitude of waiting attentively for something usually to a certain extent defined, however vaguely' (Drever *Dictionary of Psychology* 1958).	• Heightened expectations that arise out of needs and desires.
	• Heightened expectations that arise because the other party has the ability to provide a reward.
3. 'the act or an instance of expecting of looking forward; the probability of an event' (*Concise Oxford Dictionary* 1996).	

concept and to gain a clearer, systematic understanding of the differences between different types of beliefs.

One way to address this challenge is to devise a means of comparing the different types of beliefs and assess which may be the most appropriate to the psychological contract concept. In other words, given what we understand the psychological contract to be, what should be contained within beliefs about the psychological contract? In Table 7.3 we list what we believe to be four important and necessary characteristics of psychological contract beliefs.

Such beliefs should refer to or imply: (*a*) the other party to the contract; (*b*) an exchange between two parties; (*c*) strength of motivation to act; (*d*) perceived mutual agreement. How well and to what extent do promises, obligations, and expectations have these key characteristics? This is described in Table 7.3.

Table 7.3 shows that no one type of belief has all the key characteristics of psychological contract beliefs. This analysis suggests that each of these types of

Table 7.3 Key characteristics of psychological contract beliefs

The definition of the belief should include:	Promise	Obligation	Expectation
The other party to the contract	Necessary for promises	Necessary for obligations	Not necessary for expectations
Exchange	Not necessary	Necessary	Not necessary
Strength of motivation to act	More likely to be high	More likely to be high	Could range from low to high
Perceived mutual agreement	Likely to be high	Not necessary for some definitions; in other definitions, could range from low to high	Likely to be low

beliefs may be relevant to some extent and the challenge for researchers is therefore to understand how and when these different types of beliefs are relevant to the psychological contract and the different origins and functions of these more specific types of belief.

> *Specific challenges:*
>
> *1. How are promises, obligations, and expectations conceptually different?*
> *2. Which types of beliefs (promises, obligations, or expectations) are most appropriate to the psychological contract?*

7.2.2. Challenge 2: What is meant by implicit promises?

While the first challenge concerned the need to make clearer distinctions between promises, obligations, and expectations, this challenge refers specifically to the meaning of implicit promises and how its present definition means that more general beliefs (e.g. expectations) are included as part of the psychological contract.

Recall from Chapter 3 that explicit promises refer to written or verbal commitments (Rousseau and McLean Parks 1993). However, psychological contracts are thought to consist largely of implicit promises (Levinson et al. 1962; Guest 1998; Meckler, Drake, and Levinson 2003), defined as 'interpretations of patterns of past exchange, vicarious learning (e.g. witnessing other employees' experiences) as well as through various factors that each party may take for granted (e.g. good faith or fairness)' (Robinson and Rousseau 1994: 246), and beliefs 'based upon both inferences and observations of past practice' (Rousseau 1990: 390).

The implicit nature of psychological contract is arguably the most fascinating and distinctive contribution of the psychological contract concept—implicit promises are unwritten and unspoken and, as such, are much more open to interpretation making them psychological and perceptual in nature rather than tangible, externally verifiable promises. Definitions of implicit promises suggest that they can include those beliefs formed whenever an employee makes inferences from explicit promises and the past behaviours of the employer (existing implicit promises). For example, Box 7.1 illustrates some possible inferences made from an implicit promise where an employee believes they will be rewarded for special efforts.

If we accept that implicit promises can include those beliefs derived from inferences it raises three important problems. First, it becomes difficult if not impossible to make distinctions between implicit promises that are part of the psychological contract and the vast array of vague expectations, hopes, hunches, and desires individuals have anyway. In other words, how is it possible to distinguish between those implicit promises that can properly be thought of as part of the psychological contract and implicit promises that are more appropriately construed as falling outside the psychological contract? A second and related problem is that, because implicit promises can arise through endless iterations of inferences from existing explicit and implicit promises, the contents of the psychological contract becomes unbounded and perhaps infinite. Last, as beliefs arising from repeated iterations and chains of inferences are likely to be highly speculative and not strongly held, is it reasonable to consider promises that are so implicit and weak as promises?

The challenge is, therefore, to understand more precisely what implicit promises mean and specify the role that interpretation and inference play in terms of generating implicit promises.

One way to meet this challenge is to refine the definition of an implicit promise by returning to the idea of the psychological contract as a metaphor of a legal contract. To constitute a promise in employment law, the performer of the behaviour must be able to prove that their behaviour is causally related to the reward (Cheshire et al. 1991). Extending this logic to psychological

---

Box 7.1 Example of inferences made from an implicit promise

An employee believes (an implicit promise) that if he makes special efforts that go beyond his formal job description he will be rewarded by the organization. Possible inferences from this implicit promise leading to other implicit promises may include:

- 'The organization will care for me if I perform adequately.'
- 'The organization will look after me if I continue to be flexible.'
- 'I have a better chance of being promoted if I continue making these efforts over a long enough period.'
- 'The organization will tolerate occasional shortfalls in performance for tasks that form part of my job description.'

contracts, for an implicit promise to be considered as such the employee must be able to provide evidence from previous interactions with the employer showing that their belief about the implicit promise is based on actual experience and the behaviour of the employer. To take the example in Box 7.1, if the employee believes that the organization will reward special efforts over and above their job description, for this to be an implicit promise it must be based on evidence that the organization has rewarded such behaviour consistently in the past. A vital question is what constitutes evidence? We speculate that evidence in this case requires an employee to show how the promise was *made*, which involves two things: firstly, that the implicit promise has never been verbalized or expressed in writing, as this would then make it an explicit promise; and secondly, that the employee can produce an account of their employer's behaviour that shows clearly how the implicit promise was made or constructed. Such an account should be based on the employee's direct experience and witnessing of their employer's behaviour rather than, say, what others say about the employer or what the employee's friends outside the organization say about their employer.

A second way to better understand implicit promises is to consider how far removed the implicit promise is from the initial experience. In other words, a one-step inference made on the basis of a particular experience can be considered implicit and it seems reasonable to think of it as part of the psychological contract. For example, through observing another employee receiving a reward for a particular behaviour, an employee may infer an implicit promise that if they engage in the same behaviour they will also receive the same reward. However, if the employee then goes on to make another inference on the basis of this one then the implicit promise becomes even more implicit. So, for example, in a second-step of inference, the employee may then infer that engaging in a wide range of other sorts of similar behaviours will result in different kinds of reward on the basis of the initial implicit promise that if they engage in the same behaviour they observed in another employee they will receive the same reward. A chain of inferences could continue until it reached a stage at which the inferred implicit promise was very different from the initial experience or observation. In such a case it would be difficult to see that such an implicit promise is really part of the psychological contract. Furthermore, different levels of implicit promises are likely to influence behaviour in different ways.

Specific challenges:

1. How implicit or not are the implicit promises that form the psychological contract?
2. What does implicit really mean?
3. What role does interpretation and inference play in terms of generating implicit promises?

7.2.3. Challenge 3: Are psychological contract beliefs only those shaped by the employee's current organization?

Psychological contract beliefs can be shaped in various ways and through various experiences. The challenge, therefore, is whether we define psychological contract beliefs as only those that are shaped by the employee's current organization or whether we include beliefs that have been shaped by experiences that occurred before or outside the employee's current organization.

Recall from Chapter 3 that recent psychological contract definitions consider the organization to be chiefly responsible for shaping the psychological contract (Roehling 1996) giving, for instance, less emphasis to experiences predating the current employment relationship; 'if the perceived obligation is based solely on past experience in other employment relationships, then it falls outside of the psychological contract' (Morrison and Robinson 1997: 228). This suggests that it is both possible and desirable to make a firm distinction between psychological contract beliefs (such as promises) that originate only from factors or experiences outside the current employment relationships and those that originate from or are shaped by the current employment relationship.

This particular position is not the only one within the psychological contract literature. Other approaches see the psychological contract as highly perceptual and interpretive (Rousseau and McLean Parks 1993), such that it may be difficult or impossible to ascertain whether a promise originates solely from sources inside the organization, or from any number of other factors such as an individual's needs, peer influences outside work, past experience, and exposure to traditions and norms.

The extent to which an employee's psychological contract is formed by factors outside their relationship with their employer, or formed by the organization itself, is clearly central to psychological contract theory in terms of understanding what can be considered to lie inside or outside an employee's psychological contract.

While each of these approaches to defining psychological contract beliefs has strengths and limitations, rather than deciding that certain beliefs are within or outside the psychological contract on the basis of how they are shaped it may be more useful to understand how such beliefs are actually shaped and whether or not the way they are shaped influences the effects of such beliefs on behaviour. For example, do beliefs about promises that are largely shaped by the organization differ in their effects from beliefs shaped by extra-organizational factors?

Specific challenges:

1. To what extent are psychological contracts formed by factors external to the organization, such as friends, family, outside employment interests?
2. To what extent are psychological contracts formed by factors that predate the employee's current employment relationship?
3. Should distinctions be made between parts of the psychological contract that are not shaped by the organizations and those that are?

7.2.4. Challenge 4: What are the precise links in the reciprocal exchange between the employer and the employee?

The notion of exchange is central to psychological contract theory as the theory is essentially attempting to describe and explain the relationship between employer and employee in terms of what each exchanges with the other. It seems likely that employees build up perhaps quite complex and dynamic cognitive representations of these exchanges containing, for example, specific exchanges, timescales, and ways of judging when the exchange has been completed. However, these exchanges tend to be described in very general terms. For example, 'contributions' by employees are exchanged for 'inducements' from employers, or what the employee 'offers' is exchanged for what the organization 'offers'. There is little sense of how the exchanges work or what, specifically, is exchanged for what. Psychological contract research is therefore extremely vague in terms of specifying the nature of what each party exchanges and the time frames over which such exchanges may take place:

> Contracts are agreements to exchange services for compensation. The rich array of possible exchanges (such as effort, learning, sacrificed opportunities elsewhere) and their duration (a day or infinity) create a variety of potential contracts between employee and employer. (Rousseau and Wade-Benzoni 1994: 293–4)

While the variety and richness of the possible exchanges is acknowledged there has been little if any attempt to understand this variety and richness. This very general way of thinking about exchange is echoed in writing about social exchange theory:

> Social exchange generates an expectation of some future return for contributions; however the exact nature of that return is unspecified. . . . social exchange does not occur on a quid pro quo or calculated basis (like economic exchanges) [they] are based on individual's trusting that the other parties to the exchange will fairly discharge their obligation in the long run. (Konovsky and Pugh 1994: 657)

The similarly unspecified approaches taken in both the psychological contract and social exchange literatures may suggest that having only a very general insight into the exchange is unproblematic. However, social exchange theory and psychological contract theory differ critically on the issue of whether individuals are aware of the specific details of the exchange. Social exchange theory does not claim that individuals know in advance the details of the exchange: one party performs a service for another party and the recipient feels obliged to reciprocate. But how they are expected to reciprocate is at their discretion and not specified by a prior implicit or explicit agreement; as Konovsky and Pugh state above, the 'exact nature of that return is unspecified'. In contrast, psychological contract theory states that individuals are aware of the exchange and what specific returns are expected. As psychological contracts are effectively mental models of the exchange, so employees should be aware of the links between what they are expected to do and what they get in return (Shore and Tetrick 1994; Rousseau 2001). So while some level of generality is acceptable within social exchange theory it does not seem appropriate to the psychological contract.

Psychological contract theory and research has entirely neglected to focus attention on specifying the exchange. This causes three main problems. The first problem is that without specifying the exchange it is difficult to precisely validate any aspect of psychological contract theory. For instance, we cannot predict employee reactions to psychological contract breach, or whether any reactions extend beyond what would otherwise be a straightforward realignment of the previous agreement, without a more detailed understanding of the exchange. To illustrate, consider the very simple exchanges in Figure 7.1 and let us assume that an employee has a mental model where the 'working late' and 'helping out her supervisor' is exchanged for 'line manager gratitude' and 'time off at a later date', as depicted by the specific exchange. Under the specific exchange, this employee is prepared to help out her supervisor in return for line manager gratitude, and work late in return for line manager gratitude or time off at a later date. If we only understand this exchange in a general way it would not be possible to predict or understand what would happen in a situation where the employee works late, the line manager does not show gratitude but does offer time off at a later date. As a consequence of this possible breach will the employee in the future withdraw one or both of the things she offers, or none of the things she offers as the line manager is still offering time off at a later date? In contrast, if we know the specific exchange, then we can predict that if the line manager fails to express gratitude, but offers time off at a later date, we would expect the employee to not help out their supervisor on future occasions but continue to work late.

The second problem with not knowing how the exchange is specified is that we cannot understand why things are *not* done. In other words, employees may not be performing certain behaviours because the necessary inducement is missing. Returning to the exchanges in Figure 7.1, the line manager may be puzzled because while the employee always offers to work late, they are generally unwilling to help out. Knowing the more specific exchange solves this puzzle, where the

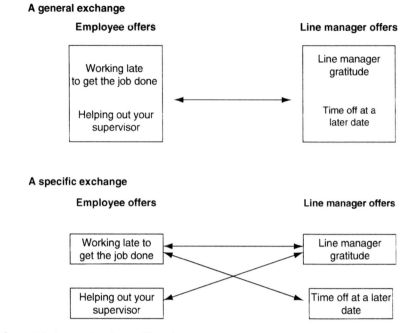

Figure 7.1 A general and a specific exchange

employee's willingness to generally help their supervisor depends specifically on line manager gratitude.

The third problem with not understanding the specific nature of the exchange is that we do not know which items may substitute or compensate for others. This may be important when psychological contracts are being negotiated or when trying to compensate employees who have had their psychological contracts breached. Returning again to the exchanges in Figure 7.1, if the line manager is no longer in a position to offer time off at a later date in exchange for the employee working late to get the job done, the line manager can substitute this inducement by offering gratitude.

The crucial challenge therefore is to specify the exchange: what is the specific exchange between employee behaviours and organizational returns? One way to address this challenge is to identify the possible specific mappings between contributions and inducements. In total, there are four possibilities: one-for-one (e.g. respect for respect); one-for-many; many-for-one; many-for-many. We now present two examples to illustrate ways of providing more accurate specification of exchanges.

The first example of an exchange is taken from Blau's early qualitative research (1955) on social exchanges, regarding an exchange of information between a supervisor (referred to as a consultant in the quote) and an employee (referred to as an agent in the quote):

A consultation [between an employee and a supervisor] can be considered as an exchange of values: both participants gain something, and both have a price to pay. The questioning agent is enabled to perform better than he otherwise could have done, without exposing his difficulties to his supervisor. By asking for advice, he implicitly pays respect to the superior proficiency of his colleague. This acknowledgement of inferiority is the cost of receiving assistance. The consultant gains prestige, in return for which he is willing to devote some time to the consultation and permit it to disrupt his work. The following remark of an agent illustrates this: 'I like giving advice. It's flattering, I suppose, if you feel that others come to you for advice.' (Blau 1955; quoted in Homans 1958: 605)

This exchange is specific in terms of its contents and time frame. The employee exchanges respect for information (one-for-one), the supervisor exchanges time and knowledge for prestige (many-for-one). The time lag between the employee's contribution and the organization's inducement is virtually zero, with the exchange of resources happening almost instantly.

The second illustration of a way of specifying exchanges is Foa and Foa's resource exchange configuration for social interactions (Foa 1971; Foa and Foa 1980), presented in Figure 7.2, where a resource is defined as anything that can be transmitted from one person to another. Foa and Foa (1980) propose a simple theory of classifying resources that are exchanged and a theory of how these resources are likely to be exchanged. The exchange of resources in social interactions can be classified into six classes (Foa and Foa 1980: 79):

- *love*—the 'expression of affectionate regard, warmth or comfort'
- *services*—'activities on the body or belongings of a person which often constitute labour for another'
- *goods*—'tangible products, objects or materials'
- *money*—'any coin, currency, or token which has some standard unit of exchange'
- *information*—'advice, opinions, instruction or enlightenment'
- *status*—'expression of evaluative judgement which conveys high or low prestige, regard or esteem'

These are configured along two dimensions. The first, concreteness versus symbolism, refers to how observable the resource is, and the second dimension, particularism versus universalism, refers to how much the value of the resource depends on the identity of the provider. For example, love occupies a midway position on the symbolic-concrete dimension as it is exchanged in both concrete forms (e.g. sex) and symbolic forms (e.g. respect); money also has a midway position as it is exchanged in both concrete (e.g. money as a standard unit of currency) and symbolic form (e.g. money as a symbol of status). On the particularism–universalism dimension, love and money occupy extreme and opposite positions as it matters a great deal from whom individuals receive love, whereas people are less particular about from whom they receive money.

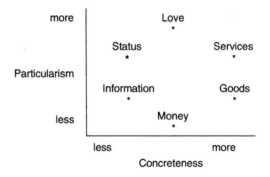

Figure 7.2 Resource exchange configuration
Note: Reprinted with permission from Foa (1971), *Science*, 171: 347. © 1971 AAAS.

Foa and Foa's empirical findings (1980) support that, in general, resources sharing similar attributes in terms of particularism and concreteness are more likely to be exchanged with one another. In terms of Figure 7.2 a resource is more likely to be exchanged with another resource from the same or neighbouring category. For example, love is most likely to be exchanged for love, and love is least likely to be exchanged for money. The explanation for this is that the value of particularistic resources are greatly influenced by who the provider is, and hence where the resource is highly particularistic, we are more likely to reciprocate in kind.

It seems likely that employee and employer resources will vary along these same dimensions and hence be configured and exchanged in similar sorts of ways.

In summary, psychological contract theory is extremely vague when it comes to specifying what the exchange is between employee and the organization. It may be that obtaining precise knowledge of the exchange is too difficult, or that such exchanges are very specific to particular contexts. If either case is true, this needs to be stated and the implications for psychological contract theory explored. We believe that it is possible to more clearly specify the exchange and illustrated two possibilities; while these may appear simplistic and also have their limitations, they at least show two ways of approaching the exchange in a more specific way.

Specific challenges:

1. *What are the specific linkages between what an employee offers and what an organization does in return? What is exchanged for what?*
2. *Over what timescales do such exchanges operate?*
3. *Are different sorts of employee contributions and employer inducements exchanged in particular ways?*

7.2.5. Challenge 5: Who, or what, do employees perceive to be the organization?

While a number of researchers acknowledge there is a problem with identifying who or what represents the organization (Guest 1998; Anderson and Schalk 1998; Turnley and Feldman 1999; Millward and Brewerton 2000) the issue has not been closely examined. Recall from Chapter 3 that it is generally assumed that employees treat the organization as if it were a single contract maker as the other party to the psychological contract. However, researchers also acknowledge that there are many other possible people and artefacts that could represent the organization, such as an employee's co-workers, supervisors, line manager, departmental manager, personnel manager, the subsidiary or parent organization, or administrative contract makers such as human resource policies, mission statements, or personnel manuals (Rousseau 1995). All could potentially communicate promises of some kind to employees or make demands from them.

If this is the case then it seems difficult to imagine how employees reduce this vast range of potential contract makers and the array of information such contract makers are transmitting into a unified, single other party to the psychological contract, as is assumed in much of the psychological contract literature. In other words, if there are so many potential contract makers or parties to the contract, is it really likely or possible that employees perceive 'the organization' as the single entity with whom they make contracts? One approach to explaining this is through suggesting that employees anthropomorphize the organization. This is discussed in Section 7.2.6. However, the issue here is who or what it is employees take to represent the organization.

Psychological contract researchers very rarely discuss who, or what, employees perceive to be the organization. Rousseau (1995) is one of the few researchers to attempt to make distinctions between different types of contract makers using the distinction between principal contract makers and agents who represent these principal contract makers.

> Organizations become party to the contract as principals who directly express their own terms or through agents who represent them. Although owner/employers create their own contracts with individual employees, most contract makers are individuals acting as the organization's agents, who communicate demands and expectations upon which employment, advancement, remuneration, and retention are predicated. (Rousseau 1995: 60)

This describes two different kinds of contract makers and also proposes a relationship between them. This is a useful distinction and we shall use it here. There are, however, unanswered questions and unresolved issues that apply generally across psychological contract research in the way researchers approach how employees perceive the organization.

First, making a distinction between principals and agents is often difficult in large organizations and it is perhaps unreasonable to suppose an employee would be sufficiently informed about representatives of the organization to be able to make such distinctions, let alone for researchers to clearly make such a distinction. Second, psychological contract theory has not sufficiently clarified how employees perceive the relationship between agents and principals and make sense of multiple agents when, for example, they communicate conflicting messages. The experience of agents sending conflicting or just different promises and demands may be common for employees with more than one line manager or for employees who are in contact with more senior managers than their immediate line manager. In such cases, it is problematic to assume that psychological contracts held with agents sending conflicting promises could be integrated into a single psychological contract held with the organization; however, most psychological contract research does assume the organization to be a single contract maker.

Third, it is unclear what the implications of having multiple agents are for psychological contract theory more generally, such as breach. For example, does a breach by one agent generalize across other agents, or does it come to be directed against the principal? Or does a breach by one agent lead to the perception of other breaches by other agents? For example, maltreatment by a line manager leading to a breach might lead to another breach if the employee perceives an implicit promise made by the organization to select and employ only competent and fair line managers. Psychological contract theory predicts that breach leads to employees withdrawing behaviours or retaliating with antisocial behaviours such as theft. However, another implication of having multiple agents is that such retaliatory behaviours are likely to affect the employee's psychological contract with a number of agents and not just their psychological contract with the perceived breaching agent. Given other research showing that employees engage in multiple exchanges in organizations (Settoon, Bennett, and Liden 1996), it seems more likely that the employee may, if multiple agents exist, direct their attention to those parties whom they perceive to be more reasonable.

The challenge then is to clarify how and if employees perceive the organization as a single party to the psychological contract and clarify the relationship between principals and agents. We suggest two ways to begin addressing this challenge.

First, as some agents are more likely to represent the organization than others, the separate and distinct psychological contracts with these agents should first be explored. Several researchers believe that the line manager is a key agent of the organization's psychological contract (Konovsky and Pugh 1994; Rousseau 1995) and this is supported by research that shows that employees perceive the line manager as responsible for 38 per cent of broken promises and 53 per cent of exceeded promises (Conway and Briner 2002a). If the supervisor is the most likely agent for the psychological contract, then a valuable source of theory and evidence to develop this idea can be found in research on leader-member-exchanges (e.g. Gerstner and Day 1997; Wayne, Shore, and Liden 1997).

CHALLENGES FOR RESEARCHERS **127**

A second way to address the challenge is to examine whether employees divide the contents of their psychological contract across different agents. For instance, it seems plausible that more transactional items of the exchange, such as pay and fringe benefits, are dealt with, by the organization as an administrative entity or through the human resources department, while the relational items of the exchange, such as respect and support, come from supervisors or line managers. Settoon, Bennett, and Liden (1996) found that employees derive different benefits from different exchange partners, where line managers were perceived as more responsible for the interpersonal aspects of the employment relationship, while the organization was perceived to be responsible for the terms and conditions of employment and the organizational recognition of an employee's contributions. This research suggests the interesting possibility that while supervisors may be the most likely agent of the psychological contract, they have relatively little control over key elements of the psychological contract, such as training and development, compensation, job security, and promotion.

In summary, how employees perceive the organization, relationships between agents and principals, and the implications of this for psychological contract theory, such as breach, need to be clarified. Rather than viewing employees as having one psychological contract with their organization, it is more plausible to imagine employees having multiple or distributed psychological contracts within their organization, where different agents deal with different items of the contents of the psychological contract, and where the agents and their roles are likely to change over time.

Challenges:

1. *Who or what represents the organization?*
2. *How can we clarify the relationships employees perceive between principals and agents?*
3. *What else and whom else could play a role in contract making?*

7.2.6. Challenge 6: How do employees anthropomorphize the organization?

While the previous section largely dealt with how employees may perceive the relationships between an organization's various principals and agents, this section looks at a related issue within psychological contract theory, where it is argued that employees anthropomorphize the organization. Researchers use the idea of anthropomorphizing the organization to explain how employees can view all the organization's possible agents, principals, and non-human contract makers as if the organization were a single, human, contract maker.

Recall from Chapter 3 that definitions of the psychological contract state that employees attribute the organization with human qualities, a process referred to as personifying or anthropomorphizing the organization (Levinson et al. 1962; Schein 1965; Eisenberger et al. 1986; Rousseau 1989; Sims 1994; Morrison and Robinson 1997). As stated by Robinson and Morrison (1995: 290): 'In a sense, the organization takes on an anthropomorphic identity as a party to the psychological contract. This personification of organizations is most likely facilitated by the fact that organizations have legal, moral, and financial responsibilities for the actions of their agents'. In psychological contract theory the organization is anthropomorphized into a 'person' who can have a relationship with an employee, who can keep and break agreements, and towards whom an employee can feel loyalty and affection. We view the assumption that employees anthropomorphize the organization as problematic and these concerns are supported both by general critiques of the use of anthropomorphism in other research areas and the more specific difficulties of explaining how the organization is anthropomorphized in psychological contract theory.

The idea of anthropomorphism has been subject to criticism in other areas such as the personification of genes (Sullivan 1995), death (Tamm 1996), animals (Mitchell and Hamm 1997), and God (Barrett and Keil 1996). For instance, the use of anthropomorphism by scientific researchers has been criticized as an imprecise use of language that should not be interpreted literally, but as a way of illustrating ideas (Sullivan 1995). It is seen as imprecise because non-human things are described in terms of human experience, as if such non-human things have motivations and intentions. Sullivan (1995) focuses on the example of the 'selfish gene' (popularized by Richard Dawkin's book *The Selfish Gene*, 1976) and reasons that genes cannot be selfish as genes are not capable of moral decision-making. Sullivan argues that anthropomorphizing non-human things is seductive to scientific researchers as a means of dramatizing and bringing to life—literally—otherwise abstract concepts that may not otherwise stimulate the interest of readers of science. The language used in psychological contract theory can also be seen as similarly 'dramatic', with organizations 'violating' promises that in turn destabilize relationships, rather than a more mundane but perhaps accurate description of where an organizational agent fails to keep a promise to an employee which, in many cases, is acknowledged and resolved in a straightforward and amicable way. Generally, then, giving non-human or abstract entities such as organizations human attributes may be interesting as a metaphor but, taken more literally, tends to obscure rather than enhance understanding.

Within the psychological contract literature the anthropomorphism of organizations can be traced back to Levinson (1965). Eisenberger et al. (1986: 500) summarize Levinson's position:

> Levinson (1965) noted that employees view actions by agents of the organization as actions by the organization itself. The personification of the organization, Levinson

suggested, is abetted by the following factors: (a) the organization has a legal, moral and financial responsibility for the action of its agents; (b) organizational precedents, traditions, policies and norms provide continuity and prescribe behaviours; and (c) the organization, through its agents, has power over individual employees. The personification of the organization was assumed to represent an employee's distillation of views concerning all the other members who control an individual's material and symbolic resources.

A closer examination of Levinson's original thesis regarding the personification of the organization reveals that his arguments, based on the concept of transference taken from psychoanalytic theory, suggest that employees perceive the organization to take on a benevolent guardian role. The organization is a place in which 'a man [*sic*] enters a work organization before he marries and remains in it long after his grandchildren are grown' (p. 373); 'the work organization is his thread of continuity and may well become a psychological anchor point for him' (p. 373); and 'if technical change eliminates a man's job, the company will often retrain him, thereby helping him to cope with the change and assuring him of long-term job security' (p. 374). Throughout, Levinson (1965) repeatedly evokes a family metaphor through which the organization can be seen as a 'symbolic parental surrogate' (p. 378).

Viewing the organization as having a benevolent parental nature appears somewhat nostalgic in the current context and may also have been overly optimistic during the period Levinson was writing. Compare Levinson's view with that of Lewis-McClear and Taylor (1997: 3) who characterize organizations as 'more focused on their own survival and profitability than on employee welfare' and employees as 'independent agents whose self-interest always takes precedence over those of the organization'. While Levinson's thesis is insightful, the validity of the argument of transference and the assumed benevolent character of the organization appear highly questionable.

The challenge, therefore, is to understand, firstly, whether organizations are anthropomorphized by employees and, if so, how this process takes place. However, it may also be helpful to consider alternative metaphors for the organization rather than the metaphor of the human being. Indeed, rather than regarding the organization as a symbolic parent any one of a number of other metaphors for the organization could be plausibly considered. Morgan's *Images of Organizations* (1986), for example, provides nine metaphors of organizations (none of which, incidentally, is a family metaphor). It seems conceivable that any one of these could also be used as a metaphor for the organization in psychological contract theory, and may result in very different theoretical predictions for the psychological contract. Taking one of Morgan's metaphors as an illustration, if an employee regarded his or her organization as a 'psychic prison' (Morgan 1986), then different concepts may be more important to psychological contract theory, such as complying with the terms of the contract.

In summary, the validity of anthropomorphizing organizations has never been considered and psychological contract theory and research would benefit from such a debate.

Challenges:

1. *Do employees anthropomorphize the organization and, if so, how?*
2. *What others metaphors could be used to understand the organization as a party to a psychological contract?*

7.3. Summary and conclusion

This chapter has presented six fundamental challenges facing psychological contract researchers. Many of the challenges refer to the imprecision and confusion relating to key terms of the psychological contract definition. We offered suggestions for ways of clarifying the key terms and for stimulating debate. Note that this chapter has not discussed all the challenges facing the psychological contract but has at least begun to interrogate some of its key concepts more closely, with the aim of more clearly specifying the psychological contract and advancing the field.

A key conclusion is that, for as long as researchers neglect to address these fundamental challenges, all theory and empirical evidence referring to the psychological will inherit current limitations in how the psychological contract concept is defined.

8 | Understanding the Psychological Contract as a Process

8.1. Introduction

Researchers broadly agree that the psychological contract represents an unfolding, dynamic process. However, we cannot think of a single piece of psychological contract research that studies process in a way that reflects recent advances in understanding how to analyse processes (see Langley 1999; Andersson and Pearson 1999). Our main aim in this chapter is to present a case for considering the psychological contract as a process. We begin by arguing why we should study the psychological contract as a process and what we mean by a process. We then consider existing theoretical approaches and empirical studies examining the psychological contract as a process, along with their limitations. Our conclusion is that there is a lack of theory and an absence of published data, leading us to speculate how it might be possible to start thinking in more detail about the processes involved in the psychological contract. We present qualitative data from one of our own studies illustrating the psychological contract as a process and offer two frameworks (self-narratives, sensemaking) that could be used to think about the psychological contract as a process. These are presented as just two examples of many more possible frameworks that may increase our understanding of the psychological contract as a process.

Our aim is not to produce a process theory of the psychological contract, but rather to present a case for a process approach and offer some examples of data illustrating the psychological contract as a process along with examples of interpretive frameworks. Taking a process perspective to phenomena is a notoriously challenging and difficult task and data are more difficult both to analyse and interpret (Langley 1999; Pentland 1999). We believe that a process perspective is necessary to gain anything more than superficial insight into how the psychological contract operates. Understanding the psychological contract as a process is also likely to have practical consequences in the form of better-informed interventions to improve psychological contracting.

We focus largely on understanding psychological contract breach, as breach is clearly defined as an event and process approaches tend to focus on events. The frameworks we propose could, however, also be applied to other areas such as ongoing reciprocation, negotiation, and development of psychological contracts.

8.2. Why should we study the psychological contract as a process?

The main reason for taking a process approach is that the psychological contract, like the contract metaphor on which it is based, is by definition a process involving a series of unfolding events and interpretations of those events. Contracts are formed, developed, changed, are met or not met, are revised to include escalated commitments, and so on. Likewise, social exchanges within an ongoing relationship are also processes in which, when one party does something for the other party, the other party then feels obligated to reciprocate to a greater or lesser extent—an act which is then carried forward into the next exchange cycle.

Schein (1980: 24) sees the psychological contract exchange as unfolding in the sense that it is in operation at all times and 'constantly renegotiated'. Employee and organization 'interact in a complex fashion that demands a systems approach capable of handling interdependent phenomena' (Schein 1980: 65). For Meckler, Drake, and Levinson (2003: 223) psychological contracts develop through reciprocation, which 'is the process of working through a series of unfolding psychological contracts in efforts to meet the expectations and concerns of the parties'. They add, 'the process has an ongoing nature extending over time and multiple episodes. Implicit in this extended time frame is the provision of feedback cycles where both parties are adjusting to changes that may enhance as well as frustrate the satisfaction of their needs. Typically this feedback is not explicitly monitored nor carefully understood, so that mutual adjustments are haphazard and often painful to both parties' (Meckler, Drake, and Levinson 2003: 225). So, for these researchers, and others, the idea of process is, as stated earlier, fundamental to the idea of the psychological contract.

More specifically, such processes can be observed in the formation of the psychological contract. While there have been plenty of recent calls to address the formation of the psychological contract (e.g. Rousseau 2001; de Vos, Buyens, and Schalk 2003), it is less often acknowledged that the psychological contract is always in a state of ongoing formation. When the psychological contract is being acted out through everyday behaviour, this behaviour and its interpretation feeds into how both parties perceive the psychological contract. Levinson et al. (1962) capture the ongoing nature of the psychological contract succinctly when observing that the psychological contract is 'affirmed, altered, or denied in day-to-day work experience' (Levinson et al. 1962: 21).

A process approach is also more likely to capture a fuller representation of the experience of being party to a psychological contract. For example, if during a conversation a friend describes an event which is essentially a breach of their psychological contract, it is likely you will start to ask questions such as who was the other party, when and where the event happened, what led up to the event, and what your friend plans to do next. In other words, you would be taking a process approach to understanding the breach event.

Indeed, one of the most appealing and powerful aspects of the psychological contract concept is that it is not about a single transaction or exchange—but rather it represents some kind of ongoing and unfolding process. That the psychological contract is an ongoing process including exchanges taking place over long periods of time (e.g. consistent performance over several years in exchange for promotion opportunities) underlines its importance to long-term relationships and hence their maintenance is of greater potential significance than theories describing more discrete, contained, and short-term transactions. One-off exchanges such as 'I'll do this for you, if you do this for me' may characterize some parts of some types of psychological contracts, but are not typical of most exchanges. Even very recent cycles of psychological contract exchanges can be shaped by events that occurred at any point during the relationship history and can, therefore, only be understood by looking at longer-term processes.

8.3. What is a 'process'?

A process has been defined as a sequence of events that precede and explain the occurrence of an outcome (Shaw and Jarvenpaa 1997). In terms of the psychological contract, we might be interested, therefore, in the process of how and why a breach of the psychological contract results in the withdrawal of certain behaviours and important intervening stages.

In a recent review of theorizing from process data, Langley (1999) describes processes as having four characteristics: first, processes are concerned with *sequences of events*, with events defined as happenings at work that cause some sort of affective, cognitive, or behavioural reaction which are often precisely located in time and space. In contrast to the concept of a variable, events either do or do not happen, whereas a variable presupposes that a phenomenon can vary in degree in some quantifiable way along a particular dimension. The second characteristic identified by Langley is that processes will often involve multiple levels of analysis, such as individuals, groups, organizations, events occurring over very short and longer time frames, and so on. Process approaches often consider multiple actors and can include multiple subjective perspectives that may conflict with one another. Third, within processes the timing between events can vary considerably, as well as the temporal boundary surrounding an event. As an example of the latter, it may only take a few minutes for a line manager to publicly humiliate an employee, but the feeling of hurt and resentment may remain with the employee for several months. Finally, processes can include a wide variety of 'events' such as changing relationships, expectations, intentions, sensemaking, and emotions.

The time span for analysing processes can vary enormously, with some process models targeted at the first few moments following social interaction (Gergen and Gergen 1988), to others which focus on time horizons spanning careers (Levinson et al. 1962), and other models which may try to synthesize activities ranging across micro and macro time horizons (e.g. Carver and Scheier 1990).

In addition to identifying the characteristics of processes Langley (1999), building on Mohr's discussion (1982) of types of organizational theory, makes a distinction between variance and process theories. Variance theories are characterized by relationships between independent and dependent variables and tend to reflect static, linear models where causation is oversimplified. Variance theories aim to explain variation in an outcome variable by looking at the effects of a range or group of independent variables. Research based on variance theories is characterized by hypotheses, models describing the relationships between variables, the use of statistical regression to test models, and no attempt to temporally order the independent variables with respect to one another or to the dependent variable. Nearly all current psychological contract research clearly falls into this category. Process theories, in contrast, deal with discrete states and events and the time ordering among them is often seen as critical to arriving at the final outcome (Mohr 1982). Mohr believes it is useful to think of a process in terms of a sequence of precursors to an outcome, rather than using the labels of independent and dependent variables taken from variance theories.

Variance models promote the view that inputs are related to outputs in a simple linear fashion. However, within process models many more types of relationships can occur such as escalation, vicious and virtuous circles, upward and downward spirals, thresholds, feedback effects, recycling between phases, parallel tracks, shifts between equilibriums, and so on (e.g. Mintzberg 1980; Masuch 1985; Langley 1999). Due to variations in the patterns of events, with individuals moving through events that are affecting them in some way while making sense of previous events, important psychological constructs relevant to processes are such things as selective attention, selective retention, anticipation of future events, sensemaking and revising previously held views (Pentland 1999).

As mentioned above, studying a phenomenon as a process can also provide more compelling and recognizable avenues for practical management and intervention. Process models highlight important events and states between a trigger and an outcome. This chain of events offers numerous possibilities for interventions and correcting negative cycles. Shaw and Jarvenpaa (1997) argue it is easier to make events and activities happen, whereas it is sometimes difficult or unclear how to change the level of an independent variable. Practitioners can more readily glean insights from a process model through seeing how they can get from A to B, compared with a variance model that omits many important intervening stages (Shaw and Jarvenpaa 1997).

While the notion of a process is not easy to define it is clear that processes and process theories are much better suited to the basic ideas contained within the psychological contract concept than are simple cause–effect ideas and variance approaches.

8.4. How do existing approaches consider the psychological contract process?

As indicated elsewhere, little theoretical or empirical attention has been directed to the idea that the psychological contract should be viewed as a process. While the studies presented below have given some consideration to process issues they have not—with the possible exception of Levinson—considered psychological contracts as unfolding sequences of events.

Dealing first with theoretical approaches to psychological contract processes, Robinson, Kraatz, and Rousseau (1994: 139) remark on how time influences the contents of psychological contracts, where the 'continued receipt and payment over time is likely to create an increasing number and diversity of obligations between the parties in an exchange relationship'. In other words, the ongoing fulfilment of obligations between parties leads to the expansion of terms to the contract, as trust develops and greater flexibility is permitted over the timing and form of repayment.

While there have been some recent attempts to explore how breach develops (most notably Morrison and Robinson 1997) these tend to regard breaches as somewhat isolated incidents and fail to explore more fully the events *leading up* to a violation *and* what happens *after* a violation occurs and how broken and exceeded promises might be related to one another and form chains of events over time.

Finally, Taylor and Tekleab (2004) present a model summarizing existing psychological contract research including feedback loops specifying that the withdrawal of employee contributions following breach may be observed by the organization and result in a counter-retaliation and that the withdrawal also leads employees to revise their cognitive representation of the obligations they believe they owe and are owed by the organization (i.e. the content). This is not a process model or process approach as such but it does contain some feedback loops.

Given the limited theoretical work on psychological contract processes it is not surprising that empirical work also tends not to examine processes. Indeed, most empirical studies of the psychological contract propose and test variance models, simply taking a small snapshot at one point in time of the extended, ongoing interaction between the employee and the employer. This is true of almost every paper that has sought to examine the effects of breach. (For instance, see the studies listed in Tables 5.2 to 5.5). These models consist of variables rather than events and are characterized by simple cause–effect models with the basic underlying principle being that breaches have negative effects on various work attitudes and behaviours.

The most explicit attempt to empirically research the psychological contract as a process was undertaken by Levinson et al. (1962), who introduced several possible psychological contract processes including increasing separation, joint decline, and joint growth. These processes were derived from their case study of workers at a utility plant in America. An example of increasing separation is described as occurring in a situation where employees were reluctant to learn new skills and their employers were increasingly adopting state-of-the-art manufacturing technology. This separation is experienced through key events, choices made by individuals, or relevant feelings and thoughts. For instance, some employees avoided new technology through refusing promotions into positions requiring its use. Ideas of Levinson et al. are helpful because they illuminate our thinking of relationships in terms of trends and trajectories, rather than snapshots, and emphasizing how relationships often involve considering whether the relationship is 'going places'. If we believe that a relationship is not 'going places', then we will feel inclined to leave this relationship, or change it considerably. Seeing relationships in terms of trajectories is explored later in the chapter.

8.5. What are the limitations of existing approaches examining the psychological contract process?

We have organized our limitations under the four headings derived from Langley's (1999) analysis of the characteristics of processes as involving sequences of events, multiple levels of analysis, time intervals between those events, and a wide range of events, experiences and phenomena.

8.5.1. The psychological contract is not interpreted as a sequence of events

Existing models depicting breach as causing changes to employee attitudes and behaviour do not consider breach as part of an ongoing social interaction. It is assumed that employees simply act out their response to the perceived breach with no attention being paid to subsequent counter-responses from the employer. It seems more likely that the breach event is preceded by many previous actions by the employee and that the employee's response to perceived breach, such as withdrawing effort, will be noticed by the employer who will react in some way, which in turn will require a response from the employee, and so on.

Existing models also omit or oversimplify intervening stages between the initial perception of breach and the employee's reaction to breach. Breach is presented as a necessary and sufficient cause for the outcome. More realistically, breach is likely to trigger a process that may or may not lead to the changes in attitudes and behaviour depending on a number of intervening stages.

8.5.2. Little attention to multiple levels of analysis

While recent psychological contract research has begun to acknowledge how multiple parties influence the employee–employer exchange, too often the psychological contract is reduced to a simple dyad of the employee and the organization, where the organization is regarded as a homogeneous entity. Organizations are, however, likely to be represented by multiple agents, with employees fulfilling their promises towards the organization through a complex network of direct and indirect exchanges.

8.5.3. No consideration of the time intervals between psychological contract events

Psychological contract theory is extremely vague when it comes to identifying time frames around which exchanges take place. We could barely find any theoretical statements regarding the role of time in relation to the psychological contract. When empirical studies have collected longitudinal data a small number of survey waves are conducted, separated by months or even years. Time elapse between surveys is not justified in any way and the selected time intervals are unlikely to provide sufficient insight into the event-based dynamic nature of psychological contracts.

8.5.4. Models of the psychological contract breach have been limited to a narrow range of experiences and outcomes

The range of outcomes considered as reactions to psychological contract breach is narrow, quite general, not theory-based, and too often concerned with the same cluster of job satisfaction, organizational commitment, OCBs, performance, and turnover intentions (Taylor and Tekleab 2004). Emotions and behaviours occurring between breach and outcomes have been overlooked. For example, an employee may experience a wide range of emotions following breach, such as surprise, curiosity to discover what has happened and why, frustration at not being able to find out, and so on. The experience and ordering of these emotions may help understand the escalation from breach to the 'hot' emotions of violation, in a similar way to that proposed by Andersson and Pearson (1999) in their analysis of how low intensity affect (e.g. annoyance) can escalate to high intensity affect (e.g. rage) in cases of spiralling incivility.

The proposed linear relationship between breach and outcomes is also too simplistic. It implies that ever-increasing levels of breach result in ever-decreasing levels of outcomes. There must, however, be limits to the extent any constructs can increase and many varieties of non-linear relationships may exist between variables. The variance models used to understand breach do not specify when the process of increasing breach stops, shifts in a non-linear manner, accelerates and decelerates, is affected by feedback loops, and so on.

In short, current approaches to understanding the psychological contract as a process are limited in several ways and do not adequately explain or deal with the fundamental characteristics of processes as described by Langley (1999).

8.6. Applying process approaches to the psychological contract

From Section 8.5 we can conclude that there is a lack of theory in this area and an absence of empirical data. So, how can we think about the processes involved in psychological contract breach? In this section we outline two examples of frameworks that can be used as starting points for developing a process-orientated understanding of the psychological contract: Weick's sensemaking (1995) and Gergen and Gergen's self-narratives (1988). We should emphasize that these are intended as just two examples of the sorts of frameworks that could be used and have been chosen to illustrate the process nature of psychological contracts and offer insights beyond existing studies and theories that are very largely restricted to variance models.

Before turning to the frameworks we first present two examples of data in Box 8.1 to illustrate psychological contract processes, taken from an unusual daily diary study of breach and exceeded promises. We will not conduct an in-depth analysis of this data, but rather use it to illustrate the nature of the psychological contract as a process of an unfolding chain of events. Daily diaries were used to collect both qualitative and quantitative data relating to the development and repercussions of broken and exceeded promises from forty-five participants over ten working days. Quantitative findings from the diary study have been published elsewhere (see Conway and Briner 2002a). The sample consisted of volunteer participants drawn from a range of mainly professional occupations who were asked to provide daily reports of whether their organization had transgressed (i.e. either violated promises or exceeded promises in a positive way). The daily schedule participants had to complete is presented in the Appendix. At the end of the two-week diary period we interviewed participants to discuss any incidents reported. The extracts from these interviews are given in Box 8.1.

Box 8.1 Interview data illustrating psychological contract processes

Interview extract 1: The case of Derek and the missing teacup

Overview

The participant, Derek, was a part-time teacher on a permanent contract who had held his current position for one month in a school in London. He had held several previous teaching positions in permanent and temporary positions at both inner city and rural schools. He had brought a new teacup into school one morning that had gone missing by lunchtime and eventually turned up four weeks later in a dirty condition. During this period and because of the incident Derek stopped bringing his milk and sugar into the staff room and started to use a flask, which he decided not to leave in the staff room and instead kept on his desk. The following extract is taken from an interview conducted with Derek three days after the incident.

While the incident at the heart of this episode may seem trivial it is important to note that it did appear to have a considerable impact on Derek's thoughts, feelings and behaviours. Derek may also appear to be a somewhat less than robust in coming to terms with and dealing with what others may regard as a relatively unimportant incident. However, the purpose of reporting these data is to illustrate processes rather than demonstrate extreme forms of breach and strong employee reactions.

I borrowed a cup off a friend and took it into school that morning with the full intention to return it to my friend's kitchen the following day, or possibly that afternoon. I only had one cup of tea from it and I went to my lesson, and I came back at break time, within an hour it had gone missing. So I was going to make my second cup of tea for the day and I couldn't find my cup anywhere. I looked in the cupboard, on the washboard, in the kitchen staff room, it wasn't there. Then I let it go, and I didn't have a cup of tea. Come lunchtime it still wasn't there and I asked someone, "Where do you think my cup may have gone?" And they said that maybe someone borrowed it, it happens all the time, things disappear and turn up again a few weeks later, or a few months later, and I was most perturbed especially because I wanted to return it to my friend and this is not the kind of behaviour I expect from my fellow staff members, because I take my milk in there for my tea, my sandwiches, and sometimes other bits of food. And that has been used in the last few weeks as well. So if I can't trust my cup in there, can I trust my milk in there? It makes you feel unsettled. This was the second cup to go missing within a few weeks.

I was under the understanding that staff members have their own specifically designated cups, as during my first two weeks I had observed how other staff members had labelled their cups and kept them in their personal pigeon-holes. I hadn't been assigned a pigeon-hole yet, and still haven't got one.

(continues)

Box 8.1. Interview data illustrating psychological contract processes (*continued*)

Well, I assumed that my fellow colleagues would bring their own cups in and I could trust them with anything in the staff room, especially when we have issues of theft around the school from pupils, one place which is supposed to be a sanctity of safety is the staff room, so I don't expect this kind of violation. The Headmaster at the school said that things would be safe in the staff room; it was always the safe place to leave anything. His word is obviously not taken too seriously.

I haven't taken anything from anyone else, so I don't expect anyone to take anything from me; you know there is a civil code of conduct. There is an implicit bond of loyalty with one's staff. It has affected the way I feel about the staff as a whole in the staff room, that obviously I can't be too trusting, I can't expect ideal relationships with teachers over even petty things. I felt that it wasn't my cup any more because anything you leave in the staff room seems to become public property, property of the school as a whole.

At the time I immediately went and borrowed someone else's cup. I thought if everyone else is going to be blasé about this then I might as well be so I borrowed someone else's. So I nonchalantly went up and took someone else's cup and made my cup of tea in it. But I feel uncomfortable about using other people's cups in the staff room just in case they feel very attached to them and I'm sure they would not say anything to me but it could be a first step in damaging relationships with them, because some people feel very close to their things and would not want my mouth on their property.

It helped to make me feel even more alienated in the place. Because if my property wasn't safe there, that kind of added to it and the milk being used as well, I didn't feel comfortable and at ease when I am there. And because I am not there so much anyway the time I am there I want to feel a part of the school so it kind of has a more distancing effect. I know that people are going to be very flippant about these things. I know what to expect from my fellow colleagues now.

Interview extract 2: The case of Beatrice and the abandoned publication

Beatrice, an editor of a news media journal, reported a sequence of transgressions of her psychological contract regarding the publication of an article. The company consisted of three employees: a Director, a Senior Editor (who is married to the Director) and Beatrice, who chiefly reports to the Senior Editor. Beatrice had been writing a paper for publication in the journal for over a year (200 hours of overtime) following a promise made by the Senior Editor that the article would be published once completed. The sequence of reported transgressed promises was as follows:

PROMISE	DESCRIPTION
Broken promise (Day 2)	Senior Editor tells Beatrice that the publication of her article will be stalled, with the intention to abandon it. Beatrice commented *'Typical. It confirmed my beliefs of the shites that work there.'*
Exceeded promise (Day 4)	Several days after the incident Beatrice, under the supervision of her Senior Editor, is allowed to watch television unrelated to her work (re-runs of *Columbo* and *Quincy*) and displays no intention of working, and eventually leaves work early. *'He actually moved the desk to make my feet more comfortable.'*
Broken promise (Day 6)	The Director treats Beatrice as a personal assistant, asking her to carry out tasks outside her job description (e.g. sending faxes), which Beatrice believes are an insult to her professional identity. *'I'm not a fucking PA. That kind of petty punishment for misdemeanours on my part or a lack of servitude is not something I take particularly well.'*
Exceeded promise (Day 9)	The Senior Editor, mindful of Beatrice's treatment by the Director earlier in the week, allows Beatrice to have half a day off.

Beatrice considered these four events as being related and as an ongoing sequence. She quit the job six months after the publication was abandoned, describing the initial event reported above as *'one too many'*. Prior to quitting she reported letting all professional standards slip; for example, she was taking three- to four-hour lunch breaks on occasions and was no longer prepared to do work overtime.

Both examples support psychological contract theory with breach resulting in some form of employee withdrawal (in Derek's case a withdrawal from colleagues, and in Beatrice's case eventually quitting the job itself). In between the initial breach and the outcome of withdrawal, the extracts illustrate a number of important intervening events. Both examples show how psychological contracts can be conceived as an ongoing chain of events where a broken promise acts as a cause and an effect, the importance of the role of time, how psychological contracts are renegotiated often involving multiple agents, and how employees attempt to make sense of their psychological contract in terms of stories and narratives.

Gergen and Gergen (1988) argue individuals use narratives to make sense of social relationships and form their identities. We first consider how their approach can be used to understand how employees make sense of their psychological contracts. The above extracts also clearly show how employees actively interpret and interrogate their environment following psychological contract breach; here we shall draw on Weick's work (1995) on sensemaking. We now present the two approaches, occasionally referring back to the above data to illustrate points.

8.6.1. Gergen and Gergen's self-narratives

Gergen and Gergen (1988) argue individuals use narratives to make sense of their social relationships and these narratives, in turn, inform how individuals understand who they are, referred to as the 'self'. In other words, sequences of social behaviour resemble a story comprising beginnings, dramatic ups and downs, an ending, and so on. Through viewing social interactions as narratives, individuals place themselves in roles and develop notions of the self. Gergen and Gergen (1988: 19) use the concept of *self-narratives* to define this process, which refers to 'the individual's accounts of the relationship among the self-relevant events across time'. These self-narratives organize self-relevant events into a coherent goal-directed sequence over time, rather than viewing life as a series of discrete, unrelated events. For example, if an individual tends to view certain events in their lives as a narrative demonstrating their successful victory over obstacles, this will bolster their self-esteem.

The concept of the story, or narrative, is central to Gergen and Gergen's approach. People use stories to understand their relationships, themselves, and how they present themselves to others. The self-narratives held by people inform their behaviour in relationships, where this behaviour in turn socially constructs the narratives. Self-narratives lend coherence and direction to an individual's life, justifying past behaviour and predicting future behaviour. Self-narratives also serve important social purposes in terms of negotiating relationships and accounting for, and calling to account, the behaviour of others.

Analysing these stories aids understanding the initiation, direction, acceleration, impediment, and conclusion of sequences of social behaviour over time. Gergen and Gergen (1988: 28) review and introduce a number of concepts—a 'basic vocabulary'—for analysing self-narratives, which are listed below:

1. The establishment of a *valued end point*. In other words, the story needs to be going somewhere. End points will often be the result of 'good' or 'bad' characters producing happy or sad outcomes.
2. The *selection of events relevant to the end point*. Events not relevant to the end point are superfluous to the story and likely to be omitted.
3. The *ordering of events*. Selected events are ordered according to a limited number of criteria. These criteria may change with time and historical and cultural fashions, but most typically may include such things as temporal sequence, importance, and recency.

4. The *establishment of causal linkages*. Events preceding the goal state are presented as being causally linked where one event or series of events leads to a subsequent event.

5. The use of *demarcation signs*. In other words, stories employ signals that indicate the beginning (e.g. 'Have I told you about what happened to me...'), key changes in narrative direction (e.g. 'Anyway, now I must tell you about what happened next...') and end of the story (e.g. 'And that was the last I heard about it').

6. Concepts to understand the direction and pace of narrative development, namely, the *stability* narrative, the *progressive*, and the *regressive* narrative. These narratives relate to the individual's emotional state (what Gergen and Gergen refer to as the 'evaluative position'). The stability narrative refers to self-narratives where the occurrence of events leaves affect unchanged, whereas the progressive and regressive narratives respectively refer to chains of events resulting in a steady increase in positive or negative affect. Gergen and Gergen argue that through combining these concepts and considering accelerating and decelerating narratives, we can generate schematic representations of many popular cultural narratives, such as those presented in Figure 8.1. Emotions accompany your current position on the narrative slope, and can also arise from anticipated future positions on the narrative curve, such as suspense and danger.

7. *Drama* can be viewed as the rapid acceleration of the narrative slope, or a turning point in the narrative slope.

8. *Macronarratives* refer to events spanning across broad periods of time (e.g. life stories) whereas *micronarratives* refer to events within close temporal proximity (e.g. 'On the way to the chemist to get my medication I was almost hit by a car...').

9. *Nested narratives* refer to narratives imbedded within one another. Consistency among narratives adds to its persuasive power.

10. *Incoherent narratives* are achieved through either discrepancies between nested narratives or where an individual's self-narrative is disputed by other actors involved in the narrative which casts doubt on its veracity. For example, I may think I am an honest and hard-working person, however, my employer disagrees and believes I am lazy.

11. Narrative inconsistencies can be resolved through *negotiations* between the parties involved. These negotiations can take place explicitly, or implicitly where the negotiation with the other party is conducted in the imagination. Given people's general tendency to avoid confrontation, Gergen and Gergen argue that implicit negotiation is particularly important to allowing social interaction to proceed without regular breakdowns.

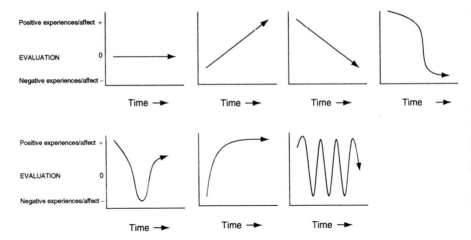

Figure 8.1 Graphing narratives

Starting with the top row and working from left to right:

- The 'stability' narrative—nothing much changes, things are reliable and predictable. These narratives can also apply to sequences, where the employees feel locked into repetitive, unchanging misery or ecstasy.
- The 'progressive' narrative—a steady series of positive events.
- The 'regressive' narrative—a steady series of negative events.
- The 'tragic' narrative—characterized by a rapid fall from grace, with a positive narrative followed by a rapid regressive narrative.
- The 'comedy-romance' narrative—seemingly insuperable problems are overcome by the romantic couple.
- The 'happily-ever-after' narrative—an individual finds their vocation or partner in life resulting in a rapid progressive narrative followed by enduring contentment.
- The 'romantic' saga narrative—the continuing cycle of ups-and-downs of a relationship.

Source: Gergen and Gergen (1988)

How can self-narratives be used to understand psychological contract breach?

One way of viewing an employee's understanding of their psychological contract is as a self-narrative to understand the ups-and-downs of the employment relationship. Self-narratives could be used in multiple ways to understand psychological contracts; here we list some examples to illustrate how self-narratives might be useful, where the list is not intended to be exhaustive. We begin by presenting general examples applying self-narratives to psychological contract concepts, followed by more specific examples by using self-narratives to analyze the data presented earlier.

The benefits of a self-narrative approach to understanding psychological contract breach and psychological contracts more generally are considerable. First, self-narratives link the ongoing evolution of an employee's psychological contract with their identity. Viewing psychological contracts in terms of employees acting out identities provides a powerful means of understanding how psychological contract breach affects employee attitudes and behaviour. The dramatic effects of breach on affect are well-documented, but there is no convincing account of why such dramatic consequences occur if the organization fails to deliver on its promises. Viewing psychological contract breach as threats to deeply held identities provides a possible explanation for why breach matters so much.

Second, self-narratives serve to predict future possible trajectories. In other words, thinking about the range of self-narratives available and their different shapes and patterns enables a broader consideration of what is likely to happen after any particular event. Such an approach may also identify when certain behaviours are necessary in order to protect or repair self-narratives.

Third, considering breach from a narrative perspective invites us to consider prominent culturally available narratives employees draw upon when understanding their psychological contract. Two likely narratives are the retaliatory narrative (e.g. 'The organization broke a promise to me, so I broke my promises in return') and the victim narrative, where the blame-free employee is viewed as a victim of the organization's behaviour and is powerless to demand the fulfilment of the original contract other than take covert action (e.g. withhold effort, lower commitment). A common aspect of these narratives is that they have no obvious positive future outcome. To alter the trajectory implied by these narratives so that they result in a positive outcome would require redirecting the narrative (a turning point in terms of the narrative curves presented in Figure 8.1). For example, instead of retaliation, the employee could redouble their efforts in an attempt to repair the relationship. Changing the direction of a regressive narrative by viewing psychological contract breach constructively is more likely to resolve conflicts successfully.

Fourth, Gergen and Gergen's narrative techniques may provide clues about how individuals use stories about psychological contract breach to justify behaviour that may otherwise be considered as self-interested or deliberately provocative. For example, an employee may use perceived breach as an opportunity to promote change, such as providing justification for exiting a relationship that they no longer find rewarding. They may also use such narratives as means of persuading others to view their behaviours and actions as reasonable and hence also to support or assist them.

Fifth, Gergen and Gergen's narrative concepts can be applied to unfolding psychological contract events. If we take an occasion where an employee perceives their organization to have breached:

- The event is likely to involve 'good' characters (the wronged, the victim) and 'bad' characters (the violator)
- Beginnings (the breach) and endings (compensation, exiting the relationship)

- The establishment of a valued end point (an apology, feeling valued again)
- Perceived causal links between events ('I did X, they did Y, in return I felt obliged to do Z . . .')
- The stability narrative (the reliable cycles of psychological contract fulfilment preceding breach)
- The drama (the sudden shock of discovery of the breach, the treachery of the other party)
- Narrative inconsistencies (disagreements between parties to the contract) resolved through negotiation
- And so on . . .

Now we offer some more specific examples using Gergen and Gergen's approach to explain Derek and Beatrice's withdrawal following breach and referring back to the interview extracts presented earlier. First, we could draw a graph of Derek's affective state over time (see Figure 8.2). His account suggests a regressive narrative where a relatively minor initial breach followed by a string of compounding negative events (attempts to find mug appear futile; headmaster's credibility called into question; trusting relationship with colleagues jeopardized; Derek's use of other's cups offers short-term satisfaction, but ultimately makes him feel uncomfortable) leading Derek to conclude that his colleagues cannot be trusted and heightening his feelings of alienation. This regressive narrative informs Derek's self-concept in important ways. The event symbolizes Derek's relationships with his staff members and his lack of identification with and independence from the school, making him aware that his values are incongruent with other school staff. The incident also reinforces his identity as a part-time and temporary employee and as someone of peripheral status in the school. He aligns the missing teacup with not having his own pigeon-hole and his comments in the last paragraph of the extract suggest that together these incidents compound his perceived peripheral part-time status.

Beatrice's account suggests a very different type of narrative in which the initial breach hastens a dramatic decline in positive regard between the two parties to a new, lowered equilibrium, which is followed by several iterations of small wins and setbacks for Beatrice (see Figure 8.2). Ultimately, however, in light of her later resignation, the relationship never recovers. For Beatrice, we can imagine that there might have been an upward trajectory before the major breach (the abandoning of the publication) where she saw herself as progressing towards an anticipated end point of a job closer to her preferred identity as a writer. The initial breach acts as a prominent relationship 'marker', along the lines of Gergen and Gergen's demarcation points.

Second, we can view the initial breach as acting as a 'tipping point'. Tipping points are the 'straw that breaks the camel's back: the point at which the last small injustice in a chain of injustices suddenly provokes a strong punitive response'

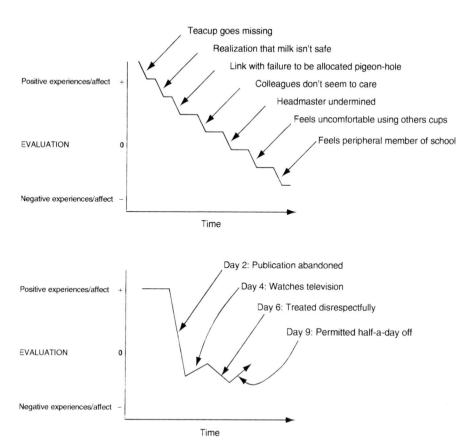

Figure 8.2 Narrative diagrams for Derek (upper diagram) and Beatrice (lower diagram)

(Andersson and Pearson 1999: 462) and are likely to be accompanied by more intense negative affect, such as rage and anger. Tipping points tend to be a much more targeted identity threat. In the case of Beatrice, while the presentation of the four incidents implies the initial breach as the starting point of a cycle, it is more likely a tipping point coming after a long series of previous niggling frustrations. Following the breach, Beatrice's desire to maintain a good relationship is at a low point. The implicit rules of orderly conduct and professionalism characterizing the relationship before the tipping point no longer apply.

Third, alternative popular narratives could also be applied. A narrative of farce is plausible, where repeated cycles of misunderstanding lead to the disintegration of the relationship between Beatrice and her employer. At the outset Beatrice feels unfairly treated and expects some kind of explanation and likely compensation following the initial breach. Rather than tackling the issue directly with her employer she decides to act out her frustration through refusing to work. Her director misreads the situation and acts to punish these behaviours, effectively compounding Beatrice's feelings of injustice.

Finally, the negotiation of the psychological contract could be seen as a game. The game in the cases presented is that neither player totally reveals their 'hand' or their psychology behind behaviours played out in the game. The behaviours are to be interpreted by the other party to propel the game forward, where the other party has various strategies to respond, although these strategies are not known or shared with the other party (see Box 8.2).

8.6.2. Weick's sensemaking

Weick's sensemaking (1995) approach focuses on how people make sense of events and situations in organizations. Sensemaking is critical for understanding the development of employee attitudes and behaviours at work (Louis 1980; de Vos, Buyens, and Schalk 2003). Sensemaking is triggered when individuals encounter surprises, shocks, or more generally a discrepancy between what they perceive to have happened and what they expected to happen. Such discrepant events trigger a need for information seeking, explanation, interpretation and consequent action constituting the sensemaking process. Weick argues that sensemaking is most likely to take place following surprises that trigger negative affect, as individuals are more motivated to seek explanations; surprises resulting

---

Box 8.2 Understanding psychological contract breach through the framework of self-narratives: some key questions

Below we list some key research questions to consider when examining psychological contract breach through self-narratives.

- Do accounts of breach resemble stories of some kind, in terms of having a beginning, dramatic ups and downs, and an end?
- How do recipients of breach depict themselves (as the wronged?) and others in their accounts of breach?
- Do accounts of breach have valued end points, where either the recipient or another character ends up with happy or sad outcomes?
- Are events in the story depicted as being causally linked?
- Can accounts of breach be described in terms of the narrative development in the recipient's emotional state? At what points is the narrative stable, progressive, regressive, rapidly changing?
- Do breach accounts resemble a common narrative such as a tragedy, or a comedy, or a heroic saga? If none of these apply, how can the narrative be described?

in positive affect are more likely to be taken for granted. Sensemaking thus seems likely to occur following psychological contract breach due to the shocking and distressing nature of such events.

We summarize Weick's seven properties (1995) of sensemaking below. It is important to note the iterative and reciprocal nature of these properties. For instance, individuals take actions that are interpreted and reinterpreted that lead to further actions, and so on. Not all steps may take place and such process features such as feedback loops and simultaneous processing may also apply.

1. Sensemaking is *grounded in identity construction* (where it bears some relation to Gergen and Gergen's ideas described earlier). In other words, how we make sense of things will be affected by and in turn affect our identity. Weick views identity as being constituted out of interaction and continually re-defined. Identity threats, a failure to confirm your self-concept, and efforts to maintain a positive self-concept motivate sensemaking, and any sense made from other properties of sensemaking will depend on the individual's identity.

2. Sensemaking is *retrospective*; in other words, in order for people to make sense of events or what they have done it needs to have already happened. Once we understand that all sensemaking is retrospective, several observations follow, such as what is occurring at the moment of sensemaking will inform what is attended to and recalled, and that those factors that affect memory will also affect sensemaking. Sensemaking is therefore likely to be a story containing discrepancies, over-looked information, and contrived consistencies.

3. Sensemaking involves *enacting sensible environments*. This means that we actively go about constructing the environment we sense. The environment is not fixed and singular and 'out there'. Individuals are part of their environment and through their actions create their environment. Weick illustrates the interdependent relationship between the individual and the environment by drawing on Follett's farming metaphor (1924) of enactment, where the farmer prunes, grafts, and fertilizes trees in order that they bear fruit, the trees become apple-bearing, which inspires further apple-bearing behaviour by the farmer, and so on. 'People create their environments as those environments create them' (Weick 1995: 34). Actors affect meaning through the consequences of their actual behaviour. Actions that are never performed but take place in the imagination can also affect meaning.

4. Sensemaking is *social* in that meaning is socially constructed and that sensemaking takes place in front of an audience of one or more people, whether they are physically present or held in the imagination.

5. Sensemaking takes place amid the *ongoing* flow of events and the act of sensemaking is an attempt to bracket continuous flows of experience and

extract cues, events, and sensations from that bracketed period. 'Sensemaking never starts. The reason it never starts is that pure duration never stops. People are always in the middle of things, which become things, only when those same people focus on the past from some point beyond it' (Weick 1995: 43). Ongoing activity is conceptualized in terms of projects, where projects are viewed as activities organized towards achieving desired goals. While immersed in these projects individuals have reasonably clear expectations as to what to expect from their environment. Interruptions to these projects result in sensemaking activity. Interruption provides the key concept linking emotion with sensemaking through preventing individuals reaching their goals and causing negative affect. Interruptions are particularly relevant in close interdependent relationships where parties come to rely on one another.

6. Sensemaking is *focused on and by extracted cues.* An extracted cue refers to 'simple familiar structures that are seeds from which people develop a larger sense of what may be occurring' (Weick 1995: 50). In other words, cues refer to the pertinent pieces of information the sensemaker selects from the flow of previous events. Cues form the building blocks of the sense made from an event and establish the frames of reference for future sensemaking. Cues are extracted from the context through a process of 'searching', 'scanning' and 'noticing' (Weick 1995: 52). Weick argues that politics shape the context, with individuals extracting cues that promote their own interests. Having influence over the possible range of cues is an important source of power. Cues tend to be selected that form a plausible story. The map of extracted cues helps 'animate and orientate people. Once people begin to act (enactment), they generate tangible outcomes (cues) in some context (social), and this helps them discover (retrospect) what is occurring (ongoing), what needs to be explained (plausibility), and what should be done next (identity enhancement)' (Weick 1995: 55). Important questions relating to extracted cues include what cues are extracted and why, and how these cues are presented and embellished as part of the sensemaker's story of the events.

7. Sensemaking is driven by *plausibility rather than accuracy.* Sensemaking is more concerned with constructing accounts of events that are pragmatic and persuasive and serving the interests of the sensemaker rather than accurately capturing events in the social world. Weick notes that in a postmodern world of multiple realities, multiple identities, with ambiguous and changing boundaries, searching for accuracy in social perceptions is a futile pursuit. The painstaking and time-consuming nature of pursuing accuracy is also off-putting to the sensemaker, who needs to act, not endlessly ponder life's complexities. Furthermore, the sensemaker, when trying to produce a compelling account, may require some poetic licence in order to string the cues into a satisfying and rounded story. 'If accuracy is nice but not necessary in sensemaking, then what is necessary? The answer is, something that

preserves plausibility and coherence, something that is reasonable and memorable, something that embodies past experience and expectations, something that resonates with other people, something that can be constructed retrospectively but also can be used prospectively, something that captures both feeling and thought, something that allows for embellishment to fit current oddities, something that is fun to construct. In short, what is necessary in sensemaking is a good story. . . . They explain. And they energise' (Weick 1995: 61).

How can sensemaking be used to understand psychological contract breach?

As with self-narratives, sensemaking could be used in multiple ways to understand psychological contracts. We first present general examples followed by more specific examples using sensemaking to analyse the data presented earlier.

Beginning with applying sensemaking to psychological contract breach with Weick's first property of sensemaking—that it is grounded in *identity construction*—employees are likely to perceive psychological contract breach in part as an *identity* threat. Identity can be expressed as the pursuit of valued goals (e.g. Emmons 1992); when organizations renege on promises this thwarts employees' progress towards goals and thus constitute an identity threat. As noted above under the self-narratives approach, viewing perceived breach as an identity threat illuminates why it is a distressing event and explains employee withdrawal from organizations following breach, in an attempt to protect their self-concept.

The *retrospective* property of sensemaking underlines the importance of cognitive biases affecting hindsight and distorting our memory of the past when making sense of breach events. For example, Schkade and Kilbourne (1991) discuss the 'disappointing effect' referring to the tendency to exaggerate the discrepancy between an individual's expectations and the received outcomes for past disappointments. This suggests individuals may exaggerate, or even invent, the extent to which a breach occurs after the event as a means of making sense of previous disappointments. In other words, employees who have experienced a breach may replay the event in their own mind or in conversation in ways that make the breach more distressing or upsetting that it was when initially experienced.

Enacting sensible environments, the third sensemaking property, suggests how employee actions following breach, and how those actions are interpreted by the organization, will critically influence the sense made of the breach event. For example, if an employee believes their manager has broken an implicit promise by not consulting them about key decisions they may then withdraw their support and refuse to do extra tasks. In response, the manager, who is unaware that the employee believes they have broken a promise, may then demand that the employee undertake the extra tasks by using her or his formal authority. The employee may then make sense of the manager's use of formal authority by seeing it as consistent with the initial broken implicit promise even though there is no relationship between these events in the mind of the manager.

One obvious role of the *social* in psychological contracting is how employees permit, resist or reproach another employee's behaviour. Social effects on employee contributions date back to the Hawthorne studies during the 1920s and Roethlisberger and Dickson's work (1939) on ratebusters, where group norms dictated the productivity levels of group members and any employee exceeding these social norms would be castigated as ratebusters, with various strategies employed to deal with the ratebuster. Ratebusting, in psychological contract terms, can be seen as exceeding the psychological contract with the employer, but breaching psychological contracts with co-workers for not respecting productivity norms.

A psychological contract is also an *ongoing* (the fifth property) sequence fulfilling and creating promises between parties. Breach corresponds to Weick's idea of interruptions to ongoing events, where breach is a shock to an employee's expectations of what they thought would happen. When ongoing cycles of psychological contract fulfilment are interrupted, the employee must decide whether to continue with their previous course of action specified by the old contract, or to pursue a different path. Interruptions are more likely to occur and arouse the strongest emotions in close interdependent relationships, making interruptions a particularly useful concept for understanding breach occurring in relational psychological contracts.

The *cues extracted* through employees scanning the environment following breach will constitute the building blocks of how they make sense of the breach. Disagreement over the terms of the psychological contract is likely to be fuelled by employees extracting cues that differ to the other party.

The final property, that sensemaking is *driven by plausibility rather than accuracy*, is apposite for psychological contract breach. The psychological contract consists of social perceptions and, as Weick notes, seeking accuracy in such perceptions is futile.

Employees cannot read their employer's mind to examine whether their behaviour was intentional or not and they may not trust their employer's account of what happened. Employees may feel insufficiently empowered to obtain the information needed to gain an accurate account of what happened and so have to rely on plausible inferences from available cues. Additionally, because breach arouses powerful negative emotions aimed at the violator, such as rage and disgust, the employee may not wish to openly and honestly confront their employer.

Considering the interview extracts presented earlier, we will use Weick's sensemaking approach to offer examples of various ways to understand Derek and Beatrice's withdrawal following breach. For illustrative purposes we have selected the most relevant of the seven properties of sensemaking to the extracts.

The incident of the missing teacup reinforced Derek's identity as a peripheral part-time worker and symbolized his alienation from the school, a feeling that was further reinforced by the school's failure to allocate him a pigeonhole. His perception of the staff room changed from regarding it as a place of safety, to a place where he now felt uncomfortable and the need to withdraw. Derek's enactment following the perceived breach was through using other cups and thus potentially committing a breach to another staff member; such behaviour is consistent with his perception that his psychological contract had been violated. His belief that a promise had been made stating that his teacup would be safe in the staff room and used only by himself is supported by three extracted cues: (1) The headmaster of the school declared the staff room as a safe place to leave things; (2) Derek's code of conduct that people—especially professionals—should not use the property of others without permission; (3) Other cups in the staff room were labelled with the owner's name and were stored in their personal pigeon-holes. The third cue demonstrates plausible rather than accurate sense-making. The labelling of cups could also be interpreted as indicating other staff members' concerns relating to the theft of their cups, hence the necessity to name and store them; however, Derek's interpretation is plausible given the set of cues he draws upon and adds power to his story of injustice.

Turning to our second extract, from Beatrice, the abandoned publication is a clear identity threat to Beatrice, in terms of how she saw her role and perceiving herself as a writer. Beatrice views the initial broken promise as an attempt by her employer to position her within an administrative role. The second broken promise by her director is a further cue that Beatrice views this incident as an attempt to keep her in a low-skill position. Once Beatrice accepts that this situation will not change, she decides to leave the organization.

The exceeded promise (allowed to watch television) following the initial breach could be viewed as enacting defiance. Beatrice's enactment is possibly misread by her director, who appears to overlook Beatrice's motivations and punishes the behaviour itself by treating Beatrice as a PA. (It would be of great use to have the employer's perspective.) The director's response effectively compounds Beatrice's feelings of injustice and increases her desire to retaliate. Beatrice is now less likely to verbalize her concerns as the relationship has already become soured. Later enacted withdrawals include intensifying efforts to look for other jobs, neglecting professional standards, taking three- to four-hour lunch breaks, and so on. Such behaviours will increase the likelihood of her employer taking further punitive measures, thus accelerating progression towards Beatrice quitting her job.

Beatrice's belief that a promise had been made regarding the publication of her article is supported by cues that in her two years at the organization the editor had expressed huge enthusiasm for the project and engaged in plentiful proof-reading (not reported in the extract). It also seems clear that the first reported broken promise sensitizes Beatrice to certain aspects of her environment, leading to more intensively scanning her environment for further transgressions relevant to the initial breach even though the events may have been independent of one another. That Beatrice selected these four events from the hundreds of possible activities and interactions occurring during the two-week diary period supports Weick's ideas that events are highly selectively extracted and bracketed from ongoing continuous flows of experience.

Finally, Beatrice's comment that her editor *'actually moved the desk to make my feet more comfortable'* could be interpreted in many ways (e.g. sarcasm); Beatrice's belief that it reflected contrition following the initial breach is plausible in light of her belief that she has been wronged.

As a concluding comment, a fuller understanding of events would clearly benefit from having the perspective of other parties to these incidents. Such information may shift our responses towards the characters involved significantly. For example, if the editor had informed us that Beatrice pursued her publication in defiance of his wishes and was using the incident to justify leaving the organization, our sympathies may shift towards the employer. Under this scenario, Beatrice becomes the wrongdoer, using the breach event to gain advantage. Relying on a single party's perspective can only provide restricted insight into psychological contract processes. Individuals are likely to frame events in such a way that promotes their own interests or enhances movement towards preferred selves (see Box 8.3).

Box 8.3 Understanding psychological contract breach through a sensemaking framework: some key questions

Below we list some key research questions to consider when examining psychological contract breach through sensemaking.

Property 1: Sensemaking is grounded in identity construction

- How does the employee see himself or herself as the victim of the breach?
- What are the cues that trigger and support the breach perception and how may they be influenced by salient identities held by the employee?
- How do employee behaviours following the breach enact various identities?

Property 2: Sensemaking is retrospective

- How might recipients of breach recall of events be affected by memorial and motivational bias (for example, through the selection of recent events, mood congruent events, events consistent with preferred selves, attribution errors, etc.)?

Property 3: Sensemaking enacts sensible environments

- Does the employee enact their environment in such a way as to confirm their suspicions of breach?
- How does the employee's action affect later interpretations?
- Do important actions take place in the employee's imagination that affect later interpretations?

Property 4: Sensemaking is social

- How do co-workers affect an employee's interpretation of breach?
- How do workplace social norms inhibit, constrain and facilitate behaviour following breach?

Property 5: Sensemaking takes place amid ongoing events

- What does the employee perceive as the key interruptions to workplace life?

Property 6: Sensemaking is focused on and by extracted cues

- What are the key pertinent pieces of information extracted by the employee from the environment that lead them to conclude a promise has been breached?
- How do these cues frame later interpretations and behaviours?

Property 7: Sensemaking is plausible rather than accurate

- What possible inaccuracies may the employee be overlooking?
- How does the employee deal with information that contradicts their account of events?
- Can you detect instances where the employee embellishes their account to make their viewpoint more plausible and compelling?

8.7. Summary and conclusion

The organizational and social sciences generally lack the conceptual tools and language to develop process theories (Monge 1990). One obvious reason for this is that the study of process is simply more difficult than studying phenomena from other perspectives.

In this chapter we began by considering the limitations of existing research. We presented a case for considering the psychological contract as a process and provided some examples of data illustrating the psychological contract as a process, along with examples of frameworks (self-narratives and sensemaking) to interpret the data and to more generally understand the psychological contract as a process.

A moment's reflection tells us that our own experience of the psychological contract is best understood as an ongoing process and we hope that the data and process frameworks presented in the chapter provide some examples of how to think about psychological contract processes. As long as the psychological contract literature neglects tackling process issues, it will, we believe, fail to capture the essence of the psychological contract and thus put a halt on future developments in our understanding.

9 | Managing the Psychological Contract

9.1. Introduction

The idea that the psychological contract could be used as a management tool was greeted by much initial enthusiasm. It was seen as a means of individualizing the employment relationship and, by making implicit beliefs explicit, it was felt that the psychological contract could be relatively easily controlled and managed.

The psychological contract appears to be used by many organizations. In a recent survey of 1,300 senior UK Human Resource managers 36 per cent reported that their organizations use it to manage the employment relationship and 90 per cent agreed that it is a useful concept (Guest and Conway 2002). Furthermore, psychological contract surveys consistently find employees report high levels of perceived promises, indicating that organizations could potentially benefit from successfully managing the psychological contract.

Given the apparent interest in the psychological contract, the lack of published research or other writing about managing the psychological contract is surprising. Within the academic community researchers tend to take a rather cursory approach to making practical recommendations from psychological contract theory and research. Those recommendations that are made often appear to be added as afterthoughts to articles in the form of speculative ideas inferred from empirical findings. Practical guides to managing the psychological contract are conspicuous by their absence. The reasons for this are difficult to establish. One possible explanation is that, as discussed in detail earlier, psychological contract theory is underspecified and somewhat weak. As Lewin (1945) famously noted, there is nothing as practical as a good theory. If the reverse of this is true—there is nothing as impractical as a weak theory—this may help account for the lack of practical guidance about the psychological contract.

As very little literature explicitly addresses managing the psychological contract most of the material in this chapter is based on our own speculations from empirical findings, or ideas drawn from areas outside the psychological contract literature. We first discuss key issues in managing the psychological contract and follow this with suggestions for managing the two key areas of the psychological contract: contents and breach. As most current recommendations for managing psychological contracts are from an employer's perspective, we then discuss what employees can themselves do to manage the psychological contract. We end the chapter with a discussion of some of the difficulties and dilemmas faced by employees and employers when attempting to manage the psychological contract.

9.2. Some key issues in managing the psychological contract

As mentioned above, the apparent absence of practical guidance suggests that managing the psychological contract is far from straightforward. Before discussing managing the psychological contract in detail it is, therefore, important to first identify some of the key issues in managing the psychological contract that may help explain why practical advice is difficult to provide. First, we consider what aspects of the psychological contract we are trying to manage. Second, as most research on managing the psychological contract deals with managing explicit promises, we examine this assumption and consider some of its limitations. Third, we examine whether, in principle, managing the psychological contract through managing implicit promises is likely to be effective. Fourth, we consider how, in principle, psychological contracts can be managed. Last, we discuss what we know currently about managing psychological contracts. We will return to several of these issues at the end of the chapter where we consider some of the dilemmas for employees and employers in managing the psychological contract.

9.2.1. What are we trying to manage and why?

As the psychological contract is multifaceted we could potentially manage any part of it. For example, we may try to manage the subjective features of psychological contracts by making terms of the psychological contract less subjective in order to reduce misunderstandings between employees and employers. Another example may be managing what or who should be regarded as 'the organization', as forming psychological contracts is more likely to be effective when both parties share a common understanding about the main contract makers.

Researchers' recommendations for managing the psychological contract tend to focus on the two main areas of psychological contract theory and research: contents and breach. The sorts of practical recommendations that can be made in relation to managing the contents of the psychological contract include such things as ways of deciding what promises should be made between parties, how the contents of psychological contracts can be managed during change, and how psychological contracts can be negotiated and renegotiated. The main reason for managing contents is, fairly obviously, that certain types of contents of psychological contracts and particular ways of changing the contents are likely to result in more or less positive outcomes for both the employee and employer. Such ideas are supported by evidence discussed elsewhere that employees with particular types of contract (e.g. relational) are more likely to feel committed to their employer and are less likely to quit.

The second area in which recommendations for managing are made is in relation to breach and fulfilment of psychological contracts. This might include the monitoring of psychological contracts to ensure both parties keep their side of the deal, trying to prevent breach happening, and designing strategies to deal with breach if it does happen. The main reason, clearly, for managing breach and fulfilment is to make sure both parties keep their side of the deal in order to maximize positive outcomes and to avoid or minimize the negative consequences of breach.

While managing the psychological contract could, therefore, mean managing almost any aspect of it, in practice, where recommendations are made they have tended to focus on managing contents or breach. This is in part a reflection of the focus of most research in the field but it may also reflect that managing these aspects of the psychological contract appear the most obvious or perhaps simple.

9.2.2. Is managing the psychological contract by making promises explicit really managing the psychological contract as such?

Many researchers assume that making psychological contracts explicit results in easier and more effective management as it reduces misunderstandings and, therefore, the chances of breach (e.g. Flood et al. 2001; Herriot and Pemberton 1997; Robinson and Morrison 2000). Furthermore, having an explicit record of the psychological contract facilitates the formation and renegotiation of psychological contracts. It is suggested that managers and agents of the organization can make psychological contracts explicit through regular, open, and honest discussion with employees. This can be done in various contexts such as during the recruitment process through realistic job previews, induction programmes, performance and development appraisal meetings, and ongoing day-to-day interactions between employees and managers.

Many of the suggestions made for how both employees and employers can manage the psychological contract, therefore, involve making the contract more explicit, discussing the contents, checking on delivery, and so on. Given that the psychological contract can be considered to consist largely of implicit promises, how is it possible to manage it in this way? Is managing explicit promises, or making implicit promises more explicit, really managing the psychological contract as such? In the first case, managing explicit promises, it could be argued that this is not actually managing the subtle, implicit, and inferred understandings about what each party is promising the other and is, therefore, not managing the psychological contract. In the second case, where implicit promises are made more explicit, it is also possible to view this approach as not managing the psychological contract as such but rather just managing it away: if implicit promises are made explicit, written down, and communicated verbally (e.g. the setting of sales targets for promotion) then this actually involves replacing implicit understanding with explicit promises.

As discussed in Chapter 3, some researchers (e.g. Rousseau 1995; Herriot and Pemberton 1997) view explicit promises as part of a psychological contract, as the terms are still subjectively perceived. For these researchers managing the psychological contract in this way would presumably not be problematic. However, other researchers (e.g. Guest 1998; Meckler, Drake, and Levinson 2003) believe that the psychological contract, by definition, does not include explicit promises and, therefore, by making psychological contracts explicit we are in fact managing a formal legal employment contract. Within this approach, managing the psychological contract would appear to involve intervening in more complex and perhaps subtle ways in order to affect and shape implicit promises.

A key issue is what constitutes managing the psychological contract. If it is anything that involves managing explicit promises or making promises more explicit, then almost any type of managerial intervention could play a role in managing the psychological contract. If, on the other hand, we restrict managing the psychological contract to managing implicit promises this raises other issues about how something that is implicit can be managed without making it explicit.

9.2.3. Is managing the psychological contract by making promises explicit likely to work?

Whether or not we consider managing explicit promises to be managing the psychological contract, is it likely to be an effective way of managing the employment relationship? There are several reasons why this approach may not be effective, and we consider four such reasons here.

First, a fundamental problem in trying to take this approach to managing the psychological contract is that there are good reasons why employees and organizations might actually prefer implicit contracts. For employees, implicit psychological contracts may give them greater control over the pace, quality, and quantity of their work. For employers, implicit psychological contracts help elicit organizational citizenship type behaviours from employees in ways that may not be achievable if turned into explicit promises. In more general terms, spelling out *exactly* what is required in an exchange relationship may also weaken many of the bonds that maintain a give-and-take relationship. Hence both employers and employees may resist attempts to make every aspect of their psychological contract explicit.

Second, those arguments in favour of making psychological contracts explicit tend to suggest that doing so will benefit both employer and employee. However, this approach makes somewhat naïve fairness assumptions as, in practice, explicit psychological contracts are much more likely to benefit employers than employees. Hiltrop (1996) believes that making psychological contracts explicit requires sophisticated and highly effective negotiation and participation not found in most organizations where command and control is more likely to characterize management style. This type of conclusion is supported by other analyses. In a critique of performance appraisal—where explicit negotiations of psychological contracts are most likely to happen—Newton and Findlay (1996) conclude that while organizations often present performance appraisals as an opportunity for employees to negotiate their side of the deal, organizations pay only lip-service to this ideal and that the individual's viewpoint is not given serious attention. The appraisal is more plausibly seen in the broader context 'of other forms of performance management, surveillance and accountability' (Newton and Findlay 1996: 58). Hence, it seems quite possible that attempts to make the psychological contract more explicit will come to be seen over time as simply another means of management control rather than being viewed as a means of making the deal fair and open for both parties.

A third problem is that available empirical evidence does not suggest that explicit psychological contracting is widespread or effective. If making psychological contracts explicit was so advantageous to management we might expect such sorts of techniques and interventions to be commonly used, written about, and researched. As indicated earlier there is little writing or research about managing the psychological contract, suggesting that no particular approach, including this one, has met with great success or enthusiasm. Also, the generally quite low levels of consultation between management and employees suggest that employers are making few attempts to adopt this approach to managing the employment relationship. In a large UK survey (Workplace Employment Relations Survey) conducted in 1998 employees were asked how often managers sought their views on the future plans for the workplace, staffing issues (including redundancy), changes to work practices, and health and safety. Only 17 per cent reported their views were sought on changes to future work practices, 14 per cent on future plans for the workplace, and 77 per cent said they were never consulted over any of the four issues (Cully et al. 1999).

Last, it is not clear that making psychological contracts more explicit will actually reduce breach. If anything, available evidence suggests that implicit promises are less likely to be breached. While Robinson and Morrison (2000) argue that implicit promises are broken more than explicit promises as both parties are more likely to hold different views of what implicit promises have been made, their study found no association between the implicitness of promises and subsequent breach. In their daily diary study of psychological contracts, Conway and Briner (2002a) found that explicit promises were more likely than implicit promises to be broken. Finally, Tekleab and Taylor (2003) found that the extent to which employees and managers agree over promises has a curvilinear relationship with employee breach, where managers are more likely to report that employees breach their psychological contract at either low levels or high levels of agreement, but not when the parties moderately agree over the terms of the contract. Assuming that implicit promises fall within the region of moderate agreement these findings also suggest that implicit promises are less likely than explicit ones to be broken. It appears, therefore, that implicit psychological contracts may allow more flexibility for adjustment and negotiation where discrepancies and disagreements can more easily be absorbed into and dealt with by ongoing sensemaking and renegotiation. Making the psychological contract more explicit may, perhaps paradoxically, increase rather than diminish the chances of breach.

To conclude this section, researchers generally assume that making psychological contracts explicit is a good way to manage psychological contracts. While such an approach seems to make sense there are a number of reasons, such as those discussed here, why it might not be effective.

9.2.4. What counts as managing the psychological contract and who does it?

Because the psychological contract can be influenced and shaped in so many ways, as mentioned earlier, nearly all human resource management practices and almost any management action could in some way affect the psychological contract. Here, however, we focus on those more explicit and direct ways of managing the psychological contract.

While certain aspects of management will be particularly influential, such as human resource management, leadership behaviour, organizational culture, and the role of line management, it is beyond the scope of this chapter to consider in any detail how all these factors contribute to managing the psychological contract. Interested readers should refer to the special issue of *Human Resource Management* (1994) journal on human resource management and the psychological contract, and Paul, Niehoff, and Turnley's (2000) analysis of human resource management approaches to managing the psychological contract.

As well as the question of what counts as managing the contract there is the question of who does such managing. A particularly important agent is the line manager who may actively use the psychological contract to motivate and reward employees and also clarify messages from human resource management practices and more remote contract makers (Rousseau 2004). While this chapter focuses largely on how the employer and agents of the employer can manage the psychological contract, we also consider how the other party to the contract, the employee, could and does manage the psychological contract.

9.2.5. What do we know about managing the PC?

The final issue is the lack of published information on managing the psychological contract. For instance, we cannot think of any studies that have explicitly researched situations in which managers or employers intentionally manage the psychological contract. As it is not possible, therefore, to report any directly relevant published evidence or theory, we instead speculate in this chapter on how the psychological contract could be managed on the basis of the theory and evidence that is available, much of which has already been discussed.

While the absence of directly relevant information is something of a limitation it does leave plenty of opportunity for speculation. However, wherever possible we have tried to base such speculation on what is currently known about the psychological contract.

9.3. Managing the contents of the psychological contract

What, in principle, does managing the contents of the psychological contract entail? Results from UK national surveys of the psychological contract discussed earlier, in Chapter 4, provide an indication of the contents of psychological contracts in terms of the promises employees and employers perceive the other party to have made. Employees perceive that organizations have promised, for example, to provide a safe and congenial work environment, job security, equitable rates of pay, and procedural fairness, and in return employees have promised to work their contracted hours and to do so diligently and honestly. Employers, on the other hand, perceive that employees have promised, for example, to work their contracted hours, to do a good job in terms of quality and quantity, and to be honest, and in return employers promise to provide employees with fringe benefits, treat employees humanely, ensure procedural fairness, and recognize special contributions.

So, if these are typical psychological contract contents, what does it then mean to manage these contents? Put simply, managing the contents means doing things that will in some way change these contents. Completely new items could be added to the psychological contract (e.g. a new choice of work schedules), some existing items could be removed (e.g. no more long-term job security) and the relative importance of existing items could be changed (e.g. increased emphasis on quality).

Here we discuss three means by which the contents of the psychological contract can be managed: through imposing change; through the communication of promises; and through negotiation.

9.3.1. Managing the contents through imposing change

Later we will discuss how the contents can be managed by communicating promises and by negotiation. Here, we are more concerned with what happens when the employer wants to impose or cannot avoid changing the psychological contract in a particular way.

While this may or may not be a particularly effective or ethical way of changing the psychological contract, there is little doubt that employers sometimes feel they sometimes must and also have the right to unilaterally take actions to make such changes. For example, pressure from shareholders may mean that organizations feel they have no choice but to reduce staff numbers and salary costs and to improve performance. These changes in turn are likely to affect the psychological contract.

There is little theory or empirical research about how such changes in turn change the psychological contract, although such changes are widely regarded as major causes of breach. For many employees the experience of change is commonplace. In the UK, for example, Guest and Conway (1999) found that 50 per cent of employees reported that some kind of change programme had taken place within the previous year, with the most likely type of change being restructuring and the introduction of new technology. More specifically, 30 per cent reported restructuring, 22 per cent the introduction of new technology, 17 per cent the reorganization of work, 17 per cent redundancies, 16 per cent a merger or acquisition, and 10 per cent a culture change programme.

Rousseau (1995, 1998) considers ways of changing psychological contracts from the organization's perspective, while trying to minimize violating psychological contracts with employees. She suggests that psychological contract change can occur either through accommodation or transformation. Accommodation consists of small changes that do not fundamentally challenge the ongoing relationship. Such changes are absorbed into the existing contract through alterations to one or a small number of psychological contract terms.

In contrast, transformations constitute 'radical surgery' (Rousseau 1998: 50), where the employee must completely change their understanding of the terms of the contract. Rousseau describes four stages that she believes organizations should go through in order to successfully transform psychological contracts:

1. *Challenge the old contract* by providing sufficient justification for change.
2. *Prepare for change* by underlining that change is definitely going to happen, communicating in advance what changes will happen, offering compensations for possible losses, and making sure transition structures are in place.
3. *Generate the new contract* by ensuring employees buy into their new roles by reapplying for positions and being involved in the design of the new role, and ensuring that organizations have contract makers readily available for discussion.

4. *Live the new contract* by ensuring consistency of treatment, delivery of new promises, and reinforcing the new contract through ongoing communication.

Rousseau's suggestions for the stages involved in the successful transformation of psychological contracts represent one of the few attempts in the literature to provide practical advice. This particular approach tends to position employees as somewhat passive and responding in fairly predictable ways. However, organizational change tends to destabilize and reduce employees' trust in the organization (Guest and Conway 2002), which may mean that any imposed changes to the psychological contract in such a context could be met with resistance.

Clearly, imposing different sorts of changes to the psychological contract may prove to be difficult and employees may respond to such changes in ways that are ultimately damaging to the organization. One particular type of imposed change to the psychological contract occurs when employees feel compelled to perform behaviours that have not in the past been considered to be a part of their role. Over time, these behaviours slowly start to be incorporated into their role such that the job gets larger. This phenomenon has been described as 'job creep' and defined as 'the slow and subtle expansion of employee job duties that is not officially recognized by the organization' (Van Dyne and Butler Ellis 2004: 181). An example of job creep is a situation in which a previously unusual, rare and discretionary behaviour, such as staying late at work to help out colleagues, becomes a more frequent occurrence and changes from being a discretionary behaviour to a behaviour which managers come to expect from employees. It is argued that job creep has negative effects on employees as they perceive that their personal freedom has been threatened.

There are numerous other ways of imposing change on the psychological contract and many other potential employee responses to such imposed change. We now turn to more subtle, ongoing, and participatory ways of changing the contents of the psychological contract.

9.3.2. Managing the contents by communicating promises

While imposing changes to the contract does also involve communication, here we focus on how organizations can communicate in a more ongoing way what promises they expect from employees and what employees can expect in return. If promises are not communicated effectively or consistently employees will not develop a clear understanding of their psychological contract and instead may be confused and uncertain about exactly what 'the deal' is. First, some of the means of communicating promises are discussed followed by a brief discussion of ways of ensuring the consistency of such communications.

Human resource management practices are one of the main ways of communicating the contents of psychological contracts. Indeed, some human resource management practices, such as performance appraisal, are used for the express purpose of communicating the psychological contract, as they provide an opportunity for the organization to establish and clarify expectations with employees (Herriot and Pemberton 1997; Rousseau 1995).

A survey by Guest and Conway (2002) of 1,300 senior UK HR managers revealed that some practices are perceived as being more effective than others in communicating the organization's promises to employees (Table 9.1). Communication about promises can take place in different ways and communicate different types of promises: communication about what the job itself involves; communication during recruitment about what employees can expect; and top-down communication from senior managers. As shown in Table 9.1, different practices are used for these different types of communication and are judged to be more or less effective as ways of communicating promises. The three practices considered to be most effective were recruitment, informal day-to-day interactions, and induction and initial training. It is worth noting that the practice rated as second most effective, day-to-day interactions, is not actually a human resource management practice as such, though may be influenced by other practices. So, while formal practices are clearly thought of by these human resource managers as very important means of communicating promises, everyday informal interactions between managers and employers are also regarded as very important.

It appears that employees pick up messages about implicit promises in various and many ways; hence there may be a range of other practices, interventions, and actions that could in some way be used to communicate promises. Whichever

Table 9.1 The effectiveness of human resource management practices in communicating the organization's promises to employees

	% of organizations rating practice as effective in communicating promises
Job communication	
Informal day-to-day interaction	56
Training and development	53
Individual objectives and targets	51
Performance appraisal	51
Briefing by line management	49
Team targets	31
Recruitment communication	
Recruitment process	66
Induction and initial training	55
Staff handbook / manual	46
Job descriptions	26
Top-down communication	
Annual company meetings with staff	34
Mission statements	27

Note: Adapted from Guest and Conway (2002).

way promises are communicated, and whatever those promises are, the consistency of the messages employees receive is likely to be key in determining communication effectiveness. Morrison and Robinson (2004) have made several suggestions for ways of ensuring that consistent promises are communicated, such as holding focus groups with psychological contract agents from across the organization.

One issue in trying to ensure that all agents are giving consistent messages is that the organization needs to be aware of who employees perceive the agents to be. In other words, employees may perceive that promises have been communicated to them from individuals who are not regarded by the organization as agents. Guest and Conway (2000), for example, found that senior managers viewed themselves as key agents of the organization and lower levels of management and non-managerial employees endorsed this perception. However, non-managerial employees also perceived lower levels of management as agents of the organization, whereas these managers did not regard themselves as significant agents to those they managed. An important implication for organizations, therefore, is that they need to find out who it is that employees perceive is an agent and ensure that all these agents are giving consistent messages. An implication for individual managers is that, even though they may not feel themselves to be an important communicator of promises, those they manage may regard them as such.

9.3.3. Managing the contents through negotiation

Imposing change on the contents of psychological contracts or simply communicating promises does not involve much, if any, negotiation. Rather, employees simply find out about imposed changes or are told what new promises are being made to them. In contrast, negotiating the psychological contract involves the employer and employee reaching agreement about the items in the contract and how much of each item should be promised. Three important considerations when negotiating psychological contracts are the needs of both parties, only making promises that can be realistically delivered, and respecting fairness issues. Each of these is now discussed in turn.

As both employees and organizations will want to be in psychological contracts that meet their needs (Levinson et al. 1962; Herriot 1992; Hilltrop 1996) it is vital that employees and the organization should consider each other's needs during negotiations. In other words, while it is possible for each party to simply negotiate for what it wants, the contract is more likely to be an effective one if needs are taken into account.

There are numerous typologies of employees needs (see Cherrington 1991 for a review) providing some guidance as to the kind of things employees want from their employer. For example, in a recent article on the psychological contract, Lambert, Edwards, and Cable (2003) identify six essential rewards that employees want from work: pay; recognition from supervisors; opportunities to form social relationships with others; task variety; career training; and skill development. However, designing an appropriate context where employees feel comfortable discussing their needs is more difficult, as employers often wield greater power during negotiations that may make employees reluctant to discuss what they want. Furthermore, as many fundamental human needs are believed to be unconscious (Kehr 2004), employees may be unable to verbalize and hence negotiate their needs.

Turning now to fairness, while legal scholars consider fairness irrelevant to employment contracts (Cheshire et al. 1991), Guest (1998) and Herriot and Pemberton (1995) believe fairness to be a central concern when negotiating psychological contracts. In other words, employees expect that what they get from the organization (e.g. pay, benefits, promotion, interesting work) should be a fair return for what they contribute to the organization (e.g. skills, effort, loyalty), that their deal should compare favourably with their colleagues, and that the procedures used to allocate rewards are transparent and fair. It is possible to negotiate a deal which one party believes to be unfair—just as it is possible to negotiate a deal without taking the other party's needs into account—but in both cases the psychological contract which is agreed is not likely to be one which will be sustainable.

The starting point for any negotiation is that parties state what they are prepared to do for one another. During negotiations it might be tempting for one party to overstate what he or she can offer in order to get more back from the other party. This may lead to one or both parties making promises they cannot keep. Clearly, in negotiating psychological contracts it is important that the promises that are made are realistic. While high levels of promises have been shown to be motivating and linked to more positive work attitudes (Guest and Conway 1997, 1998, 1999, 2000, 2001, 2002, 2004) one danger of making a greater number of promises, or more extravagant promises, is that they are more likely to be broken. Lester et al. (2002) pose an interesting dilemma in relation to this issue. Should organizations under-promise when negotiating psychological contracts during selection and risk not attracting the best staff, so that they can later overfulfil those promises and enhance motivation and satisfaction? Or, should they overpromise at the negotiation stage and attract the best staff even though they increase the chances of later breach and subsequent dissatisfaction and turnover? While there is no direct evidence about the effects of under- or overpromising in psychological contract negotiations, studies of exceeded and broken promises may indicate the potential consequences of under- or overpromising because exceeded promises are more likely to happen following underpromising and broken promises or breach are more likely to happen following overpromising.

Beginning with the consequences of underpromising, studies examining the effects of exceeding promises or overfulfilling promises find mixed results. Perceptions of exceeded promises have been found to be associated with higher employee performance (Lester et al. 2002). Exceeding promises on certain items (e.g. pay) has been found to be associated with job satisfaction; however, exceeded promises for other items (e.g. task variety) have been associated with job dissatisfaction (Lambert, Edwards, and Cable 2003). Finally, Conway and Briner (2002*a*) found exceeded promises were negligibly related to emotions and daily mood.

Evidence for the consequences of overpromising is more consistent. Breaches or broken promises are likely outcomes of overpromising and many studies show how breach detrimentally affects employee attitudes and behaviours. Furthermore, studies also find the detrimental effects of breach act over-and-above any possible beneficial effects from making the initial promise (Guest and Conway 2001, 2002, 2004).

In negotiating psychological contracts organizations should, therefore, not be tempted to promise things they cannot deliver. Setting realistic promises may be difficult to achieve in practice as factors outside the organization's control, such as individual and organizational change, may prevent delivery (Grant 1999). A further complication involves the role of deception, which is viewed as an inevitable and even morally acceptable feature of negotiation (Wokutch and Carson 1993). Early stages of psychological contract formation are particularly vulnerable to deception, with parties seeking to capitalize on the fact that the other party does not know what they are capable of, and where the potential rewards for deception are greatest (e.g. getting a job, negotiating starting salaries).

Negotiating the psychological contract may appear to be the most appropriate way to change the contents. However, conducting such negotiations is far from simple because promises may be implicit, both parties may not have realistic expectations of what it can really deliver, and external factors may mean that promises cannot be kept.

9.4. Managing breach and fulfilment

We now turn to ways of managing the second main area of psychological contract theory and research: breach and fulfilment. It is in organizations' interests to avoid breach and to ensure promises are fulfilled. But how can this be done? Here, we first consider ways of monitoring psychological contracts so that breach can be detected and managed. Second, we consider ways in which breach can be prevented. Lastly, we discuss ways of dealing with and compensating for breach.

9.4.1. Monitoring for early signs of breach

Psychological contracts can be monitored through various human resource management practices and initiatives such as questionnaire surveys, focus groups, exit interviews, and tribunals. However, these methods are more likely to detect the consequences of breach some time after the breach has occurred and may also be insufficiently fine-grained to detect the exact nature of the breach. What is required is some means of picking up perhaps relatively small shifts and movements in the operation of the psychological contract which may indicate that breach is more or less likely to occur.

Levinson et al. (1962) argue that a manager's ability to constantly monitor psychological factors is key to managing psychological contracts. While the cognitions associated with psychological contract breach are invisible to managers, managers can infer what employees think from their displayed emotions and behaviour. For example, employee frustration may reflect delays in promise delivery and anger a complete failure by the organization to deliver the promise. We illustrate various types of emotions and the possible associated problems with the psychological contract in Table 9.2. Organizations able to read these emotions can detect early warning indicators of psychological contract problems before they escalate into something more serious (Levinson et al. 1962).

Employee behaviours can also imply problems with the psychological contract. For example, if an employee suddenly becomes less willing to engage in citizenship-type behaviours, then this may be due to some underlying contractual issue that can be addressed.

While emotions and behaviours are potentially useful indicators of the state of the underlying psychological contract, there are several complicating factors. First, the psychological contract is only one of countless explanations for emotions and behaviour, so attributing emotions and behaviour to some aspect of the psychological contract is very difficult. Second, employee behaviours and display of emotions may be constrained by factors such as social norms hence

Table 9.2 Inferring employees' beliefs about their psychological contract from their displayed emotions

Good deal		Bad deal	
Displayed emotions	Inferred cognitions	Displayed emotions	Inferred cognitions
Contentment	When a promise is reliably delivered	Frustration	Forever waiting for promises to be delivered
Excitement	When a promise of future rewards is made by the employer	Helplessness	A sense that no action on your part will ever lead to the delivery of the promise
Pride	When the employee successfully executes their side of the deal	Anger	Immediate response to realizing that a promise will not be delivered
		Resentment	The wish to take back previously made contributions once it is realized that a promise will not be delivered

even where the psychological contract might potentially affect employee behaviour and emotion this may not always be apparent.

9.4.2. Preventing breach from happening

As mentioned above, in the section on managing contents, one general way for organizations to reduce the chances of breach is to not overpromise, or make promises that cannot be kept, during negotiation of the psychological contract. However, there are numerous other factors that can cause breaches to occur, such as the antecedents discussed in Chapter 5. Recall that three major forms of breach can be identified: misunderstandings between the employee and their organization; deliberate reneging; and breaches due to circumstances beyond the organization's control (referred to as disruption). We focus here on trying to prevent breach through reducing misunderstandings, as this is the main preventable way in which organizations break promises. The two other forms of breach are either within the control of management in the first place (deliberate reneging) or are outside the control of management (disruption) and hence cannot easily be prevented as such. Rather than preventing these forms of breach it is only really possible to redress the negative effects of breach, which is discussed in the next section.

Misunderstandings (sometimes referred to as incongruence or disagreements over contract terms) occur when the employee and the organization have different perceptions of key promises or the extent to which promises have been fulfilled. The two main reasons why employees and their managers disagree on the terms of the psychological contract are, first, that the parties use different frames of reference in terms of who the key contract makers are and, second, that an employee's psychological contract is based on their own idiosyncratic reading of the organization's culture, practices and management behaviour (Lester et al. 2002).

Researchers have suggested several strategies for reducing misunderstandings. First, organizations can focus employees' attention on the most important terms of the deal by promoting a common frame of reference (Rousseau 2001). As the psychological contract can contain many items, focusing on the most important may help ensure there is at least shared perception between both parties of a core set of items. Second, managers and employees could engage in critical self-reflection to reduce the effects of cognitive biases that serve to distort perceptions of the psychological contract (Morrison and Robinson 2004). The most likely biases are false consensus (i.e. the tendency to see your own judgements as relatively common and others as uncommon or inappropriate), and the self-centred bias (i.e. the tendency to overestimate your own contributions and underestimate the contributions of others). Each of these biases is likely to increase perception of breach. Third, both parties should engage in perspective taking, in other words, attempting to see situations from the other party's perspective and trying to feel and think as they would (Conway and Coyle-Shapiro 2003). Perspective taking is likely to reduce biases and can be facilitated by encouraging thinking about the unfolding of events from the other party's perspective, letting employees deputize for their managers so that they can see situations from their point of view, and clarifying job roles to define how an employee's work relates to others.

9.4.3. Redressing breach

Practical recommendations for redressing or compensating for breach can to some extent be inferred from studies exploring those factors that moderate or lessen the effects of breach on outcomes (see Chapter 5). In other words, if we know from research which factors or variables seem to reduce the impact of breach then intervening to affect these factors or variables may help redress breach. Three main methods of redress have been considered: offering explanations as to why the breach occurred, compensating for losses resulting from breach through providing more of another inducement, and ensuring procedural justice.

We saw in Chapter 5 that employees are much more likely to believe that organizations intentionally renege on promises, rather than the breach being due to a misunderstanding or factors outside the organization's control. Organizations that are able to provide plausible explanations might encourage employees to make more favourable attributions and moderate their responses to breach. Take the example of a severe delay in implementing a promised upgrade of working equipment and physical conditions. If the reasons were beyond management's control and they made every effort to ensure the upgrade was completed in time then explaining this to employees may mean that employees react less negatively to the breach. Surprisingly, however, empirical studies find that employee attributions about the causes of broken promises or breaches have little to no effect on employee reactions (Robinson and Morrison 2000; Conway and Briner 2002b; Turnley et al. 2003). In other words, employees tend to react badly to perceived breach regardless of whether or not they believe the organization intentionally reneged on its promises.

So, while it may be tempting for organizations to believe that broken promises can be dealt with simply by offering explanations, this may not be effective. Instead, organizations may choose to offer tangible forms of compensation. While compensating for breach has not been researched directly, several psychological contract studies have found that it is the loss of rewards or the removal of the contract item being exchanged that accompanies breach that matters most to employees, rather than the fact that a promise has been broken (Lambert, Edwards, and Cable 2003; Coyle-Shapiro and Conway 2004). We can infer from this that compensating for breach is likely to mitigate employee reactions that may have otherwise followed the breach. In other words, a successful tactic by organizations to redress breach is to compensate for contract item or inducement that has been removed due to the broken promise by providing something of a roughly equivalent value. So, for example, if an employer is perceived to have broken a promise to promote an employee then providing that employee with more interesting work or a pay bonus may serve as compensation for the breach.

A third method for mitigating the negative effects of breach is to ensure that employees are treated fairly once breach has occurred. In other words, employee's negative reactions to breach are likely to be reduced in intensity and duration if they believe they have been treated fairly following the breach. A crucial issue is that the type of justice they experience must match the content of the broken promise. For instance, there has been very little support for perceptions of fairness moderating the relationship between overall perceptions of breach and outcomes: Lo and Aryee (2003) found interactional justice did not moderate the relationship between breach and withdrawal behaviours; Kickul et al. (2001) found that neither procedural justice nor interactional justice moderated the relationship between breach and anti-citizenship behaviour.

However, when the content of the broken promise is matched with an appropriate type of justice, perceptions of fairness have moderated how employees react to breach. Kickul, Lester, and Finkl (2002) examined employees whose organizations had undergone large-scale change programmes and their results suggest that procedural justice is more effective at moderating employee reactions when organizations break promises relating to contract items allocated through formal rules and procedures such as pay, promotion, flexible work schedules; in contrast, interactional justice is more effective at moderating employee reactions when organizations break promises relating to interpersonal aspects of the contract such as respect, employee freedom and participation. Kickul, Lester, and Finkl (2002) conclude that organizations should establish fair procedures during any kind of organizational change and make sure employees are treated with respect in any dealings so that they can avoid the negative consequences of breach. They also recommend that managers be given training in providing adequate justification and explanations for managerial decisions and how to treat employees with respect during decision-making processes.

This research highlights the importance of understanding the specific nature of the psychological contract breach in order to effectively redress the breach. Without knowing precisely what the perceived broken promise involved and what should have been exchanged for what it is difficult to take actions that are likely to make the employee feel less negative about the broken promise. Also, more generally, redressing breach is likely to mean understanding and trying to deal with the sometimes strong negative emotions breaches evoke.

9.5. What can employees do to manage the psychological contract?

The discussion has thus far largely assumed that it is the organization, through its agents and principals (e.g. managers), that is responsible for managing the psychological contract. This to some extent reflects the managerialist bias in much research into the psychological contract. While, from a theoretical perspective, employees both individually and collectively are seen as actively engaged in shaping, changing, constructing and negotiating their psychological contracts, most empirical work tends to see the organization as the most active and relevant party in terms of managing the contract.

Note that many of the issues discussed earlier in the chapter—such as negotiating psychological contracts, monitoring, preventing, and addressing breach—can also be viewed from an employee's perspective. Taking monitoring the psychological contract as an example, employees can monitor the emotions and behaviours of managers to get an indication of the state of their psychological contract with the organization. As another example, employees can also take steps to prevent or reduce the chances of breach by clarifying as much as possible the promises that are being made and becoming more aware of situations where the organization may be overpromising.

Here we consider two additional ways in which employees can manage their psychological contract, first by developing idiosyncratic deals and second by 'crafting' their jobs.

Recent work by Rousseau (2001, 2005) on Idiosyncratic-Deals (I-Deals) considers what employees can do to manage their psychological contract. I-Deals are agreements struck between highly marketable employees, valued by their organization, who have the power to negotiate employment conditions to suit their preferences. Such employees have the opportunity to proactively manage their psychological contract on their own terms. Based on ideas by Rousseau (2001) some recommended negotiating tactics for employees are:

1. Drawing attention to their labour market value and the realistic limits to what the organization can expect to get the employee to contribute out of loyalty alone.
2. Stating the frame of reference for the negotiation. Employees should not aim for a complete overhaul of their terms and conditions, but rather to customize the contract to their requirements without jeopardizing or challenging wider perceptions of fairness among colleagues. Rousseau offers a useful framework to consider the terms and conditions reflecting *standardized* features (e.g. health care), *position-based* features (e.g. professional conduct), and *idiosyncratic* features (the terms and conditions that evolve during the course of employment, which may vary considerably by position but

could include discretion over hours and place of work, tasks performed, and extend right up to salaries and bonuses).

3. Arguing that their requests do not compromise consistency of treatment in relation to other employees, which is likely to be a major concern from the employer's perspective. Rousseau believes this can be achieved by demonstrating that the idiosyncratic deal will not jeopardize the standardized or position-based features of the job. A second key factor is whether the new deal can be openly publicized without risk of reprobation for either the employee or the organization.

4. Arguing that the new deal is also in the interest of the organization and can be shared with other employees.

I-Deals are currently one of the very few attempts by researchers to explore how employees can manage their psychological contracts. The idea of I-Deals is in its early stages of development and at present is limited to highly marketable employees and, therefore, only applies to a relatively small proportion of the workforce.

A second way in which employees can manage their psychological contract is through job crafting which has been defined as 'the physical and cognitive changes individuals make in the task or relational boundaries of their work' (Wrzesniewski and Dutton 2001: 179). Three forms of job crafting are identified which involve changing: the scope, number and type of tasks; the nature of social interaction with others in the job; the cognitive or mental boundaries and interpretation of what the job entails. Key to the notion of job crafting is that such changes are informal and thus not necessarily explicitly negotiated with or recognized by managers. Also central to the idea of job crafting is that it takes place in all types of jobs, even those where we might assume employees have very little scope to change the way they do any aspect of their job. As 'job crafters create different jobs for themselves, within the context of defined jobs' (Wrzesniewski and Dutton 2001: 180) they are also, in effect, creating different psychological contracts for themselves.

Clearly, there are many other ways in which it is possible for employees to manage their psychological contract. One additional way not yet mentioned is through collective action either undertaken informally or through Trades Unions and employee representatives.

9.6. Managing the psychological contract: difficulties and dilemmas

As is already apparent from the discussion above, managing the psychological contract is by no means easy and presents a wide range of difficulties and dilemmas. Returning to a point made earlier, it seems likely that the absence of more popular or even academic writing about how to manage the psychological contract is a reflection of such difficulties and dilemmas. Difficulties include how to manage something that is implicit, what exactly it is we are trying to manage when we manage the psychological contract, the limited evidence base we have to work with, and the external constraints faced by organizations in trying to manage the psychological contract. Dilemmas of managing the psychological contract include whether making implicit promises explicit is actually useful, and whether it is better to overpromise in order to encourage employee contributions but with the increased risk of breach or to under-promise to avoid breach but then run the risk of lower levels of employee contributions. Here, by way of illustration, we discuss two of the most important difficulties and dilemmas both of which were mentioned earlier.

Perhaps the most important difficulty is managing implicit psychological contracts. Whatever definition of the psychological contract we choose to adopt it seems likely that very important parts of 'the deal' between employer and employee are implicit in that they are either unknown or are unclear in some respect. For example, an employee may have a vague sense that if they make certain sorts of extra effort, such as being very conscientious about meeting deadlines, that this may, in time, be rewarded by being given the chance to do more responsible work of some kind such as supervising others. Such implicit promises, though not exactly consciously known or clear, seem fundamental to the psychological contract.

As discussed above, managing the implicit promises within the psychological contract has usually been taken to mean making such promises explicit. And, as argued there, this is not managing or dealing with implicit promises as such but rather it is manage them away by making them explicit. But what about trying to manage implicit promises? How could this be done and what are the difficulties involved in doing so?

Implicit promises are formed by an individual's interpretation of a wide array of signals and information such as the behaviour of co-workers, organizational symbols and artefacts, and verbal statements. From such information implicit promises are inferred and in some cases such inferences, as discussed earlier, may be complex and involve several processing stages. For example, numerous implied promises could be inferred from just a single observation of the response of a line manager to the behaviour of a co-worker. Likewise, an organizational mission statement claiming that the organization values its employees could be understood in various ways leading to inferences of many sorts of implied promises. While it is clear that many factors shape implicit promises, what is less clear is what those factors are, how such inferences are made, and, therefore, how such factors could be managed.

An important dilemma in managing the psychological contract involves the possible costs and benefits of making implicit promises explicit. On the one hand, it seems entirely plausible that trying to clarify and negotiate the terms of the psychological contract will have benefits such as reducing ambiguity and breach. On the other hand, doing so may also have considerable costs. One cost is that employees may realize the organization is not actually in a position to offer much by way of concrete inducements—particularly if it is going through or anticipating a period of significant change. In making the implicit promises explicit organizations can no longer offer 'jam tomorrow' deals in which they suggest that great rewards will follow at some unspecified point in the future.

Another cost that may follow from making implicit promises explicit is that, given the potentially very wide scope of the psychological contract, any attempt to make implicit promises explicit will only ever be capable of focusing on a relatively small number of promises. Those few that are made explicit may come to dominate how the employee and employer view the psychological contract. As a consequence far less attention will be paid to the numerous other implicit and explicit parts of the contract, thus increasing the chances of breach in relation to those other promises. In other words, as both employer and employee may become competent at managing those few parts of the psychological contract that are made explicit, little attention is given to the rest of the psychological contract making breach of promises more likely.

The difficulties and dilemmas involved in trying to manage the psychological contract present considerable challenges to those who may wish to do so. While it is clear that the psychological contract is influenced and shaped in sometimes subtle and complex ways by numerous factors, how and indeed whether it can be 'managed' as such remains an unanswered question.

9.7. Summary and conclusion

In this chapter we presented key issues in managing the psychological contract, followed by reviewing possible ways of managing the two key areas of the contents and breach of psychological contracts. Managing the psychological contract was considered from both an employer's and employee's perspective. We noted several difficulties and dilemmas when attempting to manage the psychological contract.

The current state of theory and evidence about the psychological contract means that we know surprisingly little about how the psychological contract can be managed. First, theory and empirical evidence about how the psychological contract works is in many cases quite limited or weak and hence few implications for managing the psychological contract can be drawn from such work. Second, there is virtually no research specifically about how to manage the psychological contract, which means little can be said about which management approaches work or do not work.

Making practical recommendations for managing implicit psychological contracts in particular is simply not possible at the moment. Meckler, Drake and Levinson's critique (2003) is apposite: the current preoccupation with explicit psychological contracts means we do not know enough about implicit psychological contracts. To understand implicit psychological contracts requires greater attention to how employees make sense of behaviours, gestures, and symbols.

10 Summary and Conclusions: Prospects for Psychological Contract Research and Practice

In this chapter we first provide a brief summary and discussion of what has been achieved in relation to the three aims of the book. Next, ways in which research might usefully be developed are discussed. Some methodological and theoretical issues and empirical priorities that, in our view, require some attention are discussed. Finally, we consider the direction in which the psychological contract concept may be heading.

10.1. Summary and discussion in relation to the three aims of the book

10.1.1. First Aim: To provide a comprehensive review of psychological contract research and theory

It was not our intention to review all available literature but rather to focus on research and theory relevant to the contents of the psychological contract and how the psychological contract affects behaviour. Chapter 4 dealt with contents and Chapter 5 with how the contract impacts on work behaviour.

Before this, however, we set out some historical background in Chapter 2 and discussed definitions of the psychological contract in Chapter 3. While these chapters are not reviews of research and theory as such, the material they contain provides some useful clues about the reasons for the substantial and sometimes curious limitations of the field discussed later.

In social science terms, the concept is an old one, but, as it remained largely unexplored for decades, it has had only a relatively short period of continuous development. The recent post-Rousseau period has seen a very marked growth in research and publications. One explanation for this lack of attention to theory is that, because of its age, the concept has the appearance and feel of one that is mature, well-established, and refined. Such concepts may avoid the critical scrutiny focused on newer ideas, as researchers presume that others have done the developmental work needed to elaborate and strengthen theory. So while, as we have argued, the concept has considerable limitations, these have caught the attention of very few researchers.

Psychological contract definitions, as discussed in Chapter 3, also offer some clues about some of the current theoretical and methodological challenges. Historically, different researchers adopting the term 'psychological contract' have used it in very different ways and, hence, were actually researching different phenomena. More recently also, no definition is widely accepted, and some of the key elements still vary considerably across definitions. Given such inconsistencies it is not surprising that developing theory seems difficult and basic empirical constructs are not easily assessed.

Turning now to the first of the two areas this review covered, what do we know about the contents of the psychological contract? Most of our knowledge in this area, as in all areas of psychological contract research, comes from studies that use questionnaire surveys. While there are several instruments that measure contents, it is not clear that they contain the most important or relevant items. Also, most research measuring contents only considers the employee's perspective. There have been several attempts to find different dimensions or types of psychological contracts which have had limited success.

Although many factors are likely to shape the contents of the psychological contract, little is known about what these factors are, which are most important, and how they influence contents. A number of theories have been proposed to explain the effects of psychological contract contents on outcomes such as behaviours. While there is some evidence for some of these, the weaknesses of this evidence mean that clear conclusions cannot be drawn.

In general, we suggest that our knowledge of what the contents of the psychological contract actually are, how they are formed, and how they affect various outcomes is at present quite limited.

The second area considered in this review is how the contract affects behaviour. The idea of breach is currently one of the most important within psychological contract theory, yet it remains somewhat underdeveloped. It is sometimes used interchangeably with the concept of violation and, while the concepts are distinct, there are also disadvantages in treating the two ideas separately. Very little is known about how often breach occurs or the factors likely to lead to breach.

In contrast, there are numerous studies which set out to research the consequences of breach and this topic is, by some way, the most heavily researched in the field. While there is plenty of evidence that breach is associated with attitudes and, to a lesser degree, behaviour, these studies tell us little about the causal effects of breach. Unfortunately, the vast majority of studies are cross-sectional so are not capable of revealing cause-and-effect relationships, but rather show associations between perceptions of breach and outcomes. A major problem with most studies of breach is that the construct, and the way it is assessed, overlaps to such an extent with other constructs that the meanings of any relationships that are found remain unclear.

In pursuing the first aim of this book we reviewed research and theory about the psychological contract. This review suggests that, while we do have some knowledge about contents and breach, it is difficult to answer with much confidence or sophistication some fairly basic questions about what the psychological contract is, and how it works.

This review was not as comprehensive as it could have been in two ways. First, we focused on research published in peer-reviewed journals rather than in, say, book chapters. Second, we could have looked at more areas. However, we do not believe that reviewing more research in other types of publication or in other areas would have dramatically changed the overall conclusions that have emerged. Also, in the areas we did choose to cover, we considered almost all available journal articles.

10.1.2. To critically evaluate psychological contract research and theory and suggest ways in which the field can be further developed

Most of the critical evaluation took place in Chapters 6 and 7, although critical comments also appear throughout the book. The methods and designs used in psychological contract research were critically evaluated in Chapter 6. While several methods and designs have been used in psychological contract research, the most dominant approach, in common with most organizational psychology, is the cross-sectional questionnaire survey. This method has several important weaknesses when it is used to study the psychological contract, including the inability to assess process and the assessment of between- rather than within-person effects. In addition, measures of contents and violation have considerable limitations. Existing empirical work on the psychological research is also quite narrow in terms of what is researched with most attention being paid to contents and breach.

In addition to critically evaluating research we also considered, in Chapter 7, six mainly theoretical challenges for psychological contract researchers. Some of these challenges concern the need to be a great deal clearer about key constructs within psychological contract theory. Many of these remain insufficiently defined and their relation to other constructs has not been spelled out. Other challenges involve building new theory, or elaborating existing theory, in order to provide a more detailed explanation of the workings of various aspects of the psychological contract.

Chapter 8 was the one which focused most on further developments in psychological contract research. However, suggestions for further developments and ways of improving psychological contract research and theory can be found in many other places. Chapter 8 took as its starting point our view that the psychological contract is best conceptualized as a process. Existing theoretical and empirical approaches do not treat the psychological contract as a process. In order to demonstrate how this could be achieved, two frameworks from outside psychological contract theory were taken and applied to two sets of data taken from qualitative studies.

While there are, inevitably, a number of limitations of both the critical evaluation and discussion of suggestions for future developments provided here, such limitations should be seen in the context of the generally uncritical and unquestioning nature of much research in the field.

10.1.3.   Third Aim: To consider how the psychological contract can be practically applied in organizational settings

Most of the discussion relating to this aim took place in Chapter 9, though many of the shortcomings of theory and research are also relevant to practice and were briefly discussed in other places. One problem we found in trying to address this aim is that there is almost no directly relevant literature on which to draw. Instead, we examined available theory and evidence in order to identify any implications it may have for managing the psychological contract.

It appears that organizations and human resource managers are aware of and use the concept of the psychological contract, though little is known about how exactly they use this idea in their practice. There are a number of key issues in managing the psychological contract, such as being clear about what it is we are trying to manage and whether the management strategy of making implicit promises explicit can be considered as managing the psychological contract as such. Three ways of managing the contents of the psychological contract were considered: imposing change, communicating promises, and negotiation. Some ways of managing or preventing breach were also considered, including monitoring for early signs of breach and redressing breach. Some of the ways in which employees can themselves manage the psychological contract were discussed.

While the idea of managing the psychological contract is attractive, doing it in practice is far from straightforward and raises a number of difficulties and dilemmas. Perhaps the main one is the possible cost of managing the psychological contract by making it explicit. Attempts to apply the psychological contract concept are strongly constrained by weaknesses and gaps in both theory and evidence.

Broadly speaking, we met the third aim, as we did consider ways in which the psychological contract could be applied. However, the lack of evidence about how the psychological contract is used in practice and the limitations of theory meant that this discussion was both shorter and more speculative than we would have liked.

10.2. Some key issues in developing psychological contract research and practice

Throughout the book we have mentioned in passing, and discussed in detail, numerous challenges in researching and applying the psychological contract. Rather than repeat all these here, we will identify just some the general issues we believe it is important to address if the concept and practice is to develop.

10.2.1. Methodological issues

As in all research, it is important to use methods and designs that are compatible with our theoretical assumptions about the phenomena under investigation. In most psychological contract research it seems fair to say that method and theory are strikingly mismatched. There are probably two main reasons for this. First, the sorts of methods and designs favoured and ritualized in organizational psychology research, such as cross-sectional surveys, are particularly unsuitable for examining the sort of dynamic and within-person processes suggested by psychological contract theory. Second, the lack of specification or detail within psychological contract theory means that even where researchers do want to use appropriate methods, what these may be is not always made obvious through examining theory.

We have already described in various places the sorts of methods that might be more suited to researching the psychological contract. It can sometimes seem that almost any method would be an improvement on the cross-sectional survey. However, exactly what methods we choose depends, as already discussed, on theory, but also on the particular question the research is addressing. It is to these issues we now turn.

10.2.2. Theoretical issues

Perhaps the major problems with psychological contract theory are that there simply is not enough of it, and what exists is underdeveloped and underspecified. Here we discuss four issues we believe require attention.

There is clearly considerable conceptual overlap between constructs and explanations used within psychological contract theory and other existing constructs and explanations such as the overlap between breach and justice. If the distinct and unique potential contribution of the psychological contract to understanding work behaviour is to be realized then there is much work to be done in trying to identify how the psychological contract is both different from and relates to existing ideas. Establishing the 'added value' of psychological contract theory to existing theories about behaviour at work would do much to develop the construct.

A second area that deserves theoretical attention is the confusing set of definitions and constructs that relate to the beliefs that constitute the psychological contract. Which beliefs are psychological contract beliefs and which are not? There are several components to this problem. First is the use of the terms promises, obligations, and expectations to describe psychological contract beliefs. While these are sometimes used interchangeably they also have important differences. Are all of these types of belief relevant to the psychological contract or only some? Next, is the issue of the implicitness or otherwise of psychological contract beliefs. Do beliefs have to be implicit to be considered part of the psychological contract? Finally, what are psychological contract beliefs about? Can they be about absolutely any aspect of the exchange between employer and employee? If not, what are the limits and boundaries of psychological contract beliefs?

Third, the idea of breach, or the breaking of a promise, seems quite simple. However, in this context it is made much more complicated by the difficulties of stating exactly what constitutes a promise. Even if we can state this, many promises are such that it is difficult to establish what constitutes keeping or breaking a promise. Suggesting that breach is subjective does not, in itself, resolve these sorts of theoretical issues. Can breach, in principle, take different forms? Is there a difference between breach and unmet expectations? Here too, as is the case with psychological contract beliefs, much more thought needs to be given to what breach might mean and the mechanisms underlying breach.

The last theoretical issue concerns how we can better understand the exchange processes involved in the psychological contract. It is our view that the psychological contract is best viewed as a set of unfolding and iterative exchange processes between the employer and employee. While we have made some attempt in Chapter 8 to set out what a process approach might entail, taking a process approach further means engaging in much more theoretical elaboration.

10.2.3. Empirical priorities

As suggested in several places, psychological contract research has tended to focus quite narrowly on the two areas of contents and breach. These areas are clearly central to the psychological contract concept and future work addressing these same areas and similar questions would benefit from adopting more appropriate methodologies. At the same time, there are many other areas which deserve empirical attention. In particular, we would suggest two that are likely to be rewarding, and both relate to exchange. First is the cognitive and social representation of the exchange. The psychological contract can be considered to be a mental model of exchanges involved in the employment relationship and we currently know little about how such representations are, for example, structured, encoded, and altered (see also Rousseau 2001). It seems likely that such models may be collective as well as individual. The second area that deserves empirical attention is the operation of the exchange. How does it work on a day-to-day basis? What actually happens? Researching the exchange in more detail would also shed light on psychological contract contents and breach as it is within the context of the exchange relationship that contents are formed and breach occurs.

In addition to the subjects which are researched, we believe that another empirical priority is to conduct research in contexts in which we are more likely to find the sorts of phenomena we are investigating. While conducting empirical research into the psychological contract using intervention or quasi-experimental studies does not seem easy, there are in fact many contexts and situations in which various aspects of the psychological contract, such as contents, exchange and fulfilment are being either deliberately or incidentally manipulated through, for example, changes in human resource management practices.

The final empirical priority is finding out more about how and if the psychological contract is used in practice. While such research is certainly useful for informing practice it also is likely to provide useful information about the basic workings of the psychological contract.

10.3. Conclusions

This book has identified many weaknesses and limitations in psychological contract research and has suggested ways in which they may be overcome. In developing the critical evaluation of theory and research presented here we often had the sensation that both the concept and empirical work do not stand up to much scrutiny. The discovery of one, perhaps minor, weakness seemed in many cases to lead to the discovery of more problems, and yet more issues, which in turn led to the discovery of many highly significant shortcomings. We believe that the psychological contract concept has much to offer but it has been erected on somewhat shaky conceptual and empirical foundations.

As mentioned in the introduction, the psychological contract concept has had an unusual trajectory. It is a relatively old idea that for several decades remained undeveloped. More recently, it has been on the up and up as it caught the imagination and interest of many researchers and practitioners. Where next for the concept? It is our contention that its potential contribution to understanding behaviour at work will never be known if we do not acknowledge and address some of its fundamental limitations.

Appendix
Psychological Contract Measures

We present a selection of questionnaire measures researchers use to assess the psychological contract, so as to provide some insight into how psychological contracts have been assessed. We have referred to one or more of these measures in Chapters 4, 5, 6, and 8. Table A1 describes what each measure we have included assesses (content, breach, or violation) and whether it does so from an employee or employer's perspective. Please note that measures of the psychological contract are discussed extensively in Chapter 6.

Table A.1 Psychological contract measures

	Employee's perspective	Employer's perspective
Content	• Raja, Johns, and Ntalianis (2004) • Rousseau (2000) • Tekleab and Taylor (2003)	• Tekleab and Taylor (2003)
Breach/fulfilment	• Kickul et al. (2002) • Robinson and Rousseau (1994) • Robinson and Morrison (2000) • Rousseau (2000) • Tekleab and Taylor (2003) • Conway and Briner (2002)	• Tekleab and Taylor (2003) • Guest and Conway (2002)
Violation	• Robinson and Morrison (2000)	

Note: The measure by Conway and Briner (2002) was used as part of a diary design. All other measures were used as part of questionnaire surveys.

A.1. Employee's perspective: measures of psychological contract contents

A.1.1. PCS—Transactional and relational psychological contracts

Transactional contracts

I work only the hours set out in my contract and no more.
My commitment to this organization is defined by my contract.
My loyalty to the organization is contract specific.

I prefer to work a strictly defined set of working hours.
I only carry out what is necessary to get the job done.
I do not identify with the organization's goals.
I work to achieve the purely short-term goals of my job.
My job means more to me than just a means of paying the bills. (R)
It is important to be flexible and to work irregular hours if necessary. (R)

Relational contracts

I expect to grow in this organization.
I feel part of a team in this organization.
I have a reasonable chance of promotion if I work hard.
To me working for this organization is like being a member of a family.
The organization develops/rewards employees who work hard and exert themselves.
I expect to gain promotion in this company with length of service and effort to achieve goals.
I feel this company reciprocates the effort put in by its employees.
My career path in the organization is clearly mapped out.
I am motivated to contribute 100 per cent to this company in return for future employment benefits.

Response scale—5 point scale: 1 = strongly disagree; 5 = strongly agree.
Copyright © 2001 by Academy of Management. Reproduced with permission.
Notes

1. Items with (R) denote reverse scoring.
2. The measure comes from Raja, Johns, and Ntalianis (2004) and is an abbreviated version of Millward and Hopkins (1998).
3. You can find further details on the psychometric properties of this measure in Raja, Johns, and Ntalianis (2004).

A.1.2. PCI—organization obligations to the employee

Before respondents are presented with the PCI items asking about their employer's commitments towards them, they are provided with the rating scale.

Consider your relationship with your current employer. To what extent has your employer made the following commitment or obligation to you? Please answer each question using the following scale:

1	2	3	4	5
not at all	slightly	somewhat	moderately	to a great extent

The measure's items are organized below under their respective dimensions.

Balanced psychological contracts

Support me to attain the highest possible levels of performance
Help me respond to ever greater industry standards
Support me in meeting increasingly higher goals
Enable me to adjust to new, challenging performance requirements
Opportunity for career development within this firm
Developmental opportunities with this firm
Advancement within the firm
Opportunities for promotion
Help me develop externally marketable skills
Job assignments that enhance my external marketability
Potential job opportunities outside the firm
Contacts that create employment opportunities

Transactional psychological contracts

A job only as long as the employer needs me
Makes no commitments to retain me in the future
Short-term employment
A job for a short-time only
Limited involvement in the organization
Training me only for my current job
A job limited to specific, well-defined responsibilities
Require me to perform only a limited set of duties

Relational psychological contracts

Concern for my personal welfare
Be responsive to my personal concerns and well-being
Make decisions with my interests in mind
Concern for my long-term well-being
Secure employment
Wages and benefits I can count on
Steady employment
Stable benefits for employees' families

Source: Rousseau (2000).
Copyright © 2000 by Denise M. Rousseau. Reproduced with permission.
Notes

1. You can find further details on the psychometric properties of this measure
    in Hui, Lee, and Rousseau (2004).

A.1.3. PCI—employee obligations to the organization

Before respondents are presented with the PCI items asking about their commitments towards the organization they are provided with the rating scale.

To what extent have you made the following commitment or obligation to your employer? Please answer each question using the following scale:

1	2	3	4	5
not at all	slightly	somewhat	moderately	to a great extent

The measure's items are organized below under their respective dimensions.

Balanced psychological contracts

Accept increasingly challenging performance standards
Adjust to changing performance demands due to business necessity
Respond positively to dynamic performance requirements
Accept new and different performance demands
Seek out developmental opportunities that enhance my value to this employer
Build skills to increase my value to this organization
Make myself increasingly valuable to my employer
Actively seek internal opportunities for training and development
Build contacts outside this firm that enhance my career potential
Build skills to increase my future employment opportunities elsewhere
Increase my visibility to potential employers outside the firm
Seek out assignments that enhance my employability elsewhere

Transactional psychological contracts

Quit whenever I want
I have no future obligations to this employer
Leave at any time I choose
I am under no obligation to remain with this employer
Perform only required tasks
Do only what I am paid to do
Fulfill limited number of responsibilities
Only perform specific duties I agreed to when hired

Relational psychological contracts

Make personal sacrifices for this organization
Take this organization's concerns personally
Protect this organization's image
Commit myself personally to this organization
Remain with this organization indefinitely
Plan to stay here a long time
Continue to work here
Make no plans to work anywhere else

Source: Rousseau (2000).

Notes

1. You can find further details on the psychometric properties of this measure in Hui, Lee and Rousseau (2004).

A.1.4. Employee obligations to the organization

To what extent do you feel you are obligated to provide each of the following to (company):

 (i) Volunteer to do tasks that fall outside my job description.
 (ii) Develop new skills as needed.
 (iii) Perform my job in a reliable manner.
 (iv) Deal honestly with (company).
 (v) Work extra hours if needed to get the job done.
 (vi) Follow (company) policies and procedures.

Rated on a 5-point scale: 1 = strongly disagree; 5 = strongly agree.
Source: Tekleab and Taylor (2003).
Copyright © 2003 by John Wiley & Sons Ltd. Reproduced with permission.
Notes

1. You can find further details on the psychometric properties of this measure in Tekleab and Taylor (2003).

A.1.5. Organization obligations to the employee

To what extent is (company) obligated to provide each of the following to you:

 (i) An attractive benefits package.
 (ii) Fair treatment.
 (iii) A relatively secure job.
 (iv) Feedback on performance.
 (v) Training.
 (vi) Leadership.

Rated on a 5-point scale: 1 = strongly disagree; 5 = strongly agree.
Source: Tekleab and Taylor (2003).
Copyright © 2003 by John Wiley & Sons Ltd. Reproduced with permission.
Notes

1. You can find further details on the psychometric properties of this measure in Tekleab and Taylor (2003).

A.2. Employee's perspective: measures of psychological contract breach / fulfilment

A.2.1. Psychological contract breach

This measure includes instructions to respondents before and after presenting the questionnaire items, so in this case we reproduce the entire measure as presented to respondents.

MEASURE BEGINS

Employees and their employers develop agreements, promising to provide certain things for each other. For example, to hold up your end of the relationship, you may feel obligated to work hard and do your job to the best of your ability. On the other hand, your employer (the organization and its agents) may believe it is obligated to provide you with competitive pay and benefits. In the following questions, we are interested in what you believe your organization has promised to provide to you. These obligations may have been communicated to you explicitly (verbally or in writing) or implicitly (simply implied through other statement or behaviours). Note that we are not asking what you think your organization should provide to you. *We are interested in what you believe your organization has promised to provide to you.* After reading the following list of twenty-six obligations, please place 'X' in the box of those obligations that your organization has communicated to you.

☐ Competitive salary	____	☐ Meaningful work	____
☐ Pay and bonuses tied to performance	____	☐ Participation in decision making	____
☐ Vacation benefits	____	☐ Freedom to be creative	____
☐ Retirement benefits	____	☐ A job that provides autonomy and control	____
☐ Health care benefits	____	☐ Opportunities for personal growth	____
☐ Job security	____	☐ Continual professional training	____
☐ Flexible work schedule	____	☐ Career guidance and mentoring	____
☐ Adequate equipment to perform job	____	☐ Job training	____
☐ Enough resources to do the job	____	☐ Tuition reimbursement	____
☐ Well-defined job responsibilities	____	☐ Recognition of my accomplishments	____

☐ A reasonable workload ____ ☐ Opportunity to develop ____
new skills

☐ Safe work environment ____ ☐ Increasing ____
responsibilities

☐ Challenging and ____ ☐ Opportunities for ____
interesting work promotion and
advancement

Although organizations make promises to their employees to maintain an employment relationship, the extent to which some of these promises are actually fulfilled can vary from one organization to another. We are not interested in how well your organization has fulfilled their promises to you. Please indicate the extent to which your employment has fulfilled the promises above that you have marked with 'X'. Using the scale below, place this rating to the right of each of the marked promises.

Not at all fulfilled		Somewhat fulfilled		Very fulfilled
1	2	3	4	5

MEASURE ENDS
Source: Kickul et al. (2002).
Copyright © 2002 by Springer Science and Business Media. Reproduced with permission.
Notes

1. By first asking whether the organization has communicated a promise, this scale is also a measure of the contents of psychological contract, with a simple yes/no response scale.
2. You can find further details on the psychometric properties of this measure in Kickul et al. (2002).

A.2.2. Psychological contract breach

Using the scale below, please indicate how well, overall, your first employer has fulfilled the promised obligations that they owed you: (circle one number)

Response scale: 1 = very poorly fulfilled; 5 = very well fulfilled.
Source: Robinson and Rousseau (1994).
Copyright © 1994 by John Wiley & Sons Ltd. Reproduced with permission.
Notes

1. You can find further details on the psychometric properties of this measure in Robinson and Rousseau (1994).
2. Robinson and Rousseau (1994) sampled recently employed graduates, thus their use of the words 'first employer'.

A.2.3. Psychological contract breach

Almost all the promises made by my employer during recruitment have been kept so far. (R)

I feel that my employer has come through in fulfilling the promises made to me when I was hired. (R)

So far my employer has done an excellent job of fulfilling its promises to me. (R)

I have not received everything promised to me in exchange for my contributions

My employer has broken many of its promises to me even though I've upheld my side of the deal.

Response scale: 1 = strongly disagree; 5 = strongly agree.

Source: Robinson and Morrison (2000).

Copyright © 2000 by John Wiley & Sons Ltd. Reproduced with permission.

Notes

1. Items with (R) denote reverse scoring.
2. You can find further details on the psychometric properties of this measure in Robinson and Morrison (2000).

A.2.4. Psychological contract fulfilment

Employer fulfilment

> Overall, how well does your employer fulfil its commitments to you?
> In general, how well does your employer live up to its promises to you?

Employee fulfilment

> Overall, how well have you fulfilled your commitments to your employer?
> In general, how well do you live up to your promises to your employer?

Response scale—5-point scale: 1 = not at all; 2 = slightly; 3 = somewhat; 4 = moderately; 5 = to a great extent.

Source: Rousseau (2000).

Copyright © 2000 by Denise M. Rousseau. Reproduced with permission.

A.2.5. Employee breach of contract to the organization

I have done a good job of meeting my obligations to (company). (R)

I have fulfilled the most important obligation to the (company). (R)

Rated on a 5-point scale: 1 = strongly disagree; 5 – strongly agree.

Source: Tekleab and Taylor (2003).

Copyright © 2003 by John Wiley & Sons Ltd. Reproduced with permission.

Notes

1. You can find further details on the psychometric properties of this measure in Tekleab and Taylor (2003).

A.2.6. Organization breach of contract to the employee

(Company) has done a good job of meeting its obligations to me. (R)
(Company) has repeatedly failed to meet its obligations to me.
(Company) has fulfilled the most important obligations to me. (R)

Rated on a 5-point scale: 1 = strongly disagree; 5 = strongly agree.
Source: Tekleab and Taylor (2003).
Copyright © 2003 by John Wiley & Sons Ltd. Reproduced with permission.
Notes

1. Items with (R) denote reverse scoring.
2. You can find further details on the psychometric properties of this measure in Tekleab and Taylor (2003).

A.2.7. Psychological contract breach

This measure includes instructions to respondents before and after presenting the questionnaire items, so in this case we reproduce the entire measure as presented to respondents.

MEASURE BEGINS
Has your organization broken any promises to you today?
Now I would like to ask you whether your organization (or a person acting on behalf of the organization) has broken any promises—explicit or implicit—towards you **today**.

These promises do not have to be made and broken with you all on the same day. The promise may have been made yesterday, last week, last month, or even years ago. The important thing to note is that you became aware **today** that the promise has not been kept.

Please refer to the definitions at the front of the diary if you are unsure about what an explicit or implicit promise is or would like to be reminded of some examples. Remember that a promise can be broken regarding any aspect of your job. Also note that there may be some incidents where you believe a promise has been broken but the other party is not aware of it. Such incidents should still be recorded as broken promises.

Explicit promises
Has your organization **broken** any **explicit** promises to you **today** (e.g. you were promised something in a verbal or written form that you did not receive; you have been asked to work beyond the formal requirements of your job role)?

Please record each and every broken promise in as much detail as possible.

1...
....
2...
....
3...
....

Implicit promises

Has your organization **broken** any **implicit** promises to you **today** (e.g. you didn't get the appreciation you felt you should receive for something you did; the organization behaved towards you in a way you had not come to expect; you felt that you had been exploited)?
Please record each and every broken promise in as much detail as possible.

1...
....
2...
....
3...
....

MEASURE ENDS
Source: Conway and Briner (2002).
Notes

1. You can find further details on the psychometric properties of this measure in Conway and Briner (2002).

A.3. Employee's perspective: measure of psychological contract violation

A.3.1. Psychological contract violation

I feel a great deal of anger toward my organization.
I feel betrayed by my organization.
I feel that my organization has violated the contract between us.
I feel extremely frustrated by how I have been treated by my organization.

Response scale: 1 = strongly disagree; 5 = strongly agree.
Source: Robinson and Morrison (2000).
Copyright © 2000 by John Wiley & Sons Ltd. Reproduced with permission.
Notes

1. You can find further details on the psychometric properties of this measure in Robinson and Morrison (2000).

A.4. Employer's perspective: measures of psychological contract contents

A.4.1. Employee obligations to the organization

To what extent do you feel your designated employee is obligated to provide each of the following to (company):

   (i) Volunteer to do tasks that fall outside my job description.
  (ii) Develop new skills as needed.
 (iii) Perform my job in a reliable manner.
  (iv) Deal honestly with (company).
   (v) Work extra hours if needed to get the job done.
  (vi) Follow (company) policies and procedures.

Rated on a 5-point scale: 1 = strongly disagree; 5 = strongly agree.
Source: Tekleab and Taylor (2003).
Copyright © 2003 by John Wiley & Sons Ltd. Reproduced with permission.
Notes

   1. You can find further details on the psychometric properties of this measure in Tekleab and Taylor (2003).
   2. Employer perspective was provided by line managers.

A.4.2. Organization obligations to the employee

To what extent is (company) obligated to provide each of the following to your employee:

   (i) An attractive benefits package.
  (ii) Fair treatment.
 (iii) A relatively secure job.
  (iv) Feedback on my performance.
   (v) Training.
  (vi) Leadership.

Rated on a 5-point scale: 1 = strongly disagree; 5 = strongly agree.
Source: Tekleab and Taylor (2003).
Copyright © 2003 by John Wiley & Sons Ltd. Reproduced with permission.
Notes

   1. You can find further details on the psychometric properties of this measure in Tekleab and Taylor (2003).
   2. Employer perspective was provided by line managers.

A.5. Employer's perspective: measures of psychological contract breach / fulfilment

A.5.1. Employee breach of contract to the organization

My employee has done a good job of meeting his/her obligations to (company). (R)

My employee has fulfilled the most important obligation to the (company). (R)

Rated on a 5-point scale: 1 = strongly disagree; 5 = strongly agree.
Source: Tekleab and Taylor (2003).
Copyright © 2003 by John Wiley & Sons Ltd. Reproduced with permission.
Notes

1. You can find further details on the psychometric properties of this measure in Tekleab and Taylor (2003).

A.5.2. Organization breach of contract to the employee

(Company) has done a good job of meeting its obligations to my employee. (R)

(Company) has repeatedly failed to meet its obligations to my employee.

(Company) has fulfilled the most important obligations to my employee. (R)

Rated on a 5-point scale: 1 = strongly disagree; 5 = strongly agree.
Source: Tekleab and Taylor (2003).
Copyright © 2003 by John Wiley & Sons Ltd. Reproduced with permission.
Notes

1. Items with (R) denote reverse scoring.
2. You can find further details on the psychometric properties of this measure in Tekleab and Taylor (2003).

A.5.3. Organization breach of contract to the employee

This measure includes opening instructions, so in this case we reproduce the entire measure as presented to respondents.

MEASURE BEGINS

The following questions refer to the promises or commitments your organization makes to employees and the extent to which it has met them. Please answer the questions in relation to how the organization treats its employees generally rather than any particular employee.

In column A: Indicate the extent to which the organization promises or commits itself to provide the items listed, using the scale below.

1	2	3	4
No promise made	Suggestion of a promise, nothing actually said or written down	Strong suggestion of a promise, nothing actually said or written down	Written or verbal promises have been made

In column B: Only complete column B for items where the organization has made at least a strong suggestion of a promise (i.e. a rating of **3 or more** in column A).

	A				B			
	In your opinion, to what extent has the organization made a promise or commitment to provide the following?				If **3 or more** in Column A: In your opinion, to what extent has the organization met its promise or commitment?			
	None made			Written or verbal promise			Met to some extent	
					Exceeded	Met		Not met
Training and development opportunities	1	2	3	4	4	3	2	1
Opportunities for promotion	1	2	3	4	4	3	2	1
Recognition for innovative or new ideas	1	2	3	4	4	3	2	1
Feedback on performance	1	2	3	4	4	3	2	1
Interesting work	1	2	3	4	4	3	2	1
A fair rate of pay	1	2	3	4	4	3	2	1
An attractive benefits package	1	2	3	4	4	3	2	1
Not to make unreasonable demands of employees	1	2	3	4	4	3	2	1
Fair treatment	1	2	3	4	4	3	2	1
Reasonable job security	1	2	3	4	4	3	2	1
A pleasant working environment	1	2	3	4	4	3	2	1
A safe working environment	1	2	3	4	4	3	2	1
Open two-way communication	1	2	3	4	4	3	2	1

MEASURE ENDS

Source: Guest and Conway (2002).

Notes

1. You can find further details on the psychometric properties of this measure in Guest and Conway (2002).
2. Responses to the column A were used as a measure of psychological contract contents. It is presented here because the items operate to route respondents through to the breach items.

■ REFERENCES

Anderson, N. and Schalk, R. (1998). 'The Psychological Contract in Retrospect and Prospect', *Journal of Organizational Behavior*, 19: 637–48.

Andersson, L. M. and Pearson, C. M. (1999). 'Tit-for-Tat? The Spiraling Effect of Incivility in the Workplace', *Academy of Management Review*, 24: 452–71.

Applebaum, E., Bailey, T., Berg, P., and Kalleberg, A. (2000). *Manufacturing Advantage: Why High Performance Work Systems Pay Off*. Ithaca, NY: Cornell University Press.

Argyris, C. (1960). *Understanding Organizational Behavior*. Homewood, IL: Dorsey Press.

Arnold, J. (1996). 'The Psychological Contract: A Concept in Need of Closer Scrutiny?' *European Journal of Work and Organizational Psychology*, 5: 511–20.

Barnard, C. I. (1938). *The Function of the Executive*. Cambridge, MA: Harvard University Press.

Barrett, J. L. and Keil, F. C. (1996). 'Conceptualizing a Non-natural Entity: Anthropomorphism in God Concepts', *Cognitive Psychology*, 31: 219–47.

Blau, P. M. (1955). *The Dynamics of Bureaucracy*. Chicago: University of Chicago Press.

Blau, P. (1964). *Exchange and Power in Social Life*. New York: Wiley.

Bolger, N., DeLongis, A., Kessler, R. C., and Schilling, E. A. (1989). 'Effects of Daily Stress on Negative Mood', *Journal of Personality and Social Psychology*, 57: 808–18.

Bunderson, J. S. (2001). 'How Work Ideologies Shape Psychological Contracts of Professional Employees: Doctors' Responses to Perceived Breach', *Journal of Organizational Behavior*, 22: 717–41.

Cantor, N., Norem, J., Langston, C., Zirkel, S., Fleeson, W., and Cook-Flannigan, C. (1991). 'Life Tasks and Daily Life Experience', *Journal of Personality*, 59: 425–51.

Carlson, S. (1951). *Executive Behaviour: A Study of the Work Load and the Working Methods of Managing Directors*. Stockholm: Strombergs.

Carver, C. S. and Scheier, M. F. (1990). 'Origins and Functions of Positive and Negative Affect: A Control-Process View', *Psychological Review*, 97: 19–35.

Cassar, V. (2004). 'Identifying and Investigating the Component Forms of Psychological Contract Violation'. Unpublished Ph.D. thesis, University of London.

—— and Briner, R. B. (2005). 'Psychological Contract "Breach": A Multiple Component Perspective to an Over-Researched Construct?', *Revista de Psicología Social*, 20: 146–36.

Cherrington, D. (1991). 'Need Theories: The Content of Motivation', in R. M. Steers and L. W. Porter (eds.), *Motivation and Work Behavior*. New York: McGraw-Hill, 132–47.

Cheshire, G. C., Fifoot, C. H. S., and Furmston, M. P. (1991). *Law of Contract*, 12th edn. London: Butterworths.

Cohen-Charash, Y. and Spector, P. E. (2001). 'The Role of Justice in Organizations: A Meta-analysis', *Organizational Behavior and Human Decision Processes*, 86: 278–321.

Conrath, D. W., Higgins, C. A., and McClean, R. J. (1983). 'A Comparison of the Reliability of Questionnaire Versus Diary Data', *Social Networks*, 5: 315–22.

Conway, N. (1996). 'The Psychological Contract: A Metaphor too Far?' *Proceedings of the British Academy of Management Conference*, Birmingham, 56–7.

—— and Briner, R. B. (2002*a*). 'A Daily Diary Study of Affective Responses to Psychological Contract Breach and Exceeded Promises', *Journal of Organizational Behavior*, 23: 287–302.

—— —— (2002*b*). 'Full-Time Versus Part-Time Employees: Understanding the Links between Work Status, the Psychological Contract, and Attitudes', *Journal of Vocational Behavior*, 61: 279–301.

—— —— (2004). 'More Hyperbole than Metaphor: A Critique of the Psychological Contract', *British Psychological Society Occupational Psychology Conference*, Stratford, 65–8.

—— and Coyle-Shapiro, J. (2003). 'Employee Perspective Taking and the Psychological Contract'. Paper presented at the European Association of Work and Organizational Psychology Conference, Lisbon.

Coyle-Shapiro, J. and Conway, N. (2004). 'The Employment Relationship Through the Lens of Social Exchange', in J. Coyle-Shapiro, L. Shore, M. S. Taylor, and L. Tetrick (eds.), *The Employment Relationship: Examining Psychological and Contextual Perspectives*. Oxford: Oxford University Press, 5–28.

—— —— (2005 forthcoming). 'Exchange Relationships: Examining Psychological Contracts and Perceived Organizational Support', *Journal of Applied Psychology*.

—— and Kessler, I. (1998). 'The Psychological Contract in the UK Public Sector: Employer and Employee Obligations and Contract Fulfilment'. Paper presented at the Annual Meeting of the Academy of Management, San Diego.

—— —— (2000). 'Consequences of the Psychological Contract for the Employment Relationship: A Large Scale Survey', *Journal of Management Studies*, 37: 903–30.

—— —— (2002*a*). 'A Psychological Contract Perspective on Organizational Citizenship Behavior', *Journal of Organizational Behavior*, 23: 927–46.

—— —— (2002*b*). 'Contingent and Non-Contingent Working in Local Government: Contrasting Psychological Contracts', *Public Administration*, 80: 77–101.

—— —— (2002*c*). 'Exploring Reciprocity through the Lens of the Psychological Contract: Employee and Employer Perspectives', *European Journal of Work and Organizational Psychology*, 11: 69–86.

—— and Neuman, J. (2004). 'Individual Dispositions and the Psychological Contract: The Moderating Effects of Exchange and Creditor Ideologies', *Journal of Vocational Behavior*, 64: 150–64.

Csikszentmihalyi, M. and Csikszentmihalyi, I. (eds.) (1988). *Optimal Experience: Psychological Studies of Flow in Consciousness*. New York: Cambridge University Press.

—— and LeFevre, J. (1989). 'Optimal Experience in Work and Leisure', *Journal of Personality and Social Psychology*, 56: 815–22.

Cully, M., Woodland, S., O'Reilly, A., and Dix, G. (1999). *Britain at Work*. London: Routledge.

Darden, W. R., McKee, D., and Hampton, R. (1993). 'Salesperson Employment Status as a Moderator in the Job Satisfaction Model: A Frame of Reference Perspective', *Journal of Personal Selling and Sales Management*, 13: 1–15.

Darlington, R. B. (1968). 'Multiple Regression in Psychological Research and Practice', *Psychological Bulletin*, 69: 161–82.

Dawkins, R. (1976). *The Selfish Gene*. Oxford: Oxford University Press.

DeLongis, A., Hemphill, K. J., and Lehman, D. R. (1992). 'A Structured Diary Methodology for the Study of Daily Events', in G. Bryant (ed.), *Methodological Issues in Applied Psychology*. New York: Plenum Press, 83–109.

Drever, J. (1958). *A Dictionary of Psychology*. Harmondsworth, Middlesex: Penguin.

Drigotas, S. M., Whitney, G. A., and Rusbult, C. E. (1995). 'On the Peculiarities of Loyalty: A Daily Diary Study of Responses to Dissatisfaction in Everyday Life', *Personality and Social Psychology Bulletin*, 21: 596–609.

Edwards, J. C., Rust, K. G., McKinley, W., and Moon, G. (2003). 'Business Ideologies and Perceived Breach of Contract during Downsizing: The Role of the Ideology of Employee Self-Reliance', *Journal of Organizational Behavior*, 24: 1–23.

Eisenberger, R., Rhoades, L., and Cameron, J. (1999). 'Does Pay for Performance Increase or Decrease Perceived Self-Determination and Intrinsic Motivation?', *Journal of Personality and Social Psychology*, 77: 1026–40.

—— Huntingdon, R., Hutchison, S., and Sowa, D. (1986). 'Perceived Organizational Support', *Journal of Applied Psychology*, 71: 500–7.

Eisenhardt, K. M. (1989). 'Agency Theory: An Assessment and Review', *Academy of Management Review*, 14: 57–74.

Emmons, R. A. (1992). 'Abstract Versus Concrete Goals: Personal Striving Level, Physical Illness, and Psychological Well-being', *Journal of Personality and Social Psychology*, 62: 292–300.

Etzioni, A. (1962). *Modern Organizations*. Englewood Cliffs, NJ: Prentice-Hall.

Flood, P. C., Turner, T., Ramamoorthy, N., and Pearson, J. (2001). 'Causes and Consequences of Psychological Contracts Among Knowledge Workers in the High Technology and Financial Services Industries', *International Journal of Human Resource Management*, 12: 1152–65.

Foa, U. G. (1971). 'Interpersonal and Economic Resources', *Science*, 171: 345–51.

—— and Foa, E. B. (1980). 'Resource Theory: Interpersonal Behavior as Exchange', in K. J. Gergen, M. S. Greenberg, and R. H. Willis (eds.), *Social Exchange: Advances in Theory and Research*. New York: Plenum Press, 77–94.

Follett, M. P. (1924). *Creative Experience*. New York: Longmans, Green.

Gergen, K. J. and Gergen, M. M. (1988). 'Narrative and the Self as Relationship', *Advances in Experimental Social Psychology*, 21: 17–56.

Gerstner, C. R. and Day, D. V. (1997). 'Meta-Analytic Review of Leader-Member Exchange: Correlates and Constructs Issues', *Journal of Applied Psychology*, 82: 827–44.

Gouldner, A. W. (1960). 'The Norm of Reciprocity: A Preliminary Statement', *American Sociological Review*, 25: 161–78.

Grant, D. (1999). 'HRM, Rhetoric and the Psychological Contract: A Case of "Easier Said Than Done" ', *International Journal of Human Resource Management*, 10: 327–50.

Greene, A-M, Ackers, P., and Black, J. (2001). 'Lost Narratives? From Paternalism to Team-Working in a Lock Manufacturing Firm', *Economic and Industrial Democracy*, 22: 211–37.

Guest, D. (1998). 'Is the Psychological Contract Worth Taking Seriously?', *Journal of Organizational Behavior*, 19: 649–64.

Guest, D. and Conway, N. (1997). *Employee Motivation and the Psychological Contract.* IPD Research Report. London: IPD.

—— —— (1998). *Fairness and the Psychological Contract.* IPD Research Report. London: IPD.

—— —— (1999). *Organizational Change and the Psychological Contract.* IPD Research Report. London: IPD.

—— —— (2000). *The Public Sector and the Psychological Contract.* IPD Research Report. London: IPD.

—— —— (2001). *Public and Private Sector Perspectives on the Psychological Contract.* CIPD Research Report. London: CIPD.

—— —— (2002). *Pressure at Work and the Psychological Contract.* CIPD Research Report. London: CIPD.

—— —— (2002). 'Communicating the Psychological Contract: An Employer Perspective', *Human Resource Management Journal*, 12: 22–39.

—— —— (2004). *Employee Wellbeing and the Psychological Contract.* CIPD Research Report. London: CIPD.

Guzzo, R. A., Noonan, K. A., and Elron, E. (1994). 'Expatriate Managers and the Psychological Contract', *Journal of Applied Psychology*, 79: 617–26.

Herriot, P. (1992). *The Career Management Challenge: Balancing Individual and Organisational Needs.* London: Sage.

—— and Pemberton, C. (1995). *New Deals: The Revolution in Managerial Careers.* Chichester: Wiley.

—— —— (1996). 'Contracting Careers', *Human Relations*, 49: 759–90.

—— —— (1997). 'Facilitating New Deals', *Human Resource Management Journal*, 7: 45–56.

—— Manning, W. E. G., and Kidd, J. M. (1997). 'The Content of the Psychological Contract', *British Journal of Management*, 8: 151–62.

Herzberg, F., Mausner, B., and Snyderman, B. B. (1959). *The Motivation to Work.* New York: Wiley.

Hiltrop, J. M. (1996). 'Managing the Changing Psychological Contract', *Employee Relations*, 18: 36–49.

Ho, V. T. (2005). 'Social Influences on Evaluation of Psychological Contract Fulfillment', *Academy of Management Review*, 30: 113–29.

Homans, G. C. (1958). 'Social Behavior as Exchange', *American Journal of Sociology*, 63: 597–606.

Hui, C., Lee, C., and Rousseau, D.M. (2004).'Psychological Contract and Organizational Citizenship Behavior in China: Investigating Generalizability and Instrumentality', *Journal of Applied Psychology*, 89(2): 311–21.

Johnson, J. L. and O'Leary-Kelly, A. M. (2003). 'The Effects of Psychological Contract Breach and Organizational Cynicism: Not All Social Exchange Violations are Created Equal', *Journal of Organizational Behavior*, 24: 627–47.

Kehr, H. G. (2004). 'Integrating Implicit Motives, Explicit Motives, and Perceived Abilities: The Compensatory Model of Work Motivation and Volition', *Academy of Management Review*, 29: 479–99.

Kickul, J. R., Lester, S. W., and Finkl, J. (2002). 'Promise Breaking during Radical Organizational Change: Do Justice Interventions Make a Difference?', *Journal of Organizational Behavior*, 23: 469–88.

—— Neuman, G., Parker, C., and Finkl, J. (2001). 'Settling the Score: The Role of Organizational Justice in the Relationship between Psychological Contract Breach and Anticitizenship Behavior', *Employee Responsibilities and Rights Journal*, 13: 77–94.

Konovsky, M. A. and Pugh, S. D. (1994). 'Citizenship Behavior and Social Exchange', *Academy of Management Review*, 37: 659–69.

Kotter, J. P. (1973). 'The Psychological Contract: Managing the Joining up Process', *California Management Review*, 15: 91–9.

Lambert, L. S., Edwards, J. B., and Cable, D. M. (2003). 'Breach and Fulfillment of the Psychological Contract: A Comparison of Traditional and Expanded Views', *Personnel Psychology*, 56: 895–934.

Langley, A. (1999). 'Strategies for Theorizing from Process Data', *Academy of Management Review*, 24: 691–710.

Lester, S. W., Turnley, W. H., Bloodgood, J. M., and Bolino, M. C. (2002). 'Not Seeing Eye to Eye: Differences in Supervisor and Subordinate Perceptions of and Attributions for Psychological Contract Breach', *Journal of Organizational Behavior*, 23: 39–56.

Levinson, H. (1965). 'Reciprocation: The Relationship between Man and Organization', *Administrative Science Quarterly*, 9: 370–90.

—— Price, C. R., Munden, K. J., and Solley, C. M. (1962). *Men, Management, and Mental Health*. Cambridge, MA: Harvard University Press.

Lewin, K. (1945). 'The Research Center for Group Dynamics at Massachusetts Institute of Technology', *Sociometry*, 8: 126–35.

Lewis-McClear, K. and Taylor, M. S. (1997). 'Not Seeing Eye-to-Eye: Implications of Discrepant Psychological Contracts and Contract Violation for the Employment Relationship'. Paper presented at the Annual Meeting of the Academy of Management, Boston.

Lo, S. and Aryee, S. (2003). 'Psychological Contract Breach in a Chinese Context: An Integrative Approach.' *Journal of Management Studies*, 40: 1005–20.

Louis, M. R. (1980). 'Surprise and Sense Making: What Newcomers Experience in Entering Unfamiliar Organizational Settings', *Administrative Science Quarterly*, 25: 226–51.

McLean Parks, J. M. and Kidder, D. L. (1994). ' "Till Death Us Do Part..." Changing Work Relationships in the 1990s', *Trends in Organizational Behavior*, 1: 111–36.

—— and Schmedemann, D. (1994). 'When Promises Become Contracts: Implied Contracts and Handbook Provisions on Job Security', *Human Resource Management*, 33: 403–24.

—— Kidder, D. L., and Gellagher, D. G. (1998). 'Fitting Square Pegs into Round Holes: Mapping the Domain of Contigent Work Arrangements onto the Psychological Contract', *Journal of Organizational Behavior*, 19 (Special issue): 697–730.

MacNeil, I. R. (1974). 'The Many Futures of Contract', *Southern California Law Review*, 47: 691–816.

—— (1980). *The New Social Contract*. New Haven, CT: Yale University Press.

Mac Neil,I. R. (1985). 'Relational Contract: What We Do and Do not Know', *Wisconsin Law Sociology Review*, 28: 55–69.

March, J. E. and Simon, H. A. (1958). *Organizations*. New York: Wiley.

Masuch, M. (1985). 'Vicious Circles in Organizations', *Administrative Science Quarterly*, 30: 14–33.

Meckler, M., Drake, B. H., and Levinson, H. (2003). 'Putting Psychology Back into Psychological Contracts', *Journal of Management Inquiry*, 12: 217–28.

Menninger, K. (1958). *Theory of Psychoanalytic Technique*. New York: Basic Books.

—— and Holzman, P. S. (1973). *Theory of Psychoanalytic Technique*, 2nd edn. New York: Basic Books.

Millward, L. J. and Brewerton, P. M. (2000). 'Psychological Contracts: Employee Relations for the Twenty-First Century', in C. L. Cooper and I. T. Robertson (eds.), *International Review of Industrial and Organizational Psychology*, 15. Chichester: Wiley, 1–61.

—— and Hopkins, L. J. (1998). 'Organizational Commitment and the Psychological Contract', *Journal of Social and Applied Psychology*, 28: 16–31.

Millward Purvis, L. J. and Cropley, M. (2003). 'Psychological Contracting: Processes of Contract Formation during Interviews between Nannies and their "Employers"', *Journal of Occupational and Organizational Psychology*, 76: 213–41.

Mintzberg, H. (1980). *The Nature of Managerial Work*. Englewood Cliffs, NJ: Prentice-Hall.

Mitchell, R. W. and Hamm, M. (1997). 'The Interpretation of Animal Psychology: Anthropomorphism or Behavior Reading?', *Behavior*, 134: 173–204.

Mohr, L. B. (1982). *Explaining Organizational Behavior*. San Francisco: Jossey-Bass.

Monge, P. R. (1990). 'Theoretical and Analytical Issues in Studying Organizational processes', *Organization Science*, 1: 406–30.

Morgan, G. (1986). *Images of Organizations*. Beverly Hills, CA: Sage.

Morrison, E. W. and Robinson, S. L. (1997). 'When Employees Feel Betrayed: A Model of How Psychological Contract Violation Develops', *Academy of Management Review*, 22: 226–56.

—— —— (2004). 'The Employment Relationship from Two Sides: Incongruence in Employees and Employers' Perceptions of Obligations', in J. Coyle-Shapiro, L. Shore, M. S. Taylor, and L. Tetrick (eds.), *The Employment Relationship: Examining Psychological and Contextual Perspectives*. Oxford: Oxford University Press, 161–80.

Nadin, S. (2005). 'The Social Context of the Psychological Contract', *Proceedings of BPS Occupational Psychology Conference*, Warwick, 18–20.

Newton, T. and Findlay, P. (1996). 'Playing God? The Performance of Appraisal', *Human Resource Management Journal*, 6: 42–58.

Nicholson, N. and Johns, G. (1985). 'The Absence Culture and the Psychological Contract: Who's in Control of Absence?', *Academy of Management Review*, 10: 397–407.

Organ, D. W. (1988). *Organizational Citizenship Behavior: The Good Soldier Syndrome*. Lexington, MA: Lexington Books.

Parkinson, B., Totterdell, P., Briner, R., and Reynolds, S. (1996). *Changing Moods: The Psychology of Mood and Mood Regulation*. Harlow: Longman.

Paul, R. J., Niehoff, B. P., and Turnley, W. H. (2000). 'Empowerment, Expectations, and the Psychological Contract: Managing the Dilemmas and Gaining the Advantages', *Journal of Socio-Economics*, 29: 471–85.

Pentland, B. T. (1999). 'Building Process Theory with Narrative: From Description to Explanation', *Academy of Management Review*, 24: 711–24.

Podsakoff, P. M., MacKenzie, S. B., Moorman, R. H., and Fetter, R. (1990). 'Transformational Leader Behaviors and their Effects on Followers' Trust in Leader, Satisfaction, and Organizational Citizenship Behaviors', *Leadership Quarterly*, 1: 107–42.

Raja, U., Johns, G., and Ntalianis, F. (2004). 'The Impact of Personality on Psychological Contracts', *Academy of Management Journal*, 47: 350–67.

Reichers, A. E. (1985). 'A Review and Reconceptualization of Organizational Commitment', *Academy of Management Review*, 10: 465–76.

Reis, H. T. and Wheeler, L. (1991). 'Studying Social Interaction with the Rochester Interaction Record', *Advances in Experimental Social Psychology*, 24: 269–318.

Rhoades, L. and Eisenberger, R. (2002). 'Perceived Organizational Support: A Review of the Literature', *Journal of Applied Psychology*, 87: 698–714.

Robinson, S. L. (1995). 'Violations of Psychological Contracts: Impact on Employee Attitudes', in L. E. Tetrick and J. Barling (eds.), *Changing Employment Relations: Behavioral and Social Perspectives*. Washington DC: American Psychological Association, 91–108.

—— (1996). 'Trust and Breach of the Psychological Contract', *Administrative Science Quarterly*, 41: 574–99.

—— and Morrison, E. W. (1995). 'Psychological Contracts and OCB: The Effect of Unfulfilled Obligations on Civic Virtue Behavior', *Journal of Organizational Behavior*, 16: 289–98.

—— —— (2000). 'The Development of Psychological Contract Breach and Violation: A Longitudinal Study', *Journal of Organizational Behavior*, 21: 525–46.

—— and Rousseau, D. M. (1994). 'Violating the Psychological Contract: Not the Exception but the Norm', *Journal of Organizational Behavior*, 15: 245–59.

—— Kraatz, M. S., and Rousseau, D. M. (1994). 'Changing Obligations and the Psychological Contract: A Longitudinal Study', *Academy of Management Journal*, 37: 137–52.

Roehling, M. V. (1996). 'The Origins and the Early Development of the Psychological Contract Construct'. Paper presented at the Annual Meeting of the Academy of Management, Cincinnati.

Roethlisberger, F. J. and Dickson, W. J. (1939). *Management and the Worker*. Cambridge, MA: Harvard University Press.

Roghmann, K. J. and Haggerty, R. J. (1972). 'The Diary as a Research Instrument in the Study of Health and Illness Behavior: Experiences with a Random Sample of Young Families', *Medical Care*, 10: 143–63.

Rousseau, D. M. (1989). 'Psychological and Implied Contracts in Organizations', *Employee Responsibilities and Rights Journal*, 2: 121–39.

—— (1990). 'New Hire Perceptions of Their Own and Their Employer's Obligations: A Study of Psychological Contracts', *Journal of Organizational Behavior*, 11: 389–400.

—— (1995). *Psychological Contracts in Organizations: Understanding Written and Unwritten Agreements*. Thousand Oaks, CA: Sage.

Rousseau, D. M. (1998). 'The "Problem" of the Psychological Contract Considered', *Journal of Organizational Behavior*, 19: 665–71.

——, (2000). *Psychological Contract Inventory: Technical Report* (Tech. Rep. N-. 2). Pittsburgh, PA: Carnegie Mellon University.

—— (2001). 'Schema, Promise and Mutuality: The Building Blocks of the Psychological Contract', *Journal of Occupational and Organizational Psychology*, 74: 511–41.

—— (2004). 'Psychological Contracts in the Workplace: Understanding the Ties that Motivate', *Academy of Management Executive*, 18: 120–7.

—— (2005 forthcoming). *I-Deals: Idiosyncratic Deals Employees Bargain for Themselves*. New York: M. E. Sharpe.

—— and Anton, R. J. (1991). 'Fairness and Implied Contract Obligations in Job Terminations: The Role of Contributions, Promises and Performance', *Journal of Organizational Behavior*, 12: 287–99.

—— and Greller, M. (1994). 'Human Resource Practices: Administrative Contract Makers', *Human Resource Management*, 33: 385–401.

—— and McLean Parks, J. (1993). 'The Contracts of Individuals and Organizations', *Research in Organizational Behavior*, 15: 1–43.

—— and Tijoriwala, S. A. (1998). 'Assessing Psychological Contracts: Issues, Alternatives and Measures', *Journal of Organizational Behavior*, 19: 679–95.

—— and Wade-Benzoni, K. A. (1994). 'Changing Individual and Organizational Attachments: A Two-Way Street', in A. Howard (ed.), *The Changing Nature of Work*. San Francisco: Jossey-Bass, 290–322.

Salancik, G. R. and Pfeffer, J. (1978). 'A Social Information Processing Approach to Job Attitude and Task Design', *Administrative and Science Quarterly*, 23: 224–53.

Schein, E. H. (1965, 1980). *Organizational Psychology*. Englewood Cliffs, NJ: Prentice-Hall.

Schkade, D. A. and Kilbourne, L. M. (1991). 'Expectation-Outcome Consistency and Hindsight Bias', *Organizational Behavior and Human Decision Processes*, 49: 105–23.

Schmitt, N. (1994). 'Method Bias: The Importance of Theory and Measurement', *Journal of Organizational Behavior*, 15: 393–8.

Schneider, B. and Bowen, D. E. (1999). 'Understanding Customer Delight and Outrage', *Sloan Management Review*, 41: 35–45.

Sels, L., Janssens, M., and Van den Brande, I. (2004). 'Assessing the Nature of Psychological Contracts: A Validation of Six Dimensions', *Journal of Organizational Behavior*, 25: 461–88.

Settoon, R. P., Bennett, N., and Liden, R. C. (1996). 'Social Exchange in Organizations: Perceived Organizational Support, Leader-Member Exchange, and Employee Reciprocity', *Journal of Applied Psychology*, 81: 219–27.

Shaw, T. and Jarvenpaa, S. (1997). 'Process Models in Information Systems', in A. S. Lee, J. Liebenau, and J. I. DeGross (eds.), *Information Systems and Qualitative Research: Proceedings of the IFIP International Conference on Information Systems and Qualitative Research*. London: Chapman & Hall, 70–101.

Shore, L. and Tetrick, L. (1991). 'A Construct Validity Study of the Survey of Perceived Organizational Support', *Journal of Applied Psychology*, 76: 637–43.

Shore, L. M. and Barksdale, K. (1998). 'Examining Degree of Balance and Level of Obligation in the Employment Relationship: A Social Exchange Approach', *Journal of Organizational Behavior*, 19: 731–45.

—— and Tetrick, L. E. (1994). 'The Psychological Contract as an Explanatory Framework in the Employment Relationship', in C. L. Cooper and D. M. Rousseau (eds.), *Trends in Organizational Behavior*. New York: Wiley, 91–103.

Sims, R. R. (1994). 'Human Resource Management's Role in Clarifying the New Psychological Contract', *Human Resource Management*, 33: 373–82.

Sparrow, P. R. (1996). 'Transitions in the Psychological Contract: Some Evidence from the Banking Sector', *Human Resource Management Journal*, 6: 75–92.

Stewart, R. (1967). *Managers and Their Jobs*. London: Macmillan.

Stiles, P., Gratton, L., Truss, C., Hope-Hailey, V., and McGovern, P. (1997). 'Performance Management and the Psychological Contract', *Human Resource Management Journal*, 7: 57–66.

Sullivan, L. G. (1995). 'Myth, Metaphor and Hypothesis: How Anthropomorphism Defeats Science', *Philosophical Transactions of the Royal Society of London Series: Biological Sciences*, 349: 219–24.

Sutton, G. and Griffin, M. A. (2004). 'Integrating Expectations, Experiences, and Psychological Contract Violations: A Longitudinal Study of New Professionals', *Journal of Occupational and Organizational Psychology*, 77: 493–514.

Symon, G. (1998). 'Qualitative Research Diaries', in G. Symon and C. Cassell (eds.), *Qualitative Methods and Analysis in Organizational Research*. London: Sage, 94–117.

Tamm, M. E. (1996). 'Personification of Life and Death Among Swedish Health Care Professionals', *Death Studies*, 20: 1–22.

Taylor, F. W. (1911). *The Principles of Scientific Management*. New York: Harper and Brothers.

Taylor, S. M. and Tekleab, A. G. (2004). 'Taking Stock of Psychological Contract Research: Assessing Progress, Addressing Troublesome Issues, and Setting Research Priorities', in J. Coyle-Shapiro, L. Shore, M. S. Taylor, and L. Tetrick (eds.), *The Employment Relationship: Examining Psychological and Contextual Perspectives*. Oxford: Oxford University Press, 253–83.

—— —— (2003). 'Aren't there Two Parties in an Employment Relationship? Antecedents and Consequences of Organization–Employee Agreement on Contract Obligations and Violations', *Journal of Organizational Behavior*, 24: 585–608.

Tekleab, A. G., Takeuchi, R., and Taylor, M. S. (2005). 'Extending the Chain of Relationships Among Organizational Justice, Social Exchange, and Employee Reactions: The Role of Contract Violations', *Academy of Management Journal*, 48: 146–57.

Tennen, H., Suls, J., and Affleck, G. (1991). 'Personality and Daily Experience: The Promise and the Challenge', *Journal of Personality*, 59: 313–38.

The Concise Oxford English Dictionary of Current English, 9th edn. (1996). Oxford: Clarendon Press.

Thomas, H. D. C. and Anderson, N. (1998). 'Changes in Newcomers' Psychological Contracts during Organizational Socialization: A Study of Recruits Entering the British Army', *Journal of Organizational Behavior*, 19: 745–67.

Tsui, A. and Wang, D. (2002). 'Employment Relationships from the Employer's Perspective: Current Research and Future Directions', in C. L. Cooper and I. T. Robertson (eds.), *International Review of Industrial and Organizational Psychology*, Vol. 17. Chichester: Wiley, 77–114.

Turnley, W. H. and Feldman, D. C. (1999). 'A Discrepancy Model of Psychological Contract Violations', *Human Resource Management Review*, 9: 367–86.

—— —— (1999). 'The Impact of Psychological Contract Violations on Exit, Voice, Loyalty, and Neglect', *Human Relations*, 52: 895–922.

—— —— (2000). 'Re-Examining the Effects of Psychological Contract Violations: Unmet Expectations and Job Dissatisfaction as Mediators', *Journal of Organizational Behavior*, 21: 25–42.

—— Bolino, M. C., Lester, S. W., and Bloodgood, J. M. (2003). 'The Impact of Psychological Contract Fulfillment on the Performance of In-Role and Organizational Citizenship Behaviors', *Journal of Management*, 29: 187–206.

Van Dyne, L. and Butler Ellis, J. (2004). 'Job Creep: A Reactance Theory Perspective on Organizational Citizenship Behavior as Overfulfilment of Obligations', in J. Coyle-Shapiro, L. Shore, M. S. Taylor, and L. Tetrick (eds.), *The Employment Relationship: Examining Psychological and Contextual Perspectives*. Oxford: Oxford University Press, 181–205.

Vaus, D. (2001). *Research Design in Social Research*. London: Sage.

de Vos, A., Buyens, D., and Schalk, R. (2003). 'Psychological Contract Development during Organizational Socialization: Adaptation to Reality and the Role of Reciprocity', *Journal of Organizational Behavior*, 24: 537–58.

Wanous, J. P. (1977). 'Organizational Entry: Newcomers Moving from Outside to Inside', *Psychological Bulletin*, 84: 601–18.

—— Poland, T. D., Premack, S. L., and Davis, K. S. (1992). 'The Effect of Met Expectations on Newcomer Attitudes and Behaviors: A Review and Meta-Analysis', *Journal of Applied Psychology*, 77: 288–97.

Warr, P. B. (1987). *Work, Unemployment, and Mental Health*. Oxford: Clarendon Press.

Warr, P. (1990). 'The Measurement of Well-being and Other Aspects of Mental Health', *Journal of Occupational Psychology*, 63: 193–210.

Wayne, S. J., Shore, L. M., and Liden, R. C. (1997). 'Perceived Organizational Support and Leader–Member Exchange: A Social Exchange Perspective', *Academy of Management Journal*, 40: 82–111.

Weick, K. E. (1995). *Sensemaking in Organizations*. Thousand Oaks, CA: Sage.

Weiss, H. M. and Cropanzano, R. (1996). 'Affective Events Theory: A Theoretical Discussion of the Structure, Causes and Consequences of Affective Experiences at Work', *Research in Organizational Behavior*, 18: 1–74.

Westwood, R., Sparrow, P., and Leung, A. (2001). 'Challenges to the Psychological Contract in Hong Kong', *International Journal of Human Resource Management*, 12: 621–50.

Williams, L. J. and Podsakoff, P. M. (1989). 'Longitudinal Field Methods for Studying Reciprocal Relationships in Organizational Behavior Research: Toward Improved Causal Analysis', *Research in Organizational Behavior*, 11: 247–92.

Wokutch, R. E. and Carson, T. L. (1993). 'The Ethics and Profitability of Bluffing in Business', in R. J. Lewicki, J. A. Letterer, D. M. Saunders, and J. W. Minton (eds.), *Negotiation: Readings, Exercises, and Cases*, 2nd edn. Burr Ridge, IL: Irwin, 499–504.

Wright, T. A. (2003). 'Positive Organizational Behavior: An Idea Whose Time Has Truly Come', *Journal of Organizational Behavior*, 24: 437–42.

Wrzesniewski, A. and Dutton, J. E. (2001). 'Crafting a Job: Revisioning Employees as Active Crafters of Their Work', *Academy of Management Review*, 26: 179–201.

▓ INDEX